DATE DUE

NV 26 '98		
OC 6 '98		
DE 19 '98		

DEMCO 38-296

Home Space Planning

Home Space Planning

A Guide for Architects, Designers, and Home Owners

Nancy Temple

McGraw-Hill

New York   San Francisco   Washington, D.C.   Auckland   Bogotá
Caracas   Lisbon   London   Madrid   Mexico City   Milan
Montreal   New Delhi   San Juan   Singapore
Sydney   Tokyo   Toronto

Library of Congress Cataloging-in-Publication Data

Temple, Nancy.
    Home space planning : a guide for architects, designers, and home owners / Nancy Temple.
        p.   cm.
    ISBN 0-07-063499-8 (hc)
    1. Dwellings—Remodeling.   2. Room layout (Dwellings)   I. Title.
    TH4816.T46   1995
    643'.7—dc20
                                                             95-32921
                                                               CIP

McGraw-Hill

*A Division of The **McGraw·Hill** Companies*

1 2 3 4 5 6 7 8 9 0 BKP/BKP 9 0 0 9 8 7 6

ISBN 0-07-063499-8

The sponsoring editors for this book were Joel Stein and Wendy Lochner, the editing supervisor was Virginia Carroll, and the production supervisor was Suzanne W. B. Rapcavage. This book was set in Franklin Gothic by North Market Street Graphics. Printed and bound by Quebecor/Book Press.

McGraw-Hill books are available at special quantity discounts to use as premiums and sales promotions, or for use in corporate training programs. For more information, please write to the Director of Special Sales, McGraw-Hill, 11 West 19th Street, New York, NY 10011. Or contact your local bookstore.

 This book is printed on acid-free paper containing a minimum of 10% postconsumer waste.

This book is dedicated to
Alexander R. Temple and Anna Radhika Temple.

Contents

Acknowledgments

I would like to thank Arnold Friedmann of the University of Massachusetts in Amherst, who encouraged me in my study of design and whose critiques were always enlightening. I would also like to thank my student Mary Metcalf, for taking valuable time away from her studies and work to help me in inking the plans. Special thanks to designer and colleague Larry Ryan, who produced the lively perspective sketches which illustrate this book and which give dimension to the plans.

Introduction

Home Space Planning was written for people who are thinking about reorganizing or adding to residential spaces. Architects and interior designers may be working with clients who have difficult problems to solve—or who seem difficult to please. The wide variety of plans and illustrations with explanatory text can help the designer to arrive at a satisfactory solution. This book can also be used to help client and designer work together, by enabling them to examine many options.

Teachers and students will also find the book useful as a guide to analyzing space-planning problems, as a resource for studying the process of design, and as a reference book offering an array of solutions to specific problems.

Most of all, I wrote this book for lay people who have an interest in redesigning their own spaces, whether alone or in cooperation with architects. Knowing how to draft is useful but not necessary; drawing floor plans on graph paper can be a satisfactory substitute. Having detailed understanding of home construction is also not necessary, although structural as well as economic factors will naturally help to determine the final outcome.

As the title suggests, this is a book mostly about spaces—about movement through them, relationships between them, and sense of volume—but not about finishes, furniture, or decoration. It is filled with plans of houses, descriptions of design problems and requirements, and with many more plans demonstrating a variety of solutions. All kinds of projects are included: small- and large-scale kitchen renovations, smaller projects like adding storage or a third bathroom fixture, and larger projects such as adding whole second stories. The accompanying text considers each proposed solution from the points of view of function, aesthetics, and economy, because it is clear that a solution is not acceptable unless all three concerns have been satisfactorily addressed.

The idea for the book grew out of a conversation I had with an adult student in my drafting class. This student had recently renovated her kitchen. The room was old and lacked counter surfaces; in addition, there were so many doors (and a set of stairs) opening into the room that it was hard to create a workable layout. In a general sense, if not in every particular, she faced a common set of problems: she had a space which did not function well, and she had budget constraints. Her solution (arrived at without the help of professionals) was also common, in that it was partial. The student showed me the design that was finally built and proudly explained all that she had accomplished with her layout. Then she ruefully admitted that there was not enough space to locate a range with counters on both sides. I looked at her plan, pointed to a wall abutting an unnecessary hallway, and suggested that if she had removed the wall and incorporated the hall into the kitchen, she would have had the space she needed. My student was astonished, because, although she had thought about the room and its redesign for weeks, it had never occurred to her that a very simple move—combining hall and kitchen—would accomplish so much. I, for my part, was equally surprised that she had overlooked what seemed an obvious solution.

Perhaps I should not have been surprised. In my own space-planning practice, both residential and commercial, I have often struggled for long periods of time to find a solution to a set of problems, producing plan after plan, without being completely satisfied. Frequently, I have found in the end that one move—the demolition of a single wall, the alteration of existing fenestration, moving existing plumbing—opens up unexpected possibilities and is the key to solving the puzzle and producing a perfect plan.

It occurred to me, following the exchange with my student, that the process of solving space-planning problems is not well understood, particularly by nonprofessionals. Just as important, people do not think carefully or critically enough about their needs and about the imperfections of their houses. They assume that nothing much can be done—at least, not without great expense—and they adjust to living with crowded rooms, awkward spaces, and noisy environments. Sadly, their behavior and living patterns then become driven by the very architecture which was supposed to serve them.

It is my hope that studying this book will help lay people and professionals alike to become more successful space planners by showing them how to recognize problems, how to approach the problem-solving process, how to evaluate each proposal, and how to move towards producing a plan which represents a satisfactory solution.

Home Space Planning

About Houses and How They Function

Linda is a freelance book designer who works at home. She is single, and she has bought a contemporary-style house with many combined rooms, cathedral ceilings, loft space, and few walls. On the main level, the house has a small kitchen which opens to another room used as both dining and living rooms. A loft overlooking the living room is going to be her home studio-cum-office. An open stairwell leads to the lower level, which contains a central room probably intended as a family or TV room; opening into this are a bathroom and three bedrooms. The house is built on a hill, so most of the lower-level rooms are glassy and bright. She is delighted with her purchase.

She moves in and places an ad in the paper for a roommate. It is her plan to use one bedroom, rent the second, and keep the third for guests. She meets just the right roommate: a quiet law student at a nearby campus who spends most of her day in class or the library. The two are rarely in the house at the same time.

Then, Linda's life changes. She gets married and her roommate moves out, but since there are still only two adults living in the house, the house continues to meet their needs. Sometime later, when the first child is born, minor rearrangements become necessary. The child occupies the second bedroom, and now the TV room is a playroom and is filled with toys. With the arrival of the second child, however, Linda becomes aware that exactly the same design characteristics which initially appealed to her—the open quality that made rooms appear larger and brighter—are now causing serious problems. The worst of these problems is the transmission of noise throughout the house. As Linda tries to work in her open loft, the noise of children in the playroom below (tended by a babysitter) travels up the open stairwell and throughout the upper level. It is impossible to concentrate, and there are no doors to close! In addition, the house is fuller and messier now, and any mess is clearly visible. When the kitchen is not cleaned up, the clutter can be seen from the living room, and the littered floor of the playroom is an obstacle course to be traversed between bedrooms and bathroom. Linda decides to put the children into daycare so that she can have privacy and quiet at home. She is now being forced to change her lifestyle in order to deal with problems created by the design of her house.

The specific characteristics of Linda's house—an outgrowth of architectural principles developed after the 1940s—are perhaps justifiable as an attempt to make a small house seem larger. If a kitchen is only 8' × 10' and the dining room is about the same size, it makes sense to combine the two spaces (or to combine them with the living area). This does not add storage or counter space, nor does it permit the setup of a large dining table, but at least the area will appear bigger and less oppressive. However, new houses which are in reality very large (7000 square feet or more) often utilize the same principles, even when it is neither necessary nor desirable. The result is enormous houses with big, open, flowing spaces and relatively few walls, lots of interior balconies overlooking other spaces, lofts, and so on. Although this is intended to be visually exciting and fun to live in, it in fact creates functional problems because noise is readily transmitted throughout open spaces, furniture is harder to lay out when spaces are ill defined, and the absence of many interior walls precludes the hanging of artwork, building of storage for books, CDs, toys, and so on.

Often, architects will attempt, in both small and large houses, to delineate and define rooms in an open space by changing floor levels, ceiling levels, flooring materials, and wallcoverings or paint colors. I have seen plans for houses of less than 2000 square feet in which the designer has drawn a two-story high minifoyer from which one sees a tiny kitchen with a tile floor which is open to a long, undefined space (hallway?) with hardwood flooring. This in turn

is separated from a tile-floored "library" (about 10' × 10') which is open on two sides, has a wall of windows on the third, and a huge fieldstone fireplace on the fourth—where will the books be located? How can one read when there are no doors to shut for privacy and quiet? And abutting this "library" is a compact, step-down living room with a dropped ceiling and carpet. Every room is open and visible to every other; the great variety of flooring materials, of levels, and of wall textures creates a visual cacophany.

In a similar way, architects have always borrowed features from earlier building styles—pediments, columns, pilasters, palladian windows, stucco with tile roofs, and so on—and integrated these into contemporary structures. In today's houses, these exterior elements are used in symbolic fashion, to suggest antiquity, nobility, or wealth. Their presence on the outside of a building is largely decorative and does not interfere with the use of the structure. Unfortunately, "symbolic devices" in the interior, like two-story foyers, open spaces, marble floors, lofts, and other architectural clichés, which are becoming a standard part of current house design, do not improve function and are often counterproductive.

The point here is that professional architects and builders, partly in response to the demands of home buyers interested in status, make many ill-considered decisions. This is true even when there is plenty of available floor space and enough money to build it right. This happens because builders are driven by the market, designers are

taught to think about aesthetics more than about function, and consumers are inexperienced. Later, after living in the house for some time, buyers discover all the ways in which the architecture either creates problems or fails to meet simple needs.

I have been talking about a specific group of houses in order to make a point, but, of course, there are all kinds of houses in the world, and all kinds described in this book. There are 250-year-old antiques with low ceilings, big kitchens, and lots of pantries; 150-year-old Victorians with porches and turrets; and developments filled with split-levels, raised ranches, multilevels, and colonials. Many, if not most, of these houses will be lacking in either the style or amenities desired by their owners. What are some of the most common problems? They are: spaces which are too small, insufficient storage, missing spaces (like a house without a family room), poor traffic flow (like having to go through one bedroom to get to another), inefficient layout (like rooms too spread out, or improper adjacencies), and a lack of appropriate relationship between spaces (like a kitchen too far removed from a breakfast nook).

About Redesigning

The first step in the design process is, of course, to identify the problems and establish your needs. These may be related or separate issues. In Linda's case, the births of her children changed the way she experienced her house. Her principal problems then became a noisy environment, lack of privacy, and visual clutter. Her need was for a quiet place to work and a separate room for her children to play in, so that she could close the door on the mess. Perhaps secondarily, she may have wished for a large "public" area—that is, the kitchen/living/dining room—so that the kitchen could be visually separated from the other rooms. Linda chose to put the children in daycare, which accomplished a couple of things; it gave her quiet time in the house to work, and it meant that the playroom was used less often and thus stayed neater for longer periods of time. She could have made different choices. She might have chosen to rent office space elsewhere and leave the babysitter at home with the children. If she moved her studio out of the house, she could perhaps then have turned the loft space into a playroom, so that the toy clutter was confined to an out-of-the-way space. Or, she could have redesigned her house to meet her

new requirements; for instance, she might have reorganized the interior layout by moving or adding walls or by building an addition.

The second step in the design process is to explore the possibilities for solving the problem. To do this, you need to understand the source of the problem—in particular, you have to know how the existing architecture is involved. In some cases, the difficulty may be simply that there is not enough space, for example, that a house needs another bedroom. In other cases, as in Linda's, it would be necessary to know not only that the house is noisy but also that it is the open character of the space—a lack of walls—which creates the problem. Understanding in this way can be the result of living in a space, if you are the "client," or listening carefully to what the client tells you, if you are the designer. It will require spending time in the space. Both client and designer will have to rid themselves of architectural prejudices and preconceptions in order to "see" the house with a fresh and open mind.

It will help immensely if floor plans and elevations are drawn up. This is because walking through a house gives you a mental picture of it in segments, but it is hard to visualize the whole and the ways in which its parts are interrelated. Thinking of the plan as a kind of aerial view of the layout permits the study of these interrelationships. It has often been my experience, even in redesigning spaces that I have lived in for years, that important aspects of the solution come to light only in examining the plans.

When identifying solutions, what are the most common concerns? The three principal concerns are function, aesthetics, and economy. (In my opinion, function and economy are most important. No matter how visually satisfying or exciting a house may seem at first, if it does not meet your day-to-day needs, and if you need to adjust your behavior to adapt to the space you inhabit, then the designers have failed in their primary responsibility to you. This is not to say, of course, that building a functional house precludes making it beautiful, too.) In addition, when redesigning, it is wise to look ahead and anticipate future needs—not only, say, your own need for an extra bedroom or bathroom, but the possibility of resale. When adding a fourth bedroom to a house with three bedrooms and a single bathroom, it is worthwhile considering that houses with master suites are considered desirable and, even if you don't feel you need the extra bathroom, it might be worth it, in the long run, to make the investment.

Many books which discuss the design process underline the importance of drawing and sketching. The act of sketching one idea suggests others.

It may seem, when you are trying out different solutions, that you are highly constrained and

that only a few different layouts are possible. I want to emphasize that there are always many more design possibilities than you may think, though, of course, some will be better than others. It is essential that you approach the experimental phase with a completely open mind. Do not exclude any ideas at this point; the most unlikely possibility may lead to an unexpectedly successful plan.

Analyzing a design can not only help to bring new solutions to light but usually helps to clarify one's needs. Linda might decide to solve a noisy studio problem by enclosing it with walls. In so planning, she becomes aware that the studio will lose light it borrows from skylights located over the living room; she then has to solve a second problem—perhaps by installing another skylight, perhaps by putting windows into the new walls, so that light from the living room still penetrates the studio, or perhaps by simply adding light fixtures.

In my commercial space-planning practice, it has often been the case that a client will recite a long, apparently comprehensive list of requirements: reception room to seat two, conference room to seat twelve, six private offices, kitchenette with small table, storage room to house a nearly infinite number of brochures, research area with PC, library, workstations, and so on. The presentation of a first draft, however, often reveals additional requirements: the storage space needs to accommodate an infinite number of printed forms, as well, and the client forgot to mention several necessary adjacencies. Now the client notes that Heidi needs to be closer to Joan, and that both of them spend a lot of time in the research area. At times, reworking the plan to solve a small problem, like getting Heidi and Joan closer together, can lead to extensive changes.

In general, the design process is one of educated trial and error. It is desirable to try a wide array of solutions. Progress may not be direct; you may follow a line of reasoning, a direction, only to find an obstacle at the end which precludes the actual building. This obstacle might be functional, aesthetic, or financial; it might be too expensive to move the plumbing, or the design may be beautiful but may fail to solve an important issue such as circulation. Gradually, you will eliminate those plans or aspects of plans which are unsuccessful.

The act of creating and refining a space plan is like working on a jigsaw puzzle, in that many aspects are considered both simultaneously and separately. As you put together a jigsaw puzzle, for example, you study the shape of the piece, its color, and pattern. Similarly, in redesigning a kitchen, it is necessary to consider layout of appliances, lighting, adequate counter and storage space, and, not least, the desired relationship of the space to adjacent spaces (dining room, family room, etc.). For instance, if you wanted to install a wall of glass above a long counter in your kitchen, it would affect the installation of upper cabinets and wall ovens, both of which use up wall space. In this situation, you might choose to create a pantry or other storage area outside the kitchen, and you might also decide to install an under-counter oven. It is important to remember that you will often approach the ideal solution in increments. You will often examine a plan and find some of its parts very pleasing, while other parts don't work. You may find that you need to combine areas of one plan with parts from another to come up with something that meets all of your needs.

Expanding a Basement Bathroom

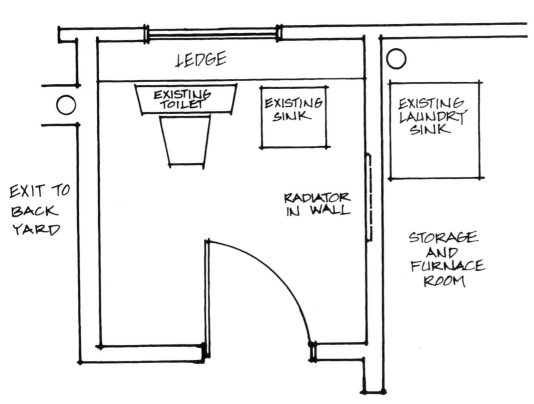

LEDGE

EXISTING TOILET

EXISTING SINK

EXISTING LAUNDRY SINK

EXIT TO BACK YARD

RADIATOR IN WALL

STORAGE AND FURNACE ROOM

1. EXISTING BATHROOM
SCALE: ½" = 1'0"

1 The existing bathroom, in the lower level of a split-level house, contains only two fixtures. It is located near the family room, and the owners of the house want to install a good-sized shower, so that the family room and bathroom can be used as a suite for an au pair. On one side of the bathroom there is a hallway and door to the backyard; on the other side is the furnace room, with storage shelving and a laundry sink. The owners want to add a shower fixture while intruding as little as possible on the adjacent storage space.

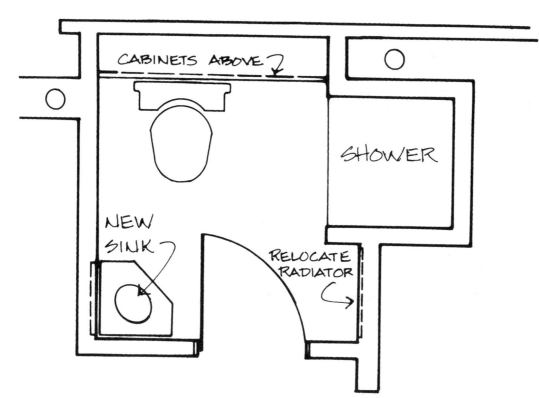

2. NEW BATHROOM
SCALE: ½" = 1'0"

2 This drawing shows the solution. The toilet is upgraded; the sink is replaced and moved; the radiator is moved slightly; a new shower uses existing space as well as space in the furnace room; the window above the toilet (which only looks out on earth below the deck and does not admit any light) is closed in and cabinets are mounted above the ledge; the laundry sink is moved.

3. PERSPECTIVE OF NEW BATHROOM

3 This perspective shows how spacious the bathroom appears at the end of the renovation.

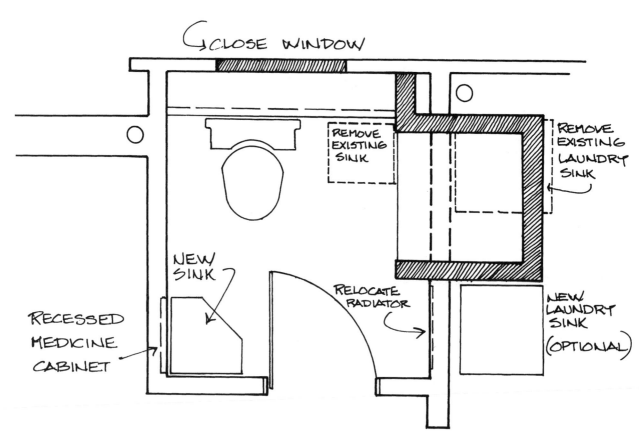

CLOSE WINDOW

REMOVE EXISTING SINK

REMOVE EXISTING LAUNDRY SINK

NEW SINK

RECESSED MEDICINE CABINET

RELOCATE RADIATOR

NEW LAUNDRY SINK (OPTIONAL)

4. DEMOLITION AND CONSTRUCTION PLAN
SCALE: ½″ = 1′0″

4 Demolition and new construction are shown in this plan.

Improving Access to an Extra Room and Adding a Studio

1 This very standard Cape was built in the 1970s. It is a well-designed house, particularly on the first floor, which has pleasantly proportioned, sun-filled rooms, a well-laid-out kitchen with good storage space, and a large family room which opens into the kitchen, garage, and a screened porch.

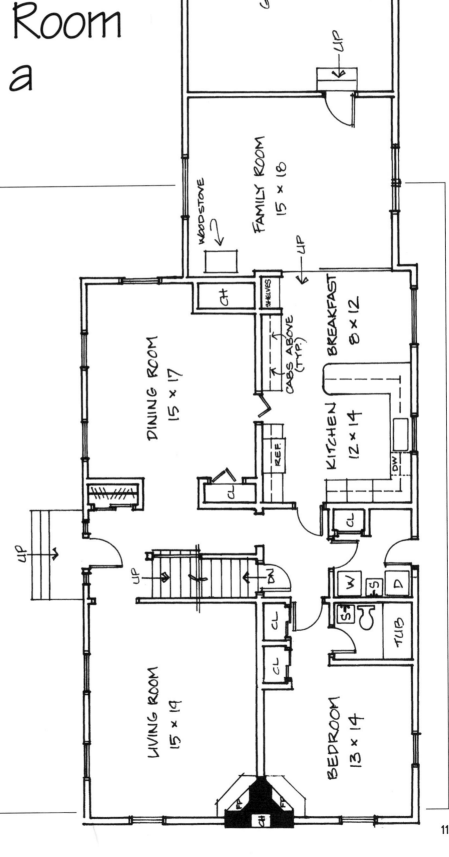

1. EXISTING FIRST-FLOOR PLAN

2 The second floor has less flexibility than the first. It suffers, like all Capes, from lack of headroom because the upper rooms are directly under the roof. Dormers bring in light but do little to add space. Nevertheless, the three bedrooms on this floor are of good size and have large closets.

If this house has a design problem, it is in the location of another room which can only be accessed from one of the bedrooms. If this room is treated as part of the adjacent bedroom, then its placement is not a problem. It is not useful as a fourth second-story bedroom, because it is fairly small, has no closet and is not convenient to any bathroom. It would be desirable as a study or play space, but then some other means of accessing this space must be created.

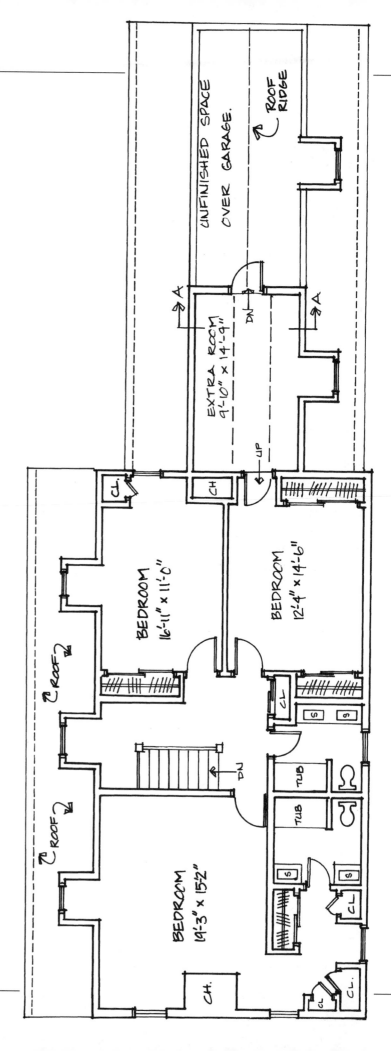

2. EXISTING SECOND-FLOOR PLAN

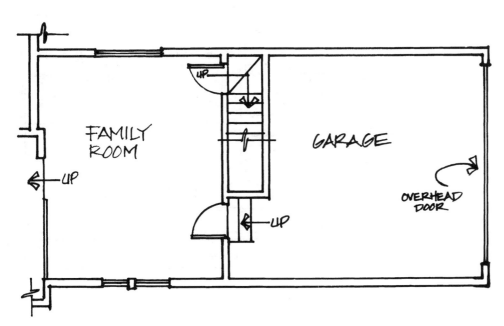

3. GARAGE WITH STAIRS TO UPPER STORY

3 This plan shows how stairs can be built into the end of the garage without disturbing the first-floor layout.

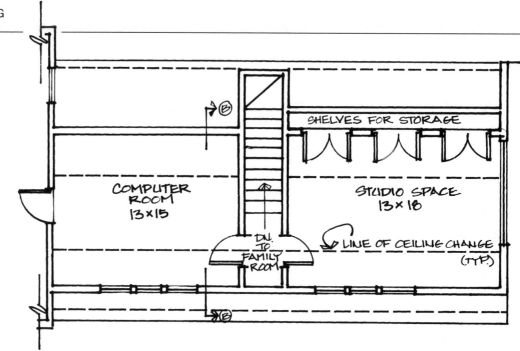

4. COMPUTER ROOM AND STUDIO ON SECOND STORY

4 The new stairs arrive behind the finished room, in the unfinished space over the garage. The plan suggests that the unfinished space could be made into a spacious studio, while the little room functions as a study. Note changes in the roofline at the back of the house.

5. SECTION THROUGH EXTRA ROOM WITH ORIGINAL ROOF

5 This is a section through the original "extra room" which clearly shows the spatial problems created by the roof pitch.

6 This section demonstrates the greater space obtained by building a long shed dormer at the back of the house.

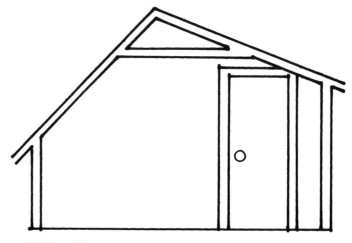

6. SECTION THROUGH EXTRA ROOM AFTER ROOF IS LIFTED

Island Vacation House

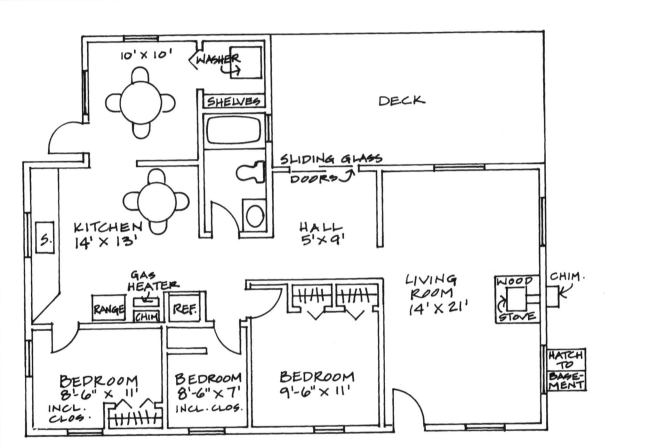

1. EXISTING FLOOR PLAN
(SCALE: ⅛″ = 1′0″)

1 This is a small one-story house built in the 1960s on a shoestring. It was originally smaller than it is shown in the plan, consisting of the 14′ × 13′ kitchen, the bathroom, and the three bedrooms. Its first owner had eight children, so he eventually added a 10′ × 10′ bedroom behind the kitchen and a living room. The second owner of the house turned the back bedroom into a second eating area and installed a washing machine in its closet. He added a deck and put sliding glass doors into the hallway. Note that the layout of the rooms is a direct result of the fact that this house has no central heat. The living room is heated by a woodstove, and the kitchen and bedrooms are all heated by a

15

BIRD'S-EYE VIEW OF ORIGINAL PLAN

vented gas heater situated between the refrigerator and the range.

The house was recently purchased by a family who plan to use it as a vacation house, largely in the summer, and as a rental property. They want to renovate the house so that it functions better for them as well as for renters and so that it will be an attractive and versatile house when it is put back on the market.

The principal problem in the current layout is related to the issue of heat. The existing bedrooms not only open onto the kitchen but in winter must leave their doors open in order to remain warm. The proximity of these bedrooms to the kitchen means that, winter or summer, the first person to wake disturbs others as he or she gets breakfast and moves about. This is a significant problem which the new owners feel is most important to correct. In addition, they would like a better kitchen in which the range and fridge are surrounded by counter and a dishwasher is installed next to the sink, a full laundry center which includes a dryer, and a master bedroom with an attached bathroom.

Note that all the renovations assume the installation of either a central heating system, whether gas, oil or electric, or individual vented or direct-vent gas heaters. This permits the necessary separation of spaces which give visual, and especially acoustical, privacy to the bedrooms.

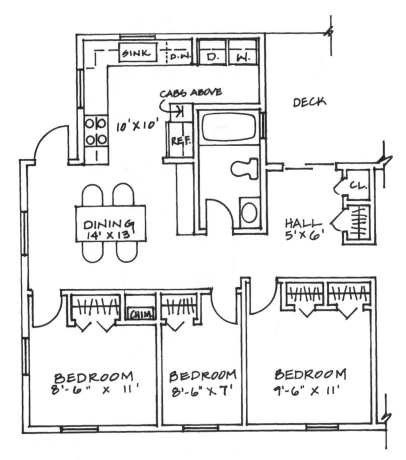

2. NEW KITCHEN AND DINING AREA
SCALE: ⅛″ = 1′0″

2 This relatively simple renovation moves the kitchen into the back room, with a well-laid-out work triangle and laundry area. The original kitchen becomes the new dining area, and because the fridge and range have been moved, the bedroom walls and closets can be moved so that the bedrooms are a bit larger. The chimney, no longer needed, is not removed but boxed in. The advantage to this plan is that it creates a much more functional kitchen and isolates it to some extent from the bedrooms; the disadvantage is that the bedrooms still open onto a public space. Children, therefore, who may go to bed early, might be disturbed by a noisy party in the dining room.

VIEW OF ORIGINAL KITCHEN

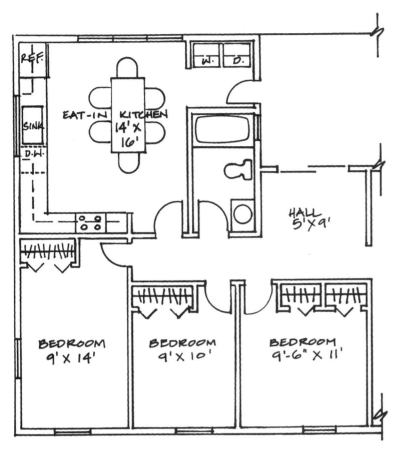

3. NEW KITCHEN
SCALE: ⅛″ = 1′0″

3 This plan duplicates some of the solutions shown in Plan #2, but the renovation is more extensive. Here, as in all subsequent plans, the chimney is shown removed, although with some alterations, it could be left in place. Again, the bedrooms are enlarged, and the kitchen is improved. An important change is the squaring off of the back end of the house, so that the 10′ × 10′ room is expanded. This expansion is small—only about 5 feet— but is very significant in permitting the installation of a big eat-in kitchen. Since the original kitchen window is removed, a wall can be extended from the bathroom, which isolates the kitchen and makes the bedrooms quieter. In this redesign, however, the two public spaces—living and dining areas—are separated by the bedrooms and bathroom. In general, a better organization would divide the house into public and private areas and would keep them distinct from one another.

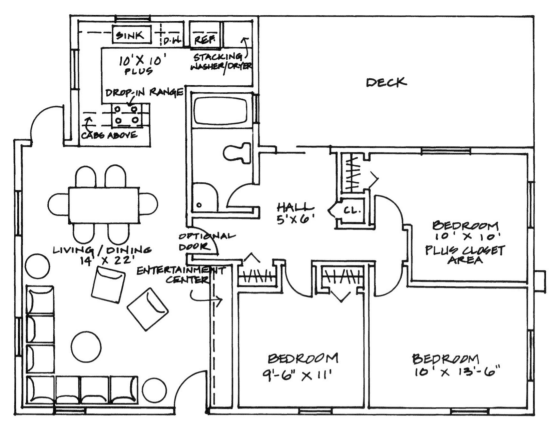

SINK · D.W. REF.

10' X 10' PLUS

STACKING WASHER/DRYER

DROP-IN RANGE

CABS ABOVE

DECK

LIVING / DINING 14' X 22'

OPTIONAL DOOR

ENTERTAINMENT CENTER

HALL 5' X 6'

CL.

BEDROOM 10' X 10' PLUS CLOSET AREA

BEDROOM 9'-6" X 11'

BEDROOM 10' X 13'-6"

4. NEW FLOOR PLAN
SCALE: ⅛" = 1'0"

4 Once again, the kitchen is located in the back room, and another variation on its layout is demonstrated. A stacking washer/dryer makes the laundry center more compact; the peninsula with cooking center makes the kitchen accessible to the dining area. The latter is now combined with a living room which has been created from two of the original bedrooms. These, in turn, have been carved out of the original living room. This plan, though it involves an extensive reorganization of the interior spaces, is less radical than might be thought. The bathroom remains intact, the house is not enlarged, and so aside from the installation of the new kitchen—which, in any case, needed to be done—the demolition of two walls and the construction of two others are really all that have been proposed.

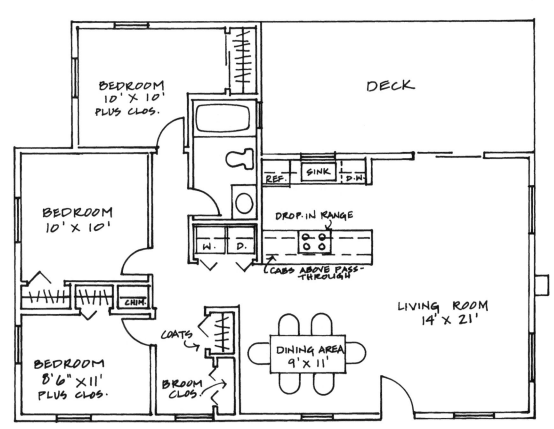

5. NEW FLOOR PLAN
SCALE: ⅛″ = 1′0″

5 This is another plan which does not involve any additions to the house but which substantially reorganizes the interior. Here, the division of public and private space is very clear, with the kitchen and dining areas moved over next to the living room; the dining area occupies the space originally given over to one of the bedrooms. Another original bedroom has been converted to closets, and the remaining space is made into three bedrooms of approximately equal size.

PERSPECTIVE OF PLAN #5, SHOWING FURNITURE

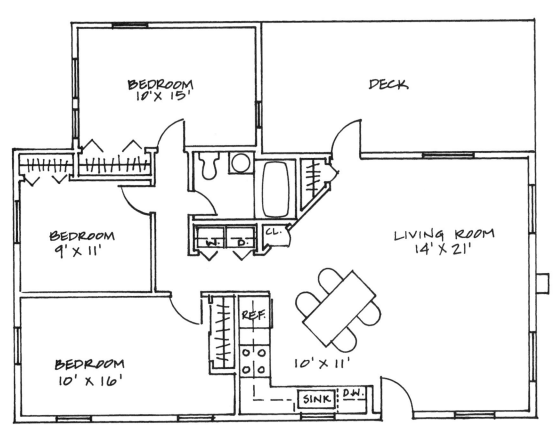

6. NEW FLOOR PLAN WITH NEW BATHROOM LAYOUT
SCALE: ⅛″ = 1′0″

6 Like Plan #5, there is a clear division of private and public areas. Here, for the first time, the existing bathroom has been reorganized, which changes the configuration and size of the back bedroom. The living/dining/kitchen again share a large space—a kind of great room—which seems appropriate for a summer home. The kitchen in this plan, as in the previous one, is small: this decision is acceptable in a vacation house in which one presumes the tenants are at the beach most of the time!

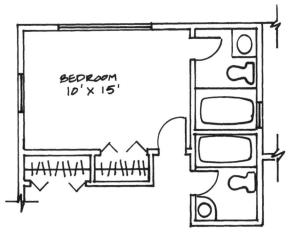

7. MASTER BEDROOM SUITE
SCALE: ⅛″ = 1′0″

7 A variation on Plan #6, this is the first time that the redesign shows a master bedroom/bathroom combination. It is accomplished by squaring off the back of the house, as was done in Plan #3.

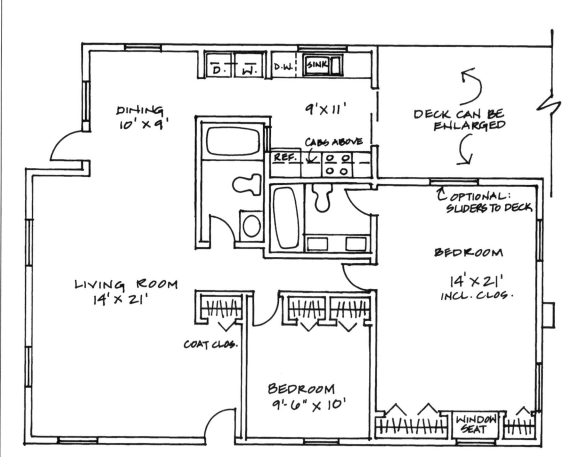

DINING
10' X 9'

9' X 11'

DECK CAN BE
ENLARGED

CABS ABOVE

REF.

OPTIONAL:
SLIDERS TO DECK

BEDROOM
14' X 21'
INCL. CLOS.

LIVING ROOM
14' X 21'

COAT CLOS.

BEDROOM
9'-6" X 10'

WINDOW
SEAT

8. FLOOR PLAN WITH TWO BEDROOMS
SCALE: ⅛" = 1'0"

8 This is the only plan in which the house is shown with only two bedrooms. This design makes all the spaces reasonably large (and the master bedroom very big), maintains the division between public and private areas, and gives a bathroom to the master bedroom. Here, a portion of the deck has been taken to accommodate a new kitchen; the original hall becomes the new bathroom, the living room is the master bedroom, and two of the bedrooms have been converted to living space, as in Plan #4. It would be desirable to enlarge the deck, wrapping it around the master bedroom.

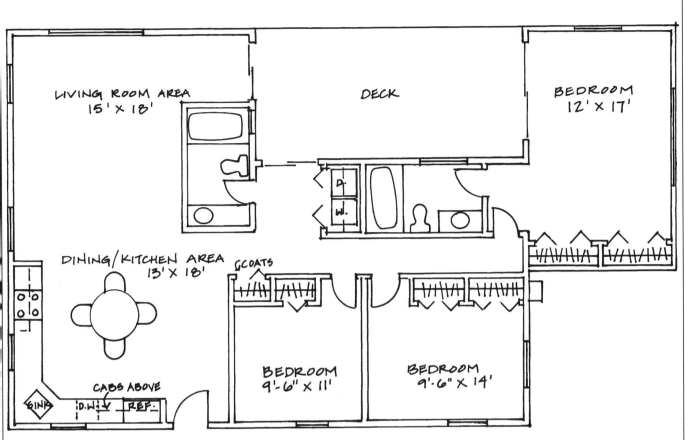

LIVING ROOM AREA
15' X 18'

DECK

BEDROOM
12' X 17'

DINING/KITCHEN AREA
13' X 18'

COATS

D.

W.

CABS ABOVE

SINK

D.W.   REF.

BEDROOM
9'-6" X 11'

BEDROOM
9'-6" X 14'

9. NEW PLAN WITH ADDITION
SCALE: ⅛" = 1'0"

9 This is one of two plans in which a substantial addition is made. In this design, the addition is the master bedroom, which could be made any size. The original bathroom is slightly changed, in order to relocate the door so that it is readily accessible to the bedrooms and not visible from the dining room. The original living room is made into a bedroom, hallway, and the master bathroom.

As in Plan #6, the living, kitchen, and dining areas are open to one another. A smaller addition—the squaring off of the corner of the house—makes the new living room more spacious. The plan works well, but there are extra plumbing costs since the second bathroom is remote from the first.

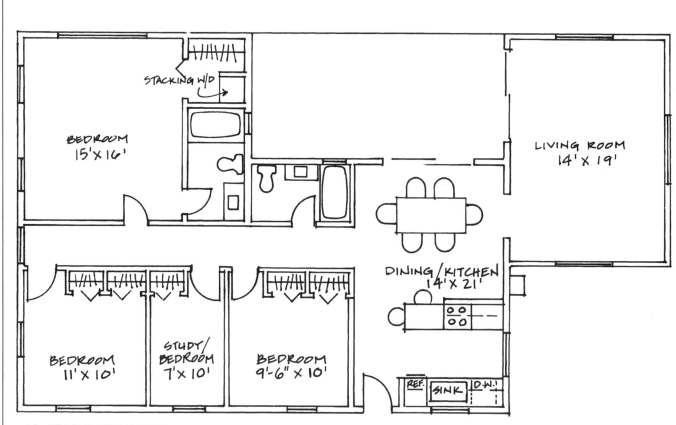

STACKING W/D

BEDROOM
15'X 16'

LIVING ROOM
14' X 19'

BEDROOM
11' X 10'

STUDY/
BEDROOM
7' X 10'

BEDROOM
9'-6" X 10'

DINING/KITCHEN
14' X 21'

REF. SINK D.W.

10. NEW PLAN WITH ADDITION

10 Like Plan #9, this one shows additions to the house—in this case, a new living room at one end, and the squaring off of the house at the other. There are a number of advantages to this plan. First, it divides the private and public areas of the house. Second, it preserves all the original bedrooms—in slightly expanded form—while it establishes a good-sized master bedroom with its own bath; here, the master bath is the original one, with its door relocated, and a second bathroom is installed in the hallway area, readily accessible to both the other bedrooms and the dining/kitchen area. The original living room is large enough to be made into an adequately sized kitchen/dining area, and there are

several ways in which this could be laid out. In this plan, the decision was made to put the dining area at the back, so that sliders to the deck could be installed. Placing the kitchen near the front with a hallway running past it also means that no cross-traffic need disturb the work triangle. An advantage to adding the living room as shown here is that, if necessary, guests could be accommodated on a sleep sofa, with doors or a curtain providing privacy.

Improving a Second Story

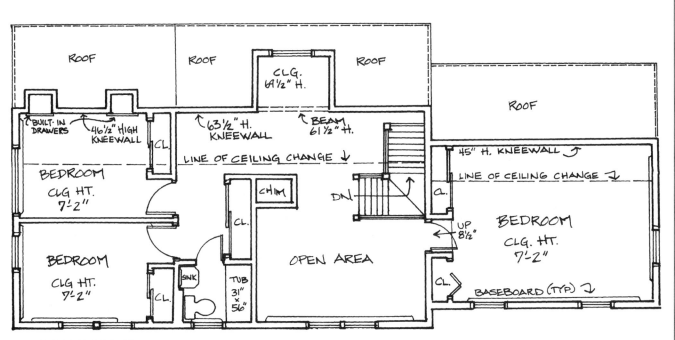

1. EXISTING FLOOR PLAN
SCALE: ⅛″ = 1′0″

1 The existing floor plan shows
the second story of a Cape,
with a steep roof pitch at the front
of the house which severely limits
floor space and headroom. The
layout of this floor is fairly hazard-
ard, and it is hard to imagine why
it was built this way, with easy
access to the bathroom from the
two very small bedrooms nearby,
with the largest bedroom remote
from the bathroom and with an ill-
defined open area at the top of
the stairs. The chimney, located in
the center of the house, makes
organization of the space on this
level more complicated.

The couple who bought this
house are active and have acquired
many possessions. Jerry is a man-
agement consultant who works
from home. Lorraine is an elemen-
tary school teacher who also does
freelance graphic design work, so
she needs a desk for grading
schoolwork as well as a place for
her drafting board, art markers,
books, and other design supplies.
They have two young children, Nina
and Michael, who have a lot of toys
and not much storage space.

Currently, the open area is furnished with a sofa (which is also
the dog's bed) and a large desk

littered with papers. The dormer at
the other side of the house,
though its ceiling is low, houses
Lorraine's drafting board and
some of her supplies. Books are
tucked in the narrow slot between
wall and stairs. The hallway leading to the children's rooms is furnished with a variety of tables and
shelves, on which games and
books are heaped.

Apart from the need for more
and better organized storage, Lorraine and Jerry would like a bigger
bathroom, with good access from
the master bedroom, and a
second-floor laundry.

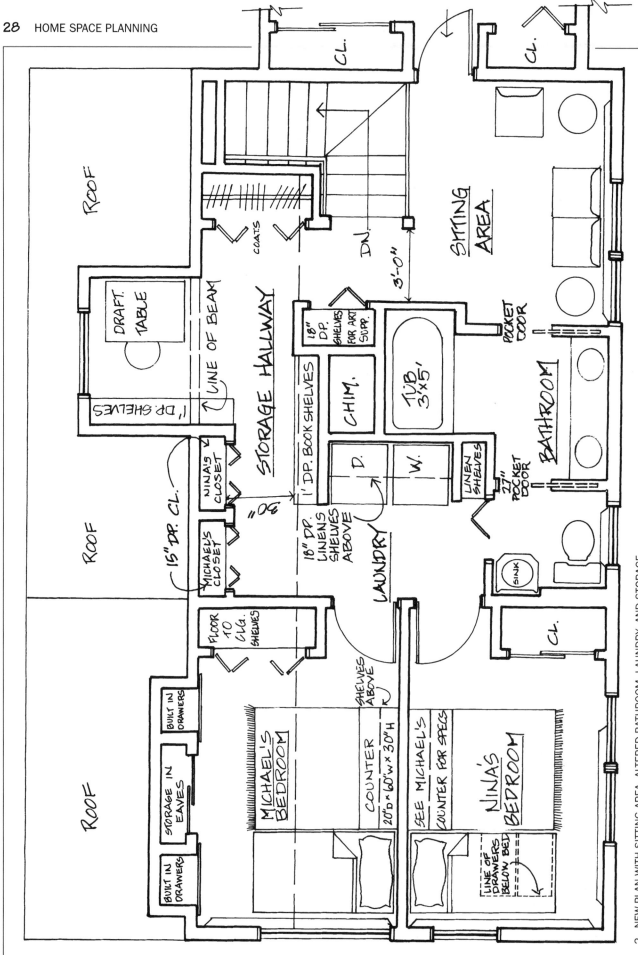

ROOF

ROOF

ROOF

CL.

CL.

DRAFT. TABLE

LINE OF BEAM

1' DP SHELVES

15" DP. CL.

NINA'S CLOSET

MICHAEL'S CLOSET

FLOOR TO CLG. SHELVES

BUILT IN DRAWERS

STORAGE IN EAVES

BUILT IN DRAWERS

MICHAEL'S BEDROOM

COUNTER 20"D × 60"W × 30"H

SHELVES ABOVE

SEE MICHAEL'S COUNTER FOR SPECS

NINA'S BEDROOM

LINE OF DRAWERS BELOW BED

COATS

STORAGE HALLWAY

18" DP. BOOK SHELVES

18" DP. SHELVES FOR ART SUPP.

CHIM.

TUB 3'×5'

D.

W.

LINEN SHELVES

18" DP. LINENS SHELVES ABOVE

LAUNDRY

30"

POCKET DOOR

27" POCKET DOOR

BATHROOM

SINK

CL.

DN.

3'-0"

SITTING AREA

2. NEW PLAN WITH SITTING AREA, ALTERED BATHROOM, LAUNDRY, AND STORAGE

SCALE: ¼" = 1'0"

2 In this plan, every square inch which could be converted to storage space has been used. At the top of the stairs, the open area remains a sitting area for reading or research. Straight ahead of the stairs is a closet for art supplies, while the coat closet which used to be located next to the bathroom has been moved to one end of the storage hallway. This makes it possible to put the washer and dryer in the space formerly used by the coat closet—a good location, since the plumbing is already nearby. There is also space enough here to build some narrow shelves next to the washer. Eighteen-inch-deep shelves for linens can be placed above the appliances.

Also in the storage hallway are a long run of bookshelves and two closets for storage of toys and other personal items, one for Michael and one for Nina. Lorraine's drafting table remains in the dormer, but the construction of shelves improves storage capacity here.

In the children's bedrooms, only one structural change has been made, which is the addition of more storage in the eaves, between Michael's two built-in dressers. The purchase of under-bed drawers for Nina's bed eliminates the need for a dresser in this small room. In both rooms, narrow counters next to the beds do double duty as night tables and as desks or hobby surfaces; shelves installed above provide more room for books.

The bathroom is substantially enlarged, with the addition of a bigger tub and double sinks for the adults. (The existing sink can remain for the use of the children.) Pocket doors are an efficient way to provide access both from the sitting area and between areas of the bathroom, so that the toilet and tub can be used separately.

VIEW OF STORAGE HALLWAY IN PLAN #3

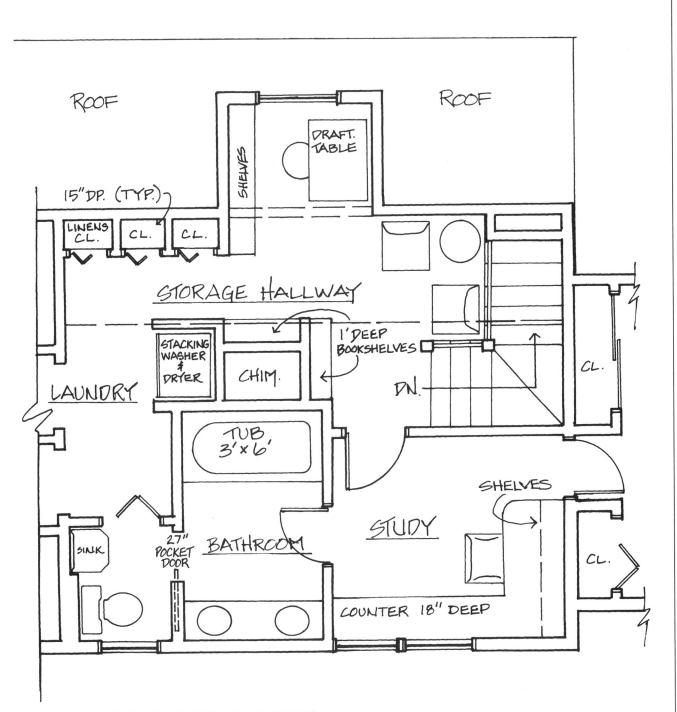

ROOF

ROOF

DRAFT. TABLE

SHELVES

15" DP. (TYP.)

LINENS CL.

CL.

CL.

STORAGE HALLWAY

STACKING WASHER & DRYER

CHIM.

1' DEEP BOOKSHELVES

DN.

CL.

LAUNDRY

TUB 3' × 6'

SHELVES

SINK

27" POCKET DOOR

BATHROOM

STUDY

CL.

COUNTER 18" DEEP

3. NEW PLAN WITH STUDY, ALTERED BATHROOM, AND STORAGE
SCALE: ¼" = 1'0"

3 Here is a variation on Plan #2. The open area is now enclosed and separated from the stairway by a wall and door, so that it can function as a quiet study; there is plenty of space for a big L-shaped work surface and for books. The bathroom is substantially the same as in Plan #2 but with a longer tub. This tub intrudes into some of the space used by the coat closet, so that there is space in this layout for stacking appliances. The sitting area, much reduced, is located at the top of the stairs. Shelves still line the dormer and are installed at the head of the stairs and along the storage hallway. Three hallway closets instead of two are shown in this plan.

Kitchen/Pantry in a 1920s House

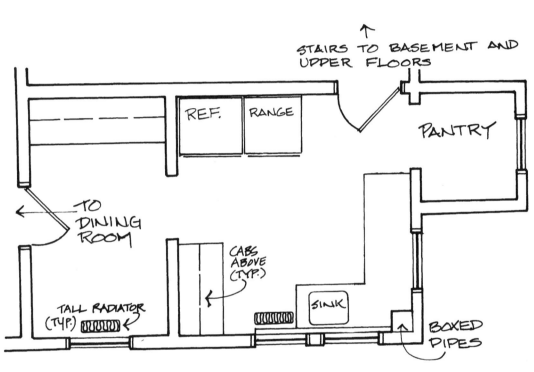

1. EXISTING FLOOR PLAN
SCALE: ¼" = 1'0"

1 This kitchen with its double pantries is located in a spacious, brick, two-family house built in the 1920s. The house as it exists today is essentially unchanged from its original construction, although a half-bath has been added behind the dining room.

As with most houses of this period, the kitchen does not meet current standards. The existing plan shows how refrigerator and range sit next to each other, with no counter space for either. There is no dishwasher, and the radiator next to the sink is 38 inches high, too high to fit below a counter.

The owner wants to make improvements in the kitchen layout without having to build an addition. She wants to install a built-in dishwasher, provide counter space adjacent to fridge and range, and establish an eating area. One of her suggestions is to continue the counter above the radiator—by bumping the counter to a 39- or 40-inch height—so that she has a place to put a stool and drink her morning coffee.

In the floor plan the following labels appear: STAIRS TO BASEMENT AND UPPER FLOORS, REF., RANGE, PANTRY, TO DINING ROOM, CABS ABOVE (TYP.), TALL RADIATOR (TYP.), SINK, BOXED PIPES.

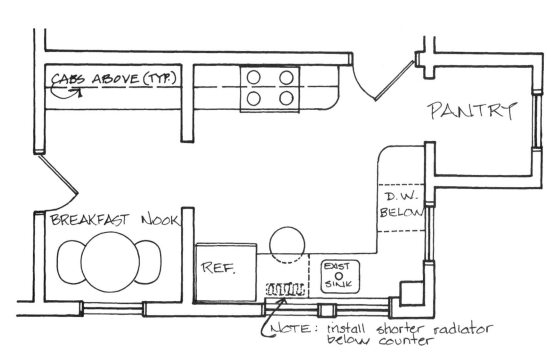

CABS ABOVE (TYP.)

PANTRY

D.W. BELOW

BREAKFAST NOOK

REF.

EXIST SINK

NOTE: install shorter radiator below counter

2. NEW KITCHEN
SCALE: ¼" = 1'0"

2 This is a simple and straight-forward solution to the owner's requirements. The existing 45½-inch-wide cabinets are removed to make space for the fridge. (These cabinets could be relocated in the pantry, though that is not shown on the plan.) A new radiator—short enough to fit below a standard 36-inch-high counter—is installed next to the sink. The sink is left in place, to conserve plumbing costs, and the dishwasher is placed around the corner. Now the wall on which the range was originally located can accommodate both range and cabinets on either side. Finally, the little anteroom can be furnished as a breakfast nook.

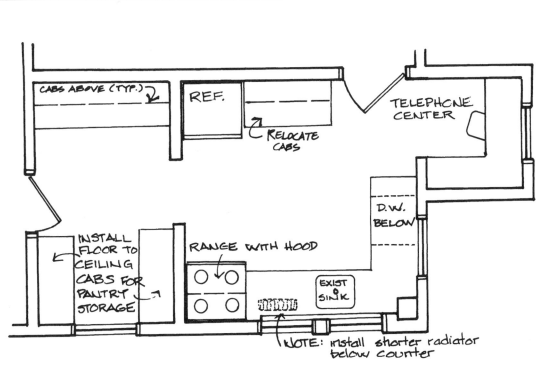

CABS ABOVE (TYP.)

REF.

RELOCATE CABS

TELEPHONE CENTER

D.W. BELOW

INSTALL FLOOR TO CEILING CABS FOR PANTRY STORAGE

RANGE WITH HOOD

EXIST SINK

NOTE: install shorter radiator below counter

3. NEW KITCHEN WITH WORK CENTER
SCALE: ¼″ = 1′0″

3 In a variation on Plan #2, the range is placed on the sink wall, the fridge stays in its original location, and the 45½-inch-wide cabinets are relocated next to the fridge. New pantry cabinets are installed in the ante-room, while the original pantry becomes a tiny home office/work center. One disadvantage to this layout is that the range has counter space on one side only.

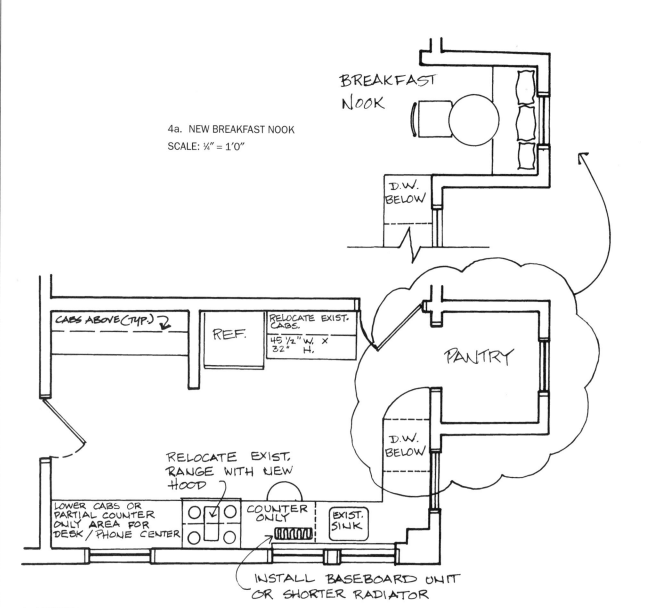

BREAKFAST NOOK

4a. NEW BREAKFAST NOOK
SCALE: ¼″ = 1′0″

D.W. BELOW

CABS ABOVE (TYP.)

REF.

RELOCATE EXIST. CABS.
45 ½″ W. × 32″ H.

PANTRY

D.W. BELOW

RELOCATE EXIST. RANGE WITH NEW HOOD

LOWER CABS OR PARTIAL COUNTER ONLY AREA FOR DESK / PHONE CENTER

COUNTER ONLY

EXIST. SINK

INSTALL BASEBOARD UNIT OR SHORTER RADIATOR

4. NEW KITCHEN
SCALE: ¼″ = 1′0″

4 In this plan, the wall separating kitchen and anteroom has been taken down. This makes counter on both sides of the range possible.

4a This partial plan shows how the pantry space can be converted to a little breakfast nook, with a built-in bench and small round table.

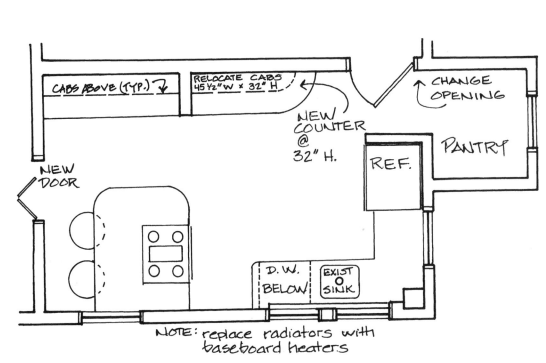

CABS ABOVE (TYP.)

RELOCATE CABS
45½" W × 32" H.

CHANGE OPENING

NEW COUNTER @ 32" H.

PANTRY

REF.

NEW DOOR

D.W. BELOW

EXIST SINK

NOTE: replace radiators with baseboard heaters

5. KITCHEN WITH PENINSULA
SCALE: ¼" = 1'0"

5 This plan also assumes the removal of one of the intervening walls and a shortening of the other, to open up the floor area. The 45½-inch cabinets are relocated. By changing the opening to the pantry, room is provided for the fridge on the window wall. The radiators are removed, and the dishwasher is located next to the sink. A drop-in range is set into a deep peninsula, with sufficient room for stools on the other side. Unlike any of the other plans, this one creates a work triangle which is isolated from traffic to the back door.

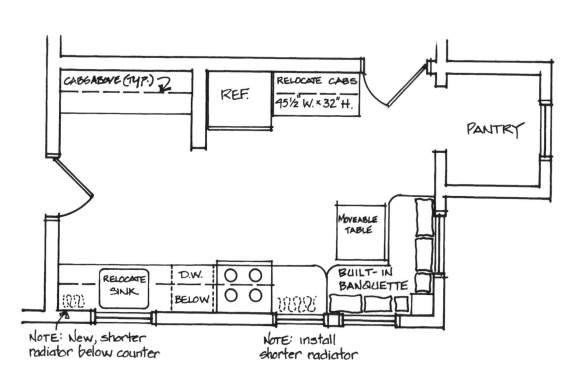

NOTE: New, shorter
radiator below counter

NOTE: install
shorter radiator

6. KITCHEN WITH BUILT-IN BANQUETTE
SCALE: ¼″ = 1′0″

6 In a variation on Plan #4, the sink and dishwasher are located nearer the dining room, and in the corner under the windows is a built-in banquette with table.

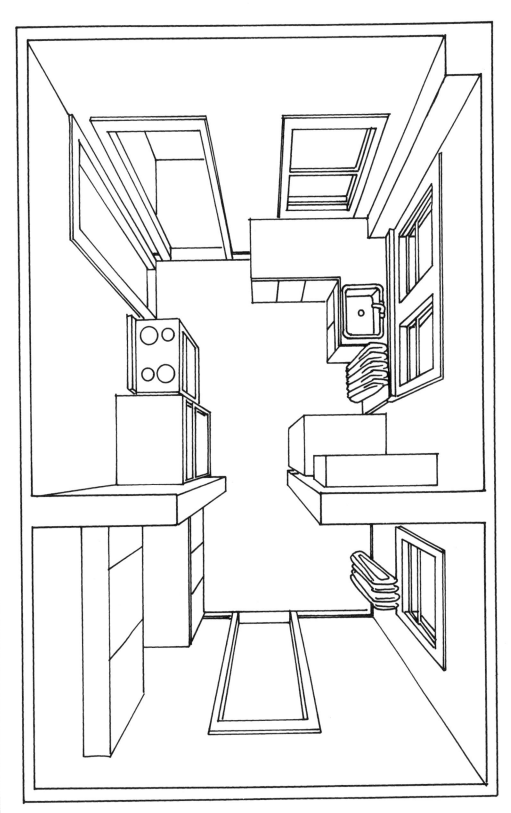

7. BIRD'S-EYE VIEW OF ORIGINAL KITCHEN

7 This bird's-eye view of the original kitchen shows how chopped up and irregular are the placements of appliances and cabinets.

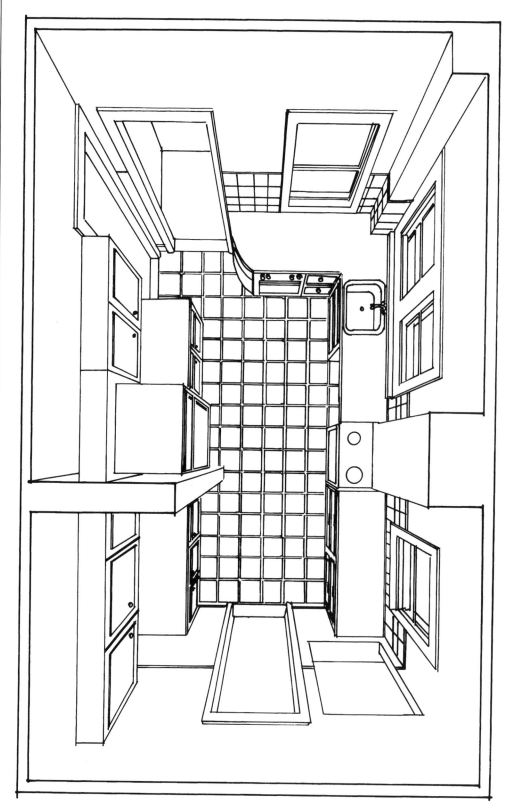

8. BIRD'S-EYE VIEW OF PLAN #4

 Bird's-eye view of Plan #4.

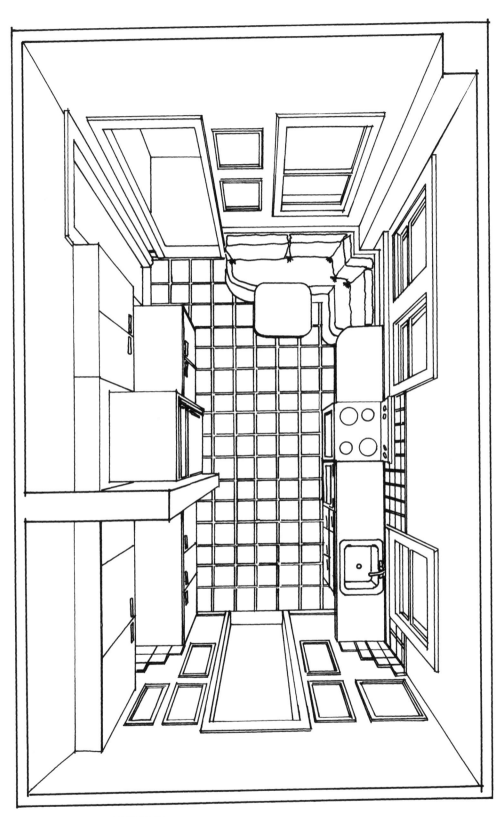

9. BIRD'S-EYE VIEW OF PLAN #6

 Bird's-eye view of Plan #6.

Making a Single-Family from a Two-Family House

T his turn-of-the-century farmhouse was at some point converted from a single-family into a two-family house, with one apartment on the first and the other on the second floor. The owner of the house would like to sell it, but there seem to be no buyers for the house as it is. He has asked the real estate broker to find a designer who will draw plans which show how the house might be reconverted into a single-family house and at the same time correct some of its existing faults, such as a lack of closet space in the bedrooms.

1 This plan shows the existing first-floor apartment. The main entrance is into the living area, which is a narrow room with a dining area at one end. The couple living here have a small child, whose crib has been set up in a narrow space which was once a porch. The kitchen has adequate counter space, but the dishwasher is remote from the sink, and there is a cooktop but no oven. There are also no upper cabinets. The parents' bedroom is awkward to access; one goes either through the kitchen or the bathroom to get in. In addition, it has no closet.

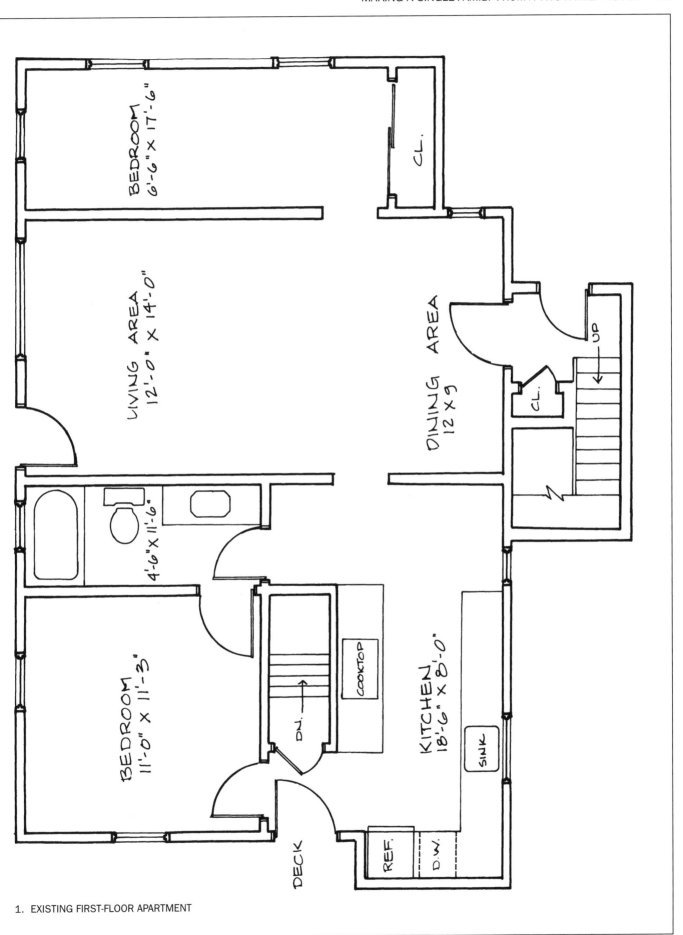

1. EXISTING FIRST-FLOOR APARTMENT

2 The second-floor apartment is accessed by means of a stairway which opens directly to the outside. (These are the only stairs to the second floor.) This stairway comes up into a hallway with two closets, facing the room used as a living room. The glassed "porch" abutting the living room is used as a study. The large kitchen is an eat-in space which also contains the washer and dryer. The bedroom is small, and its closet is located in the hallway.

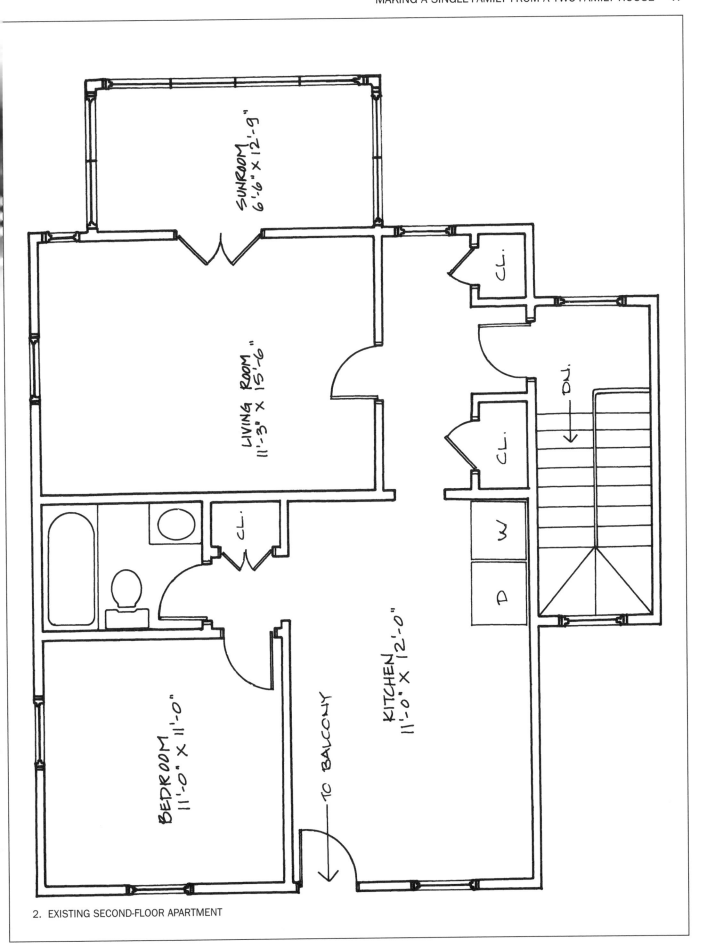

SUNROOM
6'-6" X 12'-9"

CL.

LIVING ROOM
11'-3" X 15'-6"

DN.

CL.

CL.

W

D

BEDROOM
11'-0" X 11'-0"

TO BALCONY

KITCHEN
11'-0" X 12'-0"

2. EXISTING SECOND-FLOOR APARTMENT

3 Here, the main entrance to the house is moved to the staircase entry, so that the door at the back of the living room can be made into a window. This way, traffic does not cross the living room, and furniture is easier to place. The wall between the dining area and kitchen is removed, so that the dining table can be moved over, and new walls are built to separate the kitchen. The appliances are better distributed, with the dishwasher located next to the sink and a range replacing the cooktop; upper cabinets have been installed for additional storage. The first-floor bedroom is now a TV room, and one door can be eliminated in order to contain noise and separate it from the more formal living room. Note that in this redesign, the full bath has been converted to a half-bath; this makes room for more storage. An office is laid out in the "porch" area which was the child's bedroom.

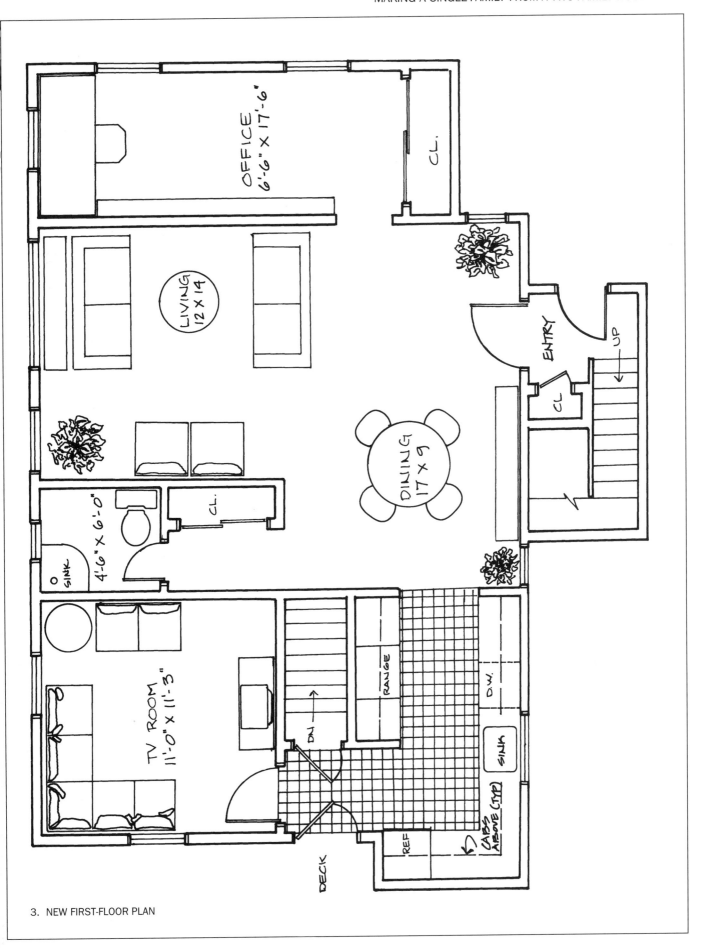

OFFICE
6'-6" × 17'-6"

CL.

LIVING
12 × 14

ENTRY

UP

CL.

DINING
17 × 9

CL.

SINK
4'-0" × 6'-0"

CL.

TV ROOM
11'-0" × 11'-3"

DN

RANGE

D.W.

SINK

REF

(ABS ABOVE (TYP))

DECK

3. NEW FIRST-FLOOR PLAN

4 Once again, the main entry is at the staircase; this time, a little vestibule with coat closet creates a better sense of entry and of transition from outside to inside. The wall separating living area from "porch" is opened up to make a large room for entertaining. The closet on the "porch" is removed and perfectly accommodates an upright piano. The kitchen is reorganized as it is in Plan #3 and also contains a small table, while the back bedroom is used as a formal dining room. The full bath is made into a half-bath, which permits the space to be opened up so that the dining room is open to the living area.

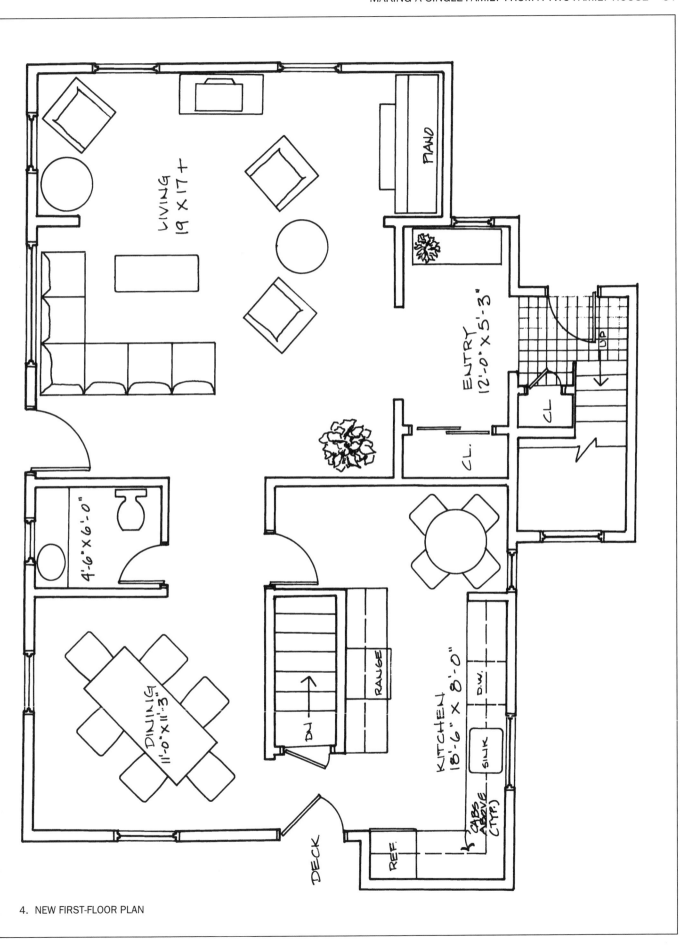

4. NEW FIRST-FLOOR PLAN

5 Perspective view of living room in Plan #4.

5. PERSPECTIVE VIEW OF LIVING ROOM IN PLAN #4

6 This is the more conservative of two redesigns of the second floor. In this plan, the bathroom and laundry are left intact. The living room and study become master bedroom and sitting room with TV. A new wall makes a bedroom out of the previous kitchen; this room has a door to the balcony. Note that all bedrooms have closets and that another closet has been added in the hallway. Though not shown, shelves or cabinets could be installed over the washer and dryer.

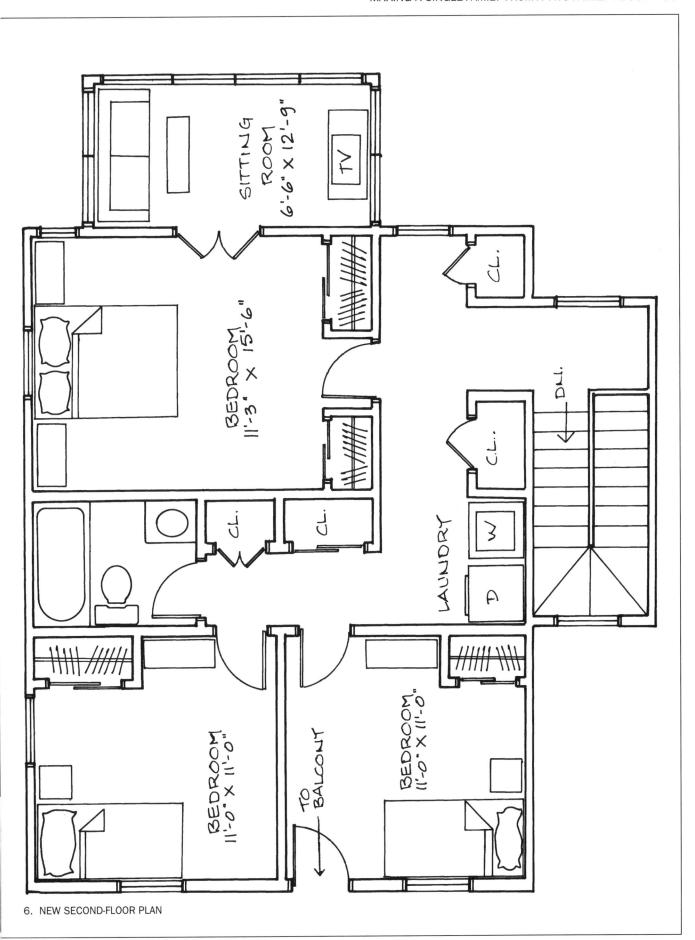

SITTING ROOM 6'-6" × 12'-9"

TV

CL.

DN.

W

D

LAUNDRY

CL.

CL.

BEDROOM 11'-3" × 15'-6"

CL.

CL.

BEDROOM 11'-0" × 11'-0"

TO BALCONY

BEDROOM 11'-0" × 11'-0"

6. NEW SECOND-FLOOR PLAN

7 By making one bedroom smaller, a second bathroom can be installed upstairs. This allows the master bedroom to have its own bathroom and to maintain its size, with sitting room attached. The disadvantage here, of course, is that the third bedroom is very small and does not provide much room for storage or floor space for childrens' play.

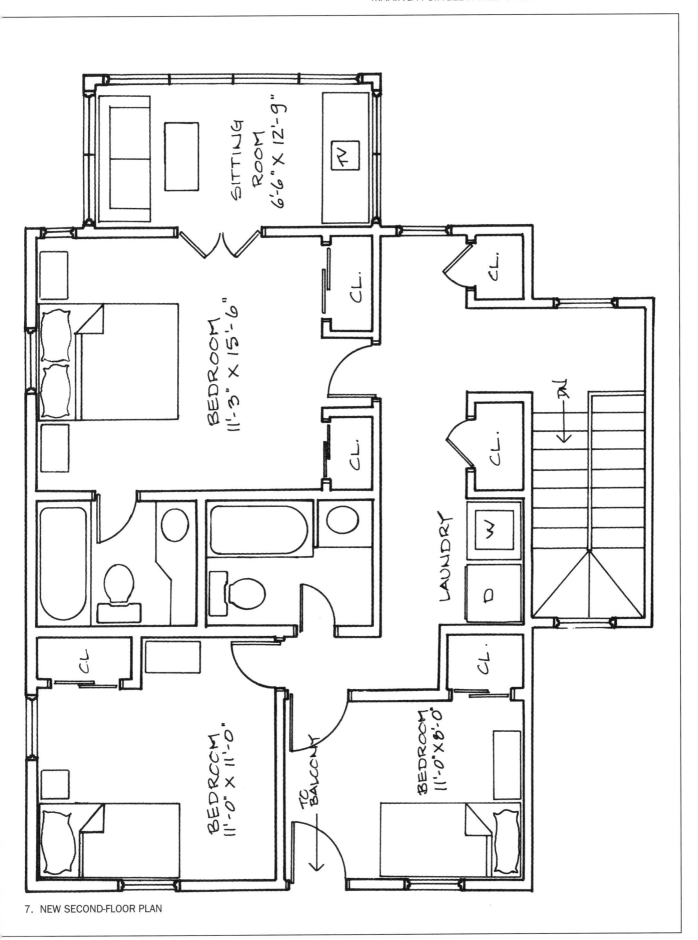

SITTING ROOM 6'-6" X 12'-9"

TV

CL.

CL.

BEDROOM 11'-3" X 15'-6"

CL.

CL.

DN

LAUNDRY

W

D

CL.

CL.

BEDROOM 11'-0" X 11'-0"

TO BALCONY

BEDROOM 11'-0" X 8'-0"

7. NEW SECOND-FLOOR PLAN

8 An alternative layout for the second floor maintains the sizes of the secondary bedrooms. Here, the master bathroom is placed into the "porch," which is large, and the openings of the hall closets are made to face the big bedroom. The two existing hall closets near the stairs could be linen closets.

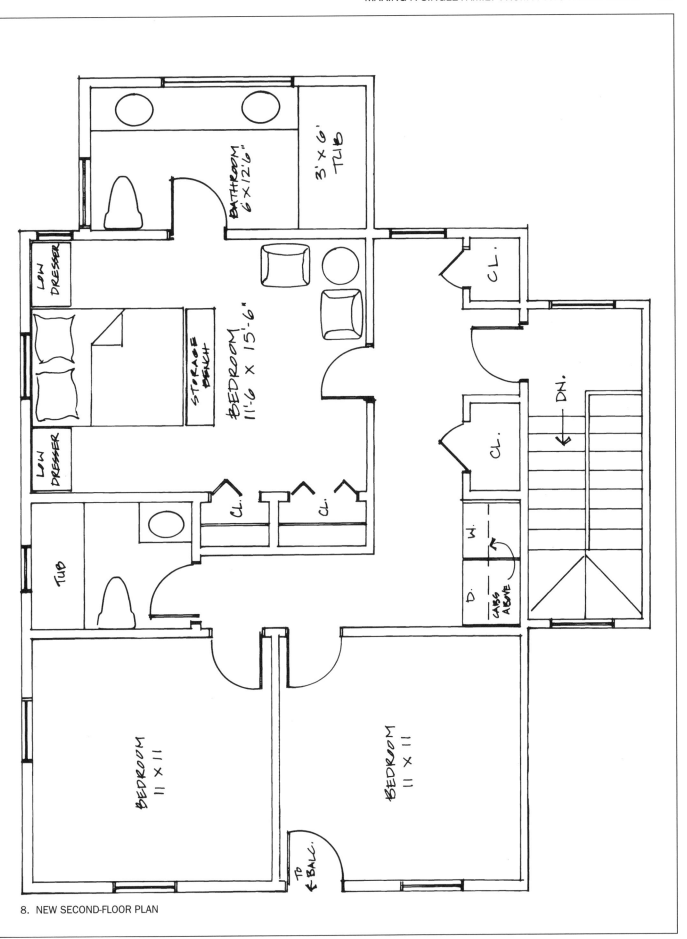

BATHROOM
6' × 12'6"

3' × 6'
TUB

LOW
DRESSER

LOW
DRESSER

BEDROOM
11'6 × 15'6"

STORAGE
BENCH

CL.

CL.

DN.

CL.

CL.

W.

D.

CABS
ABOVE

TUB

BEDROOM
11 × 11

BEDROOM
11 × 11

TO
BALC.

8. NEW SECOND-FLOOR PLAN

A Kitchen for Cooking Classes

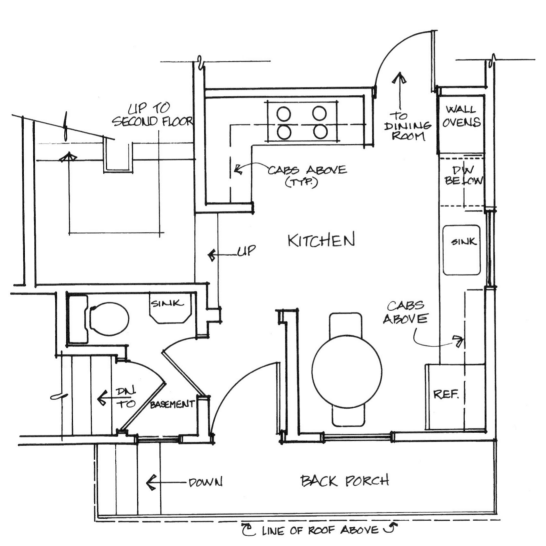

UP TO SECOND FLOOR

TO DINING ROOM

WALL OVENS

D/W BELOW

CABS ABOVE (TYP.)

UP

KITCHEN

SINK

SINK

CABS ABOVE

DN TO BASEMENT

REF.

DOWN

BACK PORCH

LINE OF ROOF ABOVE

1. EXISTING FLOOR PLAN
SCALE: ¼" = 1'0"

1 A colonial house of indeterminate style and age—probably built in the 1950s—still has its original kitchen. One long wall contains most of the appliances: refrigerator, sink, dishwasher, and wall ovens; a shorter wall has the cooktop. The drawbacks to this kitchen from the point of view of most contemporary homeowners is that little space is allocated for "eating in." The number of doors and openings in the space create another problem. With doors into the dining room, basement stairs, bathroom (a later addition), back porch, and stairs going up to the bedrooms, the kitchen becomes a Grand Central Station for the house.

The owner of this house has an unusual requirement for her new kitchen. In addition to an efficient and attractive space, she needs a room in which she can conduct small cooking classes. This

means that both the cooktop and some counter space (where preparation is done) must be visible to a small group. In institutional kitchens, this is accomplished by providing a tilted mirror over the cooktop, but even when this is present, students must cluster around the cooking center to hear the teacher speak.

2 For any redesign of this space, it is necessary to take the cooktop out of its existing location to make room for

observers. In this plan, the back porch is modified to create a new back entrance. A wall projecting into the kitchen is removed to make space for a long peninsula which houses the cooktop. The wall which held the original cooktop is redesigned to accommodate refrigerator and storage cabinets. The sink, dishwasher and wall ovens remain in place. Note that the two steps leading to the landing, which facilitate access to the kitchen from the second floor, could be removed.

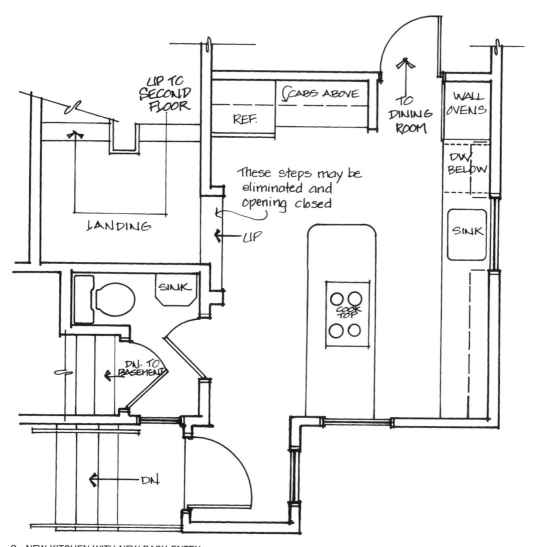

2. NEW KITCHEN WITH NEW BACK ENTRY
SCALE: ¼" = 1'0"

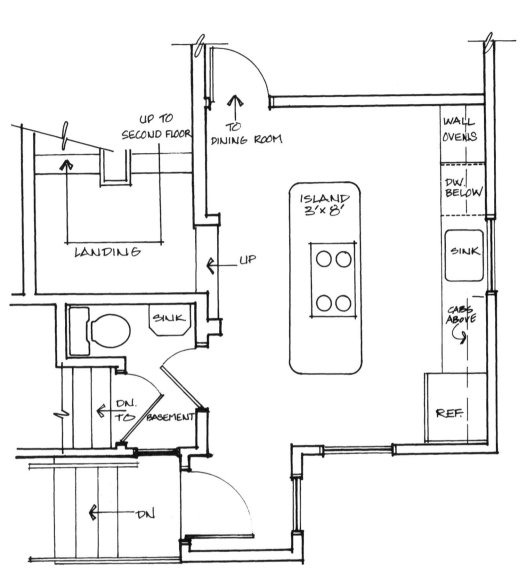

UP TO
SECOND FLOOR

TO
DINING ROOM

LANDING

UP

SINK

DN.
TO BASEMENT

DN

ISLAND
3' x 8'

WALL
OVENS

DW.
BELOW

SINK

CABS
ABOVE

REF.

3. NEW KITCHEN WITH ISLAND
SCALE: ¼" = 1'0"

3 To create this "galley" plan with its large central island, the entrance to the dining room is moved. This has the great advantage of creating a private, "dead-end" kitchen which does not do double duty as a hallway.

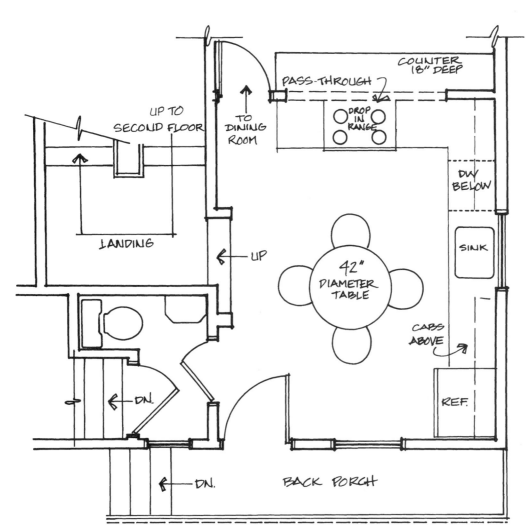

4. NEW KITCHEN WITH PASS-THROUGH
SCALE: ¼" = 1'0"

4 Here is a very different approach to the cooking class problem. The original back porch is unchanged, although the short wall is removed; the entrance to the dining room is moved. The fridge, sink, and dish-washer remain in place. The big structural change to the space is in the partial demolition of the wall which separates dining room and kitchen to create a large pass-through with deep counter which can serve as preparation counter, observation area, and serving counter. This plan permits the kitchen itself to accommodate a table which can be used both for eating and for demonstration and preparation. The disadvantage of this plan, from the point of view of the cooking students, is that movement from kitchen to dining room is slightly awkward. Another disadvantage might be that the cook considers the kitchen too open to the dining area. People have differing opinions on how separate the two rooms should be. Many architects and designers advocate open spaces and enjoy the airy aesthetic created when walls are removed or omitted. They also make assumptions about communal activity in the kitchen or about gatherings and parties in which guests chat with the cook or help with the cooking. Homeowners, on the other hand, sometimes like greater privacy in the kitchen, and they often wish that the mess in the kitchen were not visible in the dining area!

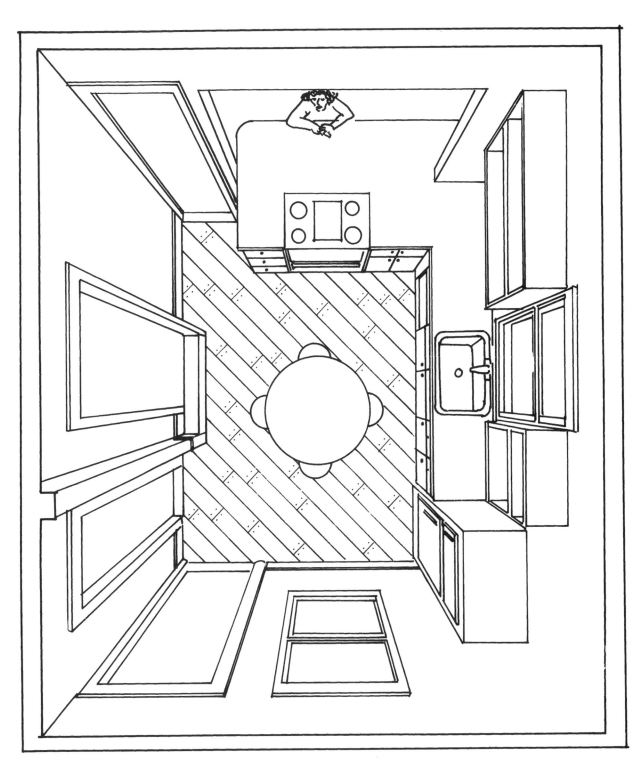

BIRD'S-EYE VIEW OF PLAN #4

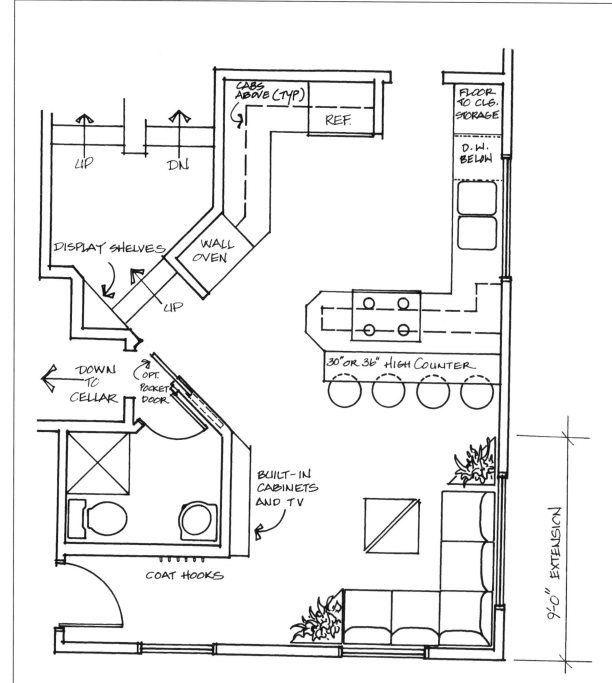

CABS ABOVE (TYP)

REF.

FLOOR TO CLG. STORAGE

D.W. BELOW

UP   DN

DISPLAY SHELVES

WALL OVEN

UP

30" OR 36" HIGH COUNTER

DOWN TO CELLAR

OPT. POCKET DOOR

BUILT-IN CABINETS AND TV

9'-0" EXTENSION

COAT HOOKS

5. NEW KITCHEN WITH ADDITION
SCALE: ¼" = 1'0"

5 If an addition is built at the back of the house, and if money is spent on structural modifications of the interior, exciting changes can be made. In this plan, a tension between rectilinear and diagonal planes creates a dramatic interior space. The room now functions as a cooking class center and as a family room, with sectional and TV in the extension. The bathroom is relocated, and this makes it possible to modify the stairs leading from the kitchen to the landing. The introduction of an angled wall gives new form to the whole space, improves the flow of traffic, and makes the kitchen feel much larger than it really is.

VIEW OF KITCHEN IN PLAN #5

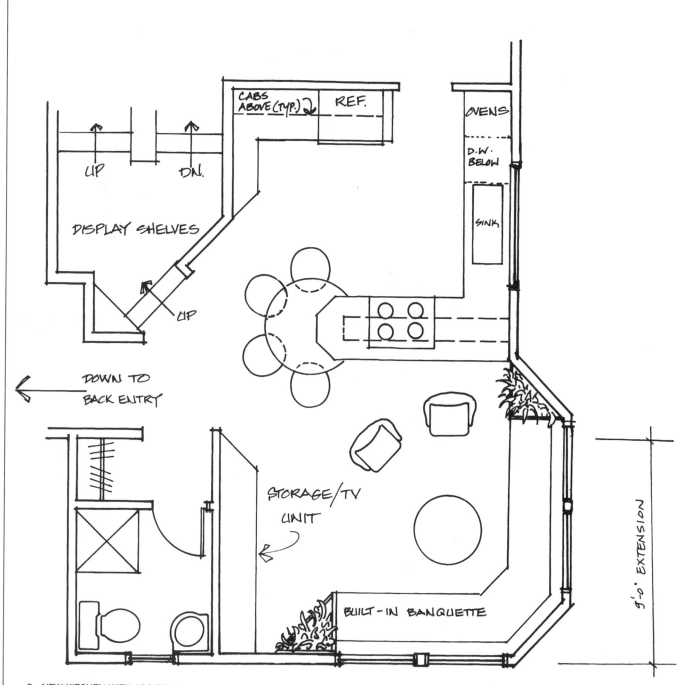

UP

DN.

CABS ABOVE (TYP.)

REF.

OVENS

D.W. BELOW

SINK

DISPLAY SHELVES

UP

DOWN TO BACK ENTRY

STORAGE/TV UNIT

9'-0" EXTENSION

BUILT-IN BANQUETTE

6. NEW KITCHEN WITH ADDITION
SCALE: ¼″ = 1′0″

6 This is a variation on Plan #5. The changes in the kitchen and family room area are relatively minimal. A small table-height extension to the peninsula is a place for informal dining as well as seating for students. More significant, access to the backyard has changed; stairs lead down towards the basement, and halfway down, a backdoor opens directly to the yard. This plan makes the family room space more self-contained.

A Typical Cape
to Be Expanded

The family living in this house is busy and active, with diverse interests. Juan, the father, is a prominent scientist and teacher; his wife Maria is an opera singer and piano teacher. She likes to entertain informally, and her screened porch and garden are important to her. Their two children, Tomas and Juliana, have many toys and books. Juan's mother visits often, and she needs a place to stay.

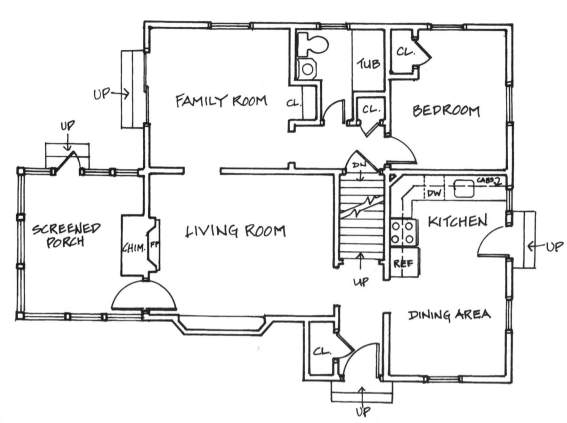

1. EXISTING FIRST FLOOR
SCALE: ⅛" = 1'0"

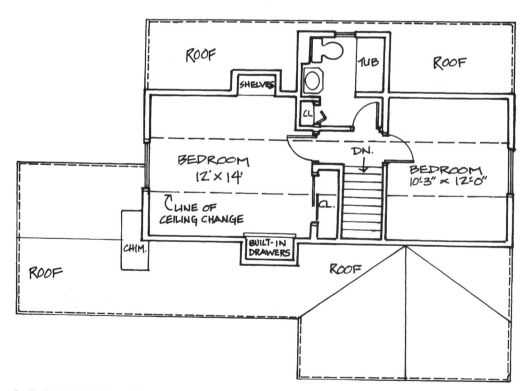

2. EXISTING SECOND FLOOR
SCALE: ⅛" = 1'0"

1 & 2

The house as it exists barely meets this family's needs. On the ground floor, Tomas' room is behind the kitchen. The living room is somewhat too small; the family room has a fold-out couch for visitors. On the second floor there are two bedrooms and one bathroom; bedrooms have inadequate storage space. Maria says that the family "lives" on the porch in summer, but its distance from the kitchen is inconvenient.

Maria would like a larger dining room which is separate from the kitchen, so that kitchen mess need not be visible to guests. She would like space for a baby grand piano on which she can teach; Juan would like room for a home office with computer. These two spaces could be combined. She would like three bedrooms—but not necessarily a second bathroom—on the upper floor. Storage space should be improved.

Maria's idea was that a full, two-story addition be put onto the back of the house, encompassing its entire width. The rather complicated roof structure—with shed dormer at the back and gable end extension in front—make this solution somewhat awkward. Such an addition would also create interior bathroom spaces, which is undesirable.

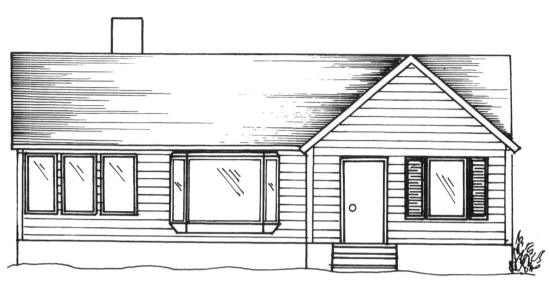

3. EXISTING FRONT ELEVATION

SCALE: ⅛″ = 1′0″

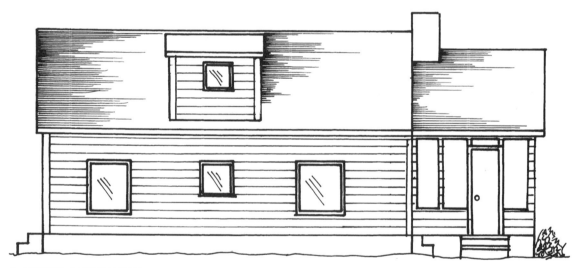

4. EXISTING BACK ELEVATION

SCALE: ⅛″ = 1′0″

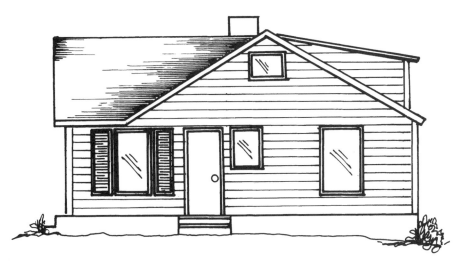

5. EXISTING SIDE ELEVATION (KITCHEN DOOR)
SCALE: ⅛″ = 1′0″

6. SIDE ELEVATION (FAMILY ROOM)
SCALE: ⅛″ = 1′0″

3-6

These drawings show the elevations of this house.

7. AXONOMETRIC VIEW OF FRONT AND PORCH SIDE OF HOUSE

7 This drawing shows an axonometric view of the front and porch side of the house.

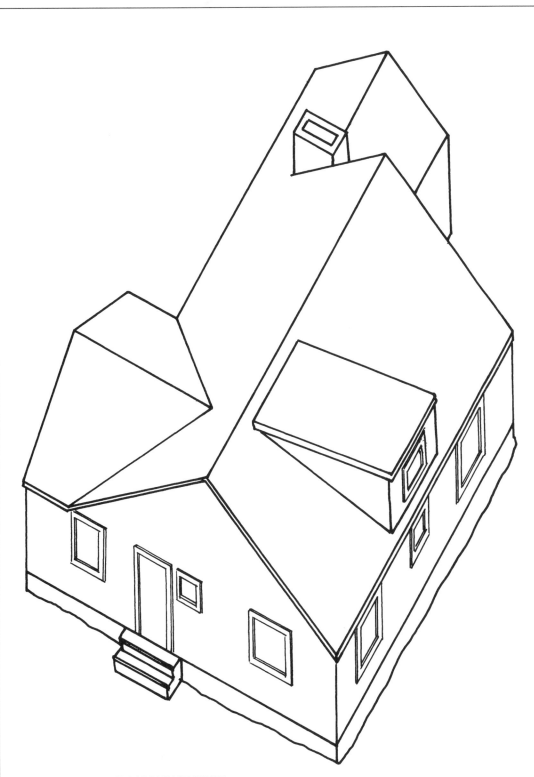

8. AXONOMETRIC VIEW OF BACK OF HOUSE

8 This drawing shows an axo-nometric view of the back of the house, with the shed dormer housing the second-story bathroom.

PERSPECTIVE VIEW OF LIVING ROOM SHOWN IN PLAN #9

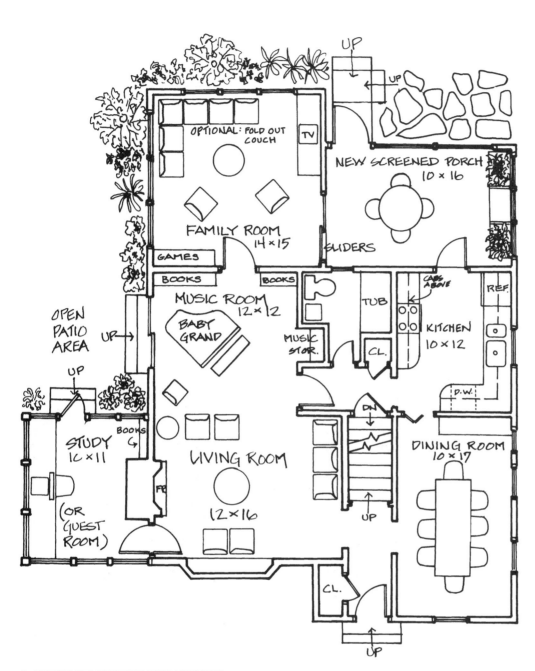

OPTIONAL: FOLD OUT COUCH

TV

NEW SCREENED PORCH
10 × 16

FAMILY ROOM
14 × 15

GAMES

BOOKS

SLIDERS

BOOKS

MUSIC ROOM
12 × 12

BABY GRAND

MUSIC STOR.

TUB

CABS ABOVE

KITCHEN
10 × 12

REF

CL.

OPEN PATIO AREA

UP

UP

BOOKS

STUDY
12 × 11

(OR GUEST ROOM)

FP

LIVING ROOM
12 × 16

DN

UP

DINING ROOM
10 × 17

D.W.

CL.

UP

UP   UP

9. FIRST-FLOOR REDESIGN WITH ADDITIONS
SCALE: ⅛″ = 1′0″

9 This is an extensive first-floor redesign which involves many changes to the house. First, the dining room is enlarged because the kitchen is moved into the room behind it (the bedroom). This also allows the kitchen to be planned more efficiently, with better placement for the appliances and with generous counter space. There are several possibilities for the kitchen layout, but since the space is only 10 feet wide, the cabinets should line the walls. The wall which separated the living and family rooms has been removed, in order to make a large room which could be furnished as a big living room for entertaining large crowds or, as here, made into a combined living and music room. This arrangement is a good one if the piano is an integral part of family life and entertaining, or if Maria wants to give student recitals.

A new family room has been added onto the back of the house, along with a big screened porch which is conveniently located between kitchen and garden. With the new porch in place, the origi-nal screened porch could be glassed in and provided with heat and would then be a pleasant study or even guest room.

PERSPECTIVE VIEW OF KITCHEN SHOWN IN PLAN #9

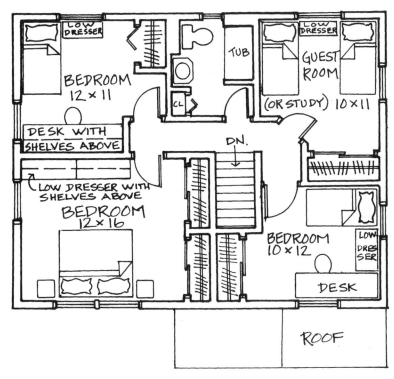

LOW DRESSER

BEDROOM
12 × 11

DESK WITH
SHELVES ABOVE

TUB

CL

DN.

LOW DRESSER WITH
SHELVES ABOVE

BEDROOM
12 × 16

LOW DRESSER

GUEST
ROOM

(OR STUDY) 10 × 11

BEDROOM
10 × 12

LOW
DRES
SER

DESK

ROOF

10. SECOND-FLOOR REDESIGN
SCALE: ⅛″ = 1′0″

10 On the second floor, the roof has been removed and the house turned from a Cape into a colonial. There is a large variety of possible floor plans. In this one, the single bathroom remains intact; four bedrooms of varying sizes, all with good closet space, are provided.

One approach to the redesigns shown in Plans #9 and #10 is to expand the house in stages. First, the roof could be raised and a full second story created. Next, the existing first floor could be reorganized. Following that, the first-floor additions at the back could be built.

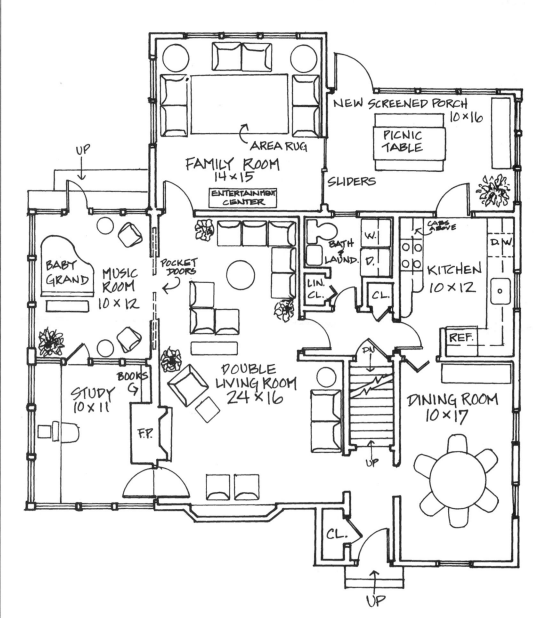

NEW SCREENED PORCH 10×16

PICNIC TABLE

SLIDERS

AREA RUG

FAMILY ROOM 14×15

ENTERTAINMENT CENTER

UP

BABY GRAND

MUSIC ROOM 10×12

POCKET DOORS

BATH & LAUND.

W.

D.

CABS ABOVE

D.W.

KITCHEN 10×12

LIN. CL.

CL.

REF.

BOOKS

STUDY 10×11

F.P.

DOUBLE LIVING ROOM 24×16

DN

UP

DINING ROOM 10×17

CL.

UP

11. ALTERNATE FIRST-FLOOR PLAN WITH ADDITION
SCALE: ⅛″ = 1′0″

11 This plan shows alternative ways of furnishing the spaces already shown in Plan #9. The kitchen is laid out a little differently. The most significant change, however, is the enlargement of the newly glassed-in porch to include space for the piano. If the sliders which were in the origi-nal family room (now the enlarged living room) are replaced with pocket doors, the music room can be opened up to the living space, creating a nice environment for entertaining or recitals.

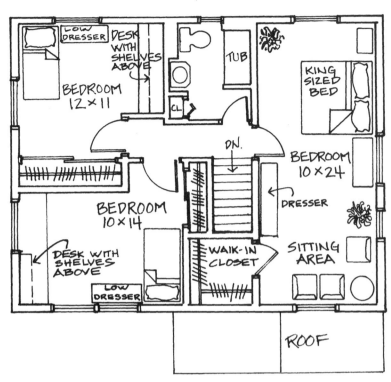

12. SECOND-FLOOR REDESIGN WITH THREE BEDROOMS
SCALE: ⅛″ = 1′0″

12 In this second-story plan, the single bathroom remains, but only three bedrooms are shown. This makes it possible to make a large master bedroom with walk-in closet and sitting area.

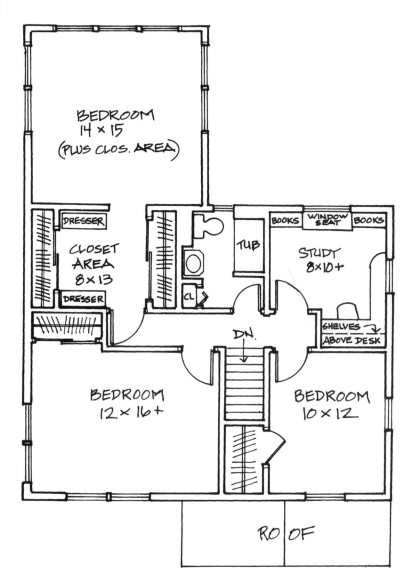

13. SECOND-FLOOR PLAN WITH ADDITION
SCALE: ⅛″ = 1′0″

13 Plan #13 represents a substantial enlargement of the second floor, since a second story is now built over the new family room on the first floor. Once again, only the existing bathroom is shown; however, with this extra expansion of the second story space, a large master with extensive closet storage can be provided, as well as a second bedroom which is 12′ × 16′ and two more bedrooms.

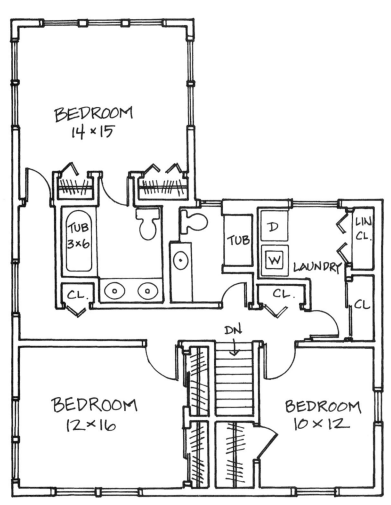

BEDROOM
14 × 15

TUB
3×6

CL.

TUB

D

W

LAUNDRY

LIN
CL.

CL

CL.

DN

BEDROOM
12×16

BEDROOM
10 × 12

14. SECOND-FLOOR PLAN WITH MASTER BEDROOM SUITE
SCALE: ⅛″ = 1′0″

14 Here, the expanded space shown in Plan #13 is utilized somewhat differently. The master bedroom now has its own large bathroom; there are, in addition, two bedrooms with good closet space, the original bathroom, and a laundry room with plenty of storage.

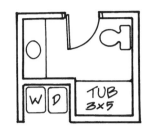

15A. ALTERNATIVE LAYOUT FOR MASTER
BATHROOM

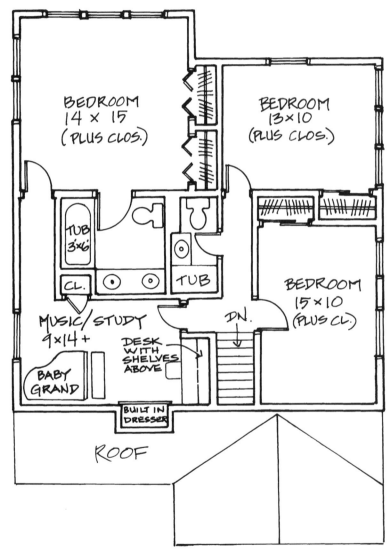

15. SECOND-FLOOR PLAN WITH ADDITION AND MASTER SUITE
SCALE: ⅛″ = 1′0″

15 In yet another expansion of the second story, both the family room and screened porch below have been enlarged to two stories. The master bedroom has a private bath and big closets. Two more bedrooms are good-sized rooms with adequate storage. Another room can be used as a study or combination study/music room (though getting the piano upstairs would not be easy!). Note that the original bathroom has been made smaller in order to accommodate a hallway to the back bedroom. This could, of course, be altered by changing the configuration and size of the master bedroom.

15a In this alternate layout for the master bathroom, the room is made slightly smaller, so that an alcove can be created for the washer and dryer; these appliances face into the music/study room.

16. FRONT ELEVATION BASED ON PLAN #9
SCALE: ⅛″ = 1′0″

17. BACK ELEVATION BASED ON PLAN #9
SCALE: ⅛″ = 1′0″

16 & 17
These drawings show the back
and front elevations of the house
as they would look if redesigned
according to Plans #9 and #10.

PERSPECTIVE OF REAR OF HOUSE BASED ON PLAN #11

Colonial Townhouse

1 This four-story Georgian-style rowhouse was probably built in about 1820, although the simplicity of its style and materials is like that of houses built fifty years earlier in many eastern cities. Sandwiched between others of similar type, its layout suffers from the constraints imposed by its narrow lot. It is only two rooms deep on each floor, so there is little space for either adequate storage or for some of the desired features of modern life, such as additional bathrooms. The interior finishes are plain but attractive and versatile, with the brick of the party walls exposed, the old wooden floors refinished and gleaming, and, in some cases, later ceiling additions removed to reveal the beams above.

The first floor shown here has a number of problems. One enters directly into the living room; there is no vestibule, no transition space, and no coat closet. In addition, the half-bath which was obviously added at some point in the history of the house opens directly into the living room.

The kitchen layout has many flaws. Most important, the range

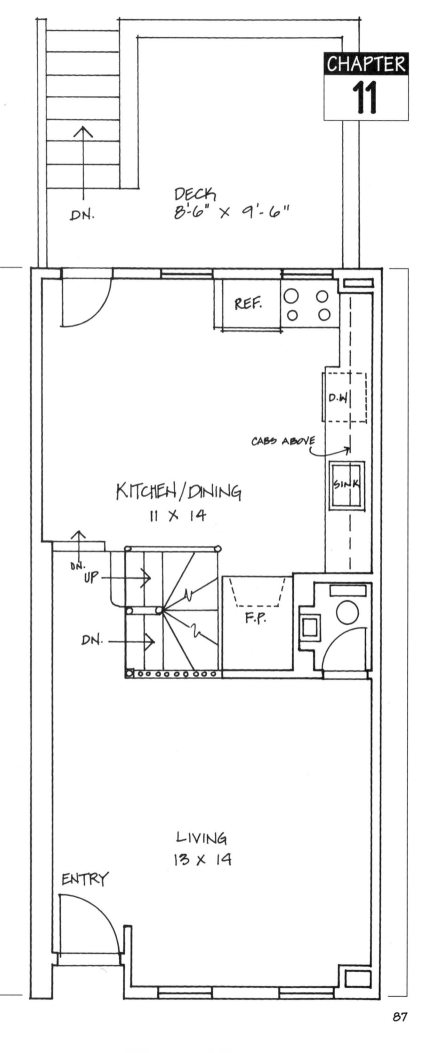

1. EXISTING FIRST-FLOOR PLAN
SCALE: ¼″ = 1′0″

is shoved directly under a window, which creates a potential fire hazard, makes opening the window a risky venture, and means that cooking grease must be cleaned off the window. Secondly, in order to open the oven door, the countertop and cabinetry had to be notched. The three major appliances—refrigerator, stove, and dishwasher—are crowded together so that there is a serious bottleneck at that end of the kitchen. The location of the range precludes installing a useful lazy Susan cabinet in the corner, and there is a shortage of counter space. Ideally, there should be a minimum of 15 to 18 inches of counter beside the refrigerator for unloading, counter on both sides of the range, and the range, if located near a corner, should be positioned with a minimum of 12

inches of counter between it and the corner.

The owner of this house, a professional single woman, would like to correct these flaws in the layout while preserving the kitchen as an eat-in space. No matter what the solution, she would like to leave the fireplace intact and visible.

2 In this kitchen rehab, the problems in the existing kitchen are solved without great expense. An important part of keeping costs down here is leaving the plumbing relatively intact; in order to accommodate the refrigerator in its new location, as well as counter for unloading, the sink and dishwasher are moved slightly. In the center of the room is an island, which can accommodate either a range (slide-in or

drop-in type) or a cooktop. If a cooktop is set into the island, an under-counter oven can be located either below the cooktop or under the counter near the dishwasher on the window wall. There is plenty of counter space throughout the kitchen, and a breakfast counter is installed near the windows with a view of the deck and backyard. The disadvantage to this layout is that there is no dining table. In this situation, it might be possible to make the front (living) room of the house into an all-purpose room furnished with comfortable seating and with a gateleg or other folding table tucked against a wall which could be pulled out for meals.

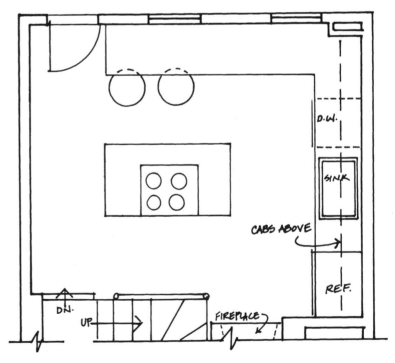

2. NEW KITCHEN
SCALE: ¼" = 1'0"

3 This is a variation on the first layout. The sink and dishwasher have been moved farther along the wall in order to accommodate not only the fridge but also the wall ovens. The cooking center is now a peninsula—larger than the island—which is deep enough to provide a counter for eating and long enough to seat four.

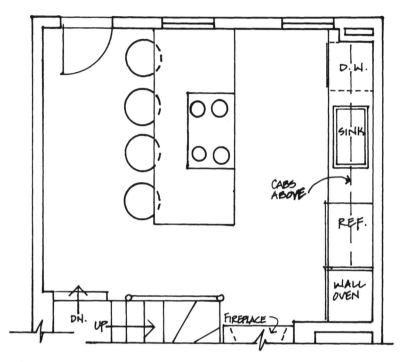

3. NEW KITCHEN
SCALE: ¼″ = 1′0″

VIEW OF KITCHEN IN PLAN #2

VIEW OF KITCHEN IN PLAN #3

4 In a slight variation on Plan #3, the peninsula has become an island; in addition, a wall of 9-inch-deep, floor-to-ceiling shelves is installed on the wall opposite the kitchen.

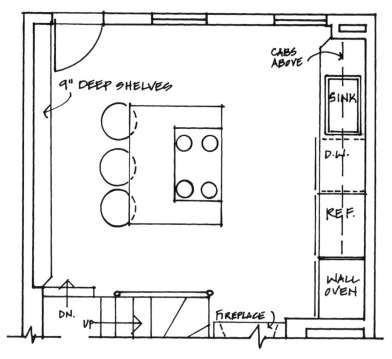

9" DEEP SHELVES

CABS ABOVE

SINK

D.W.

REF.

WALL OVEN

DN.

UP

FIREPLACE

4. NEW KITCHEN
SCALE: ¼″ = 1′0″

5 This L-shaped plan provides lots of counter space, a good layout for the appliances, and space for a small table. Some additional expense is involved in relocating the plumbing onto the exterior wall.

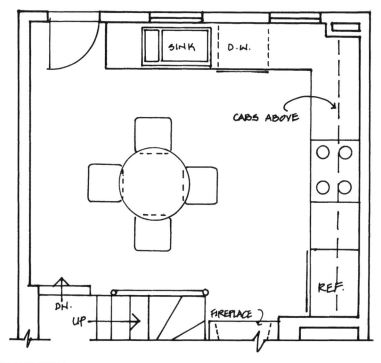

SINK

D.W.

CABS ABOVE

REF.

DN.

UP

FIREPLACE

5. NEW KITCHEN
SCALE: ¼" = 1'0"

VIEW OF KITCHEN IN PLAN #5

6 In this galley plan, there is the possibility for solving another problem: the opening of the existing bathroom into the living room. Here, by moving the toilet to the opposite bathroom wall, the opening can be moved into the kitchen. Behind the refrigerator there is a floor-to-ceiling gypsum board wall which partially hides the entry to the bathroom; if desired, the wall could be extended behind the cooktop as well. This would create a hallway to the bathroom but would cut off the view of the fireplace. This plan shows a hood mounted above the cooktop, but a down-draft cooktop could be installed instead. Most of the storage here is in lower cabinets, which has some disadvantages.

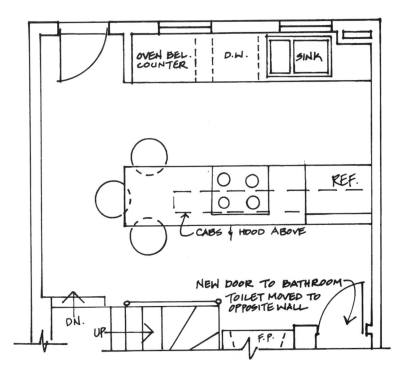

6. NEW KITCHEN
SCALE: ¼″ = 1′0″

7 Another L-shaped layout leaves the sink and fridge in their original locations but moves the dishwasher and range. The table, placed as it is against the wall, could extend if necessary. In a variation on Plan #7, the door to the deck is moved—not too expensive if it is located where there is an existing window. By filling in the original door, wall space is obtained for a much-needed coat closet!

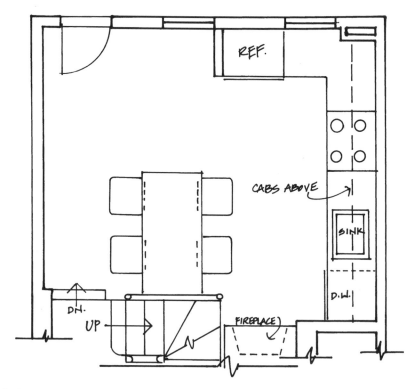

7. NEW KITCHEN
SCALE: ¼″ = 1′0″

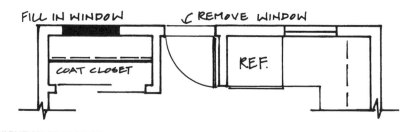

VARIATION ON PLAN #7
SCALE: ¼″ = 1′0″

8 Again, the door to the deck is relocated, but in its place a window is installed. Here, two walls are used for floor-to-ceiling storage cabinets.

9 This variation on Plan #8 leaves the door in its new location. This time, the corner space created by moving the door is used for a table and built-in banquette. This has the advantage of placing the table near the window, for natural light and perhaps a view, rather than in the interior of the kitchen. The appliances are somewhat altered: there is a peninsula with cooktop and either wall ovens or under-counter oven next to the sink.

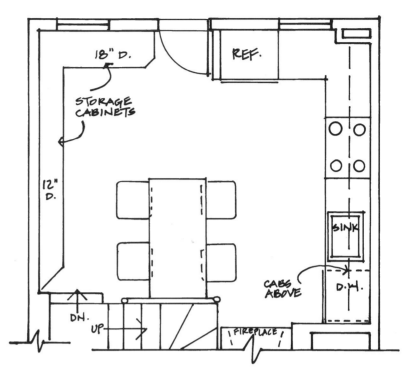

8. NEW KITCHEN
SCALE: ¼″ = 1′0″

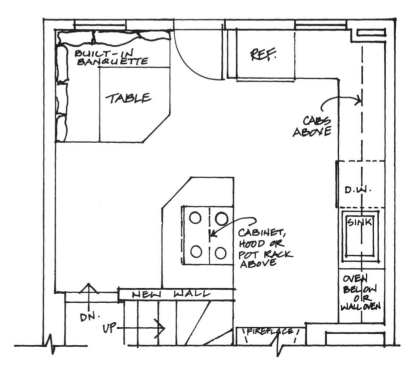

9. NEW KITCHEN
SCALE: ¼″ = 1′0″

VIEW OF KITCHEN IN PLAN #8

10 What happens if the door is moved to the opposite side of the kitchen? This creates new opportunities for cabinet and appliance layout. In this plan, the appliances are spread out and occupy both sides of the space; this, unfortunately, makes movement from one appliance to another somewhat difficult, because the table is in the way.

11 One solution to the problems in Plan #10 would be to place the table differently, so that it interrupts traffic flow less.

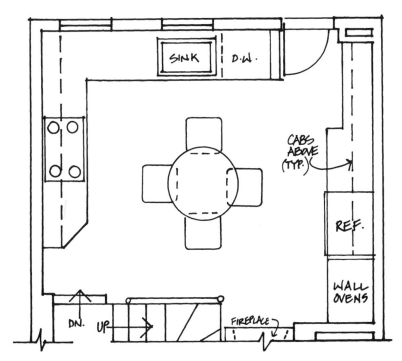

10. NEW KITCHEN
SCALE: ¼″ = 1′0″

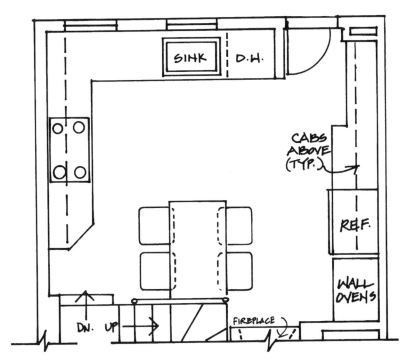

11. NEW KITCHEN
SCALE: ¼″ = 1′0″

12 Another solution to the traffic flow problems in Plan #10 is to change the arrangement of the appliances and to make one wall serve as a storage center.

13 In a variation on Plan #12, cabinetry is eliminated and a larger table accommodated.

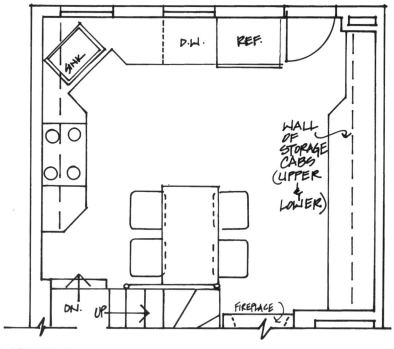

12. NEW KITCHEN
SCALE: ¼" = 1'0"

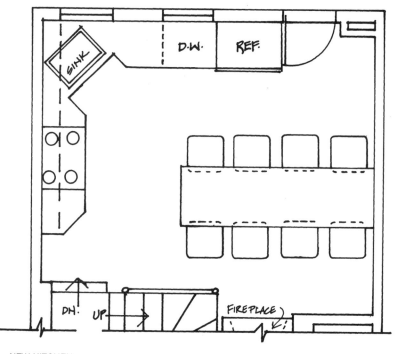

13. NEW KITCHEN
SCALE: ¼" = 1'0"

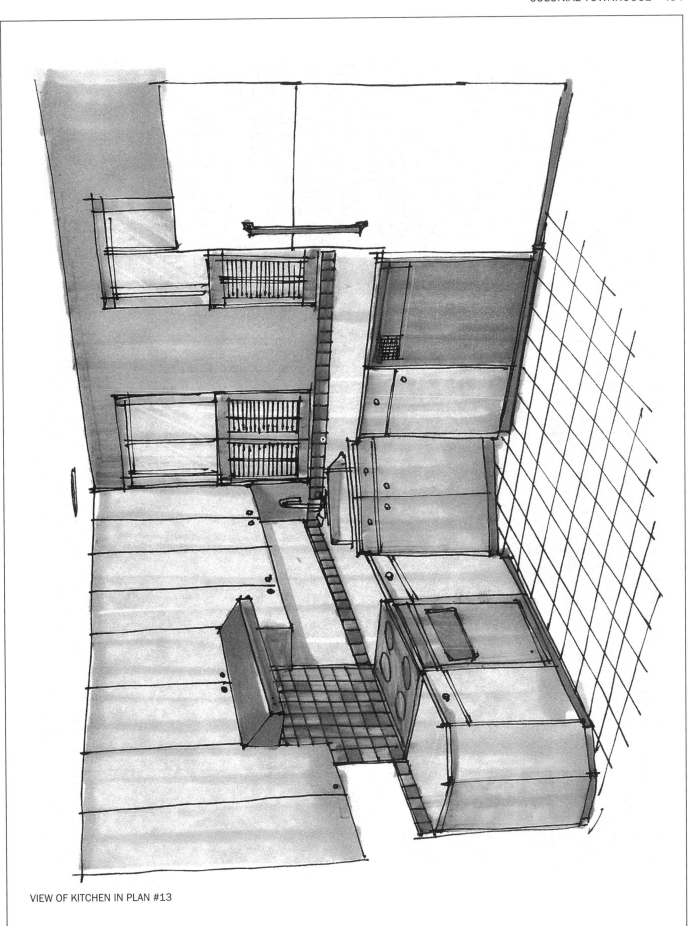

VIEW OF KITCHEN IN PLAN #13

14 Another variation on Plan #12 confines all appliances to two walls but extends the cabinets along the lefthand wall. The bathroom is removed to permit new access to the kitchen.

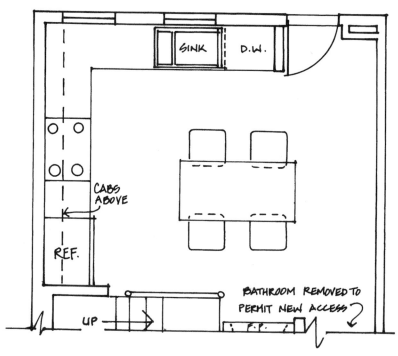

14. NEW KITCHEN
SCALE: ¼″ = 1′0″

15 Here is the first plan which incorporates the deck into the design. In this one, the kitchen remains in its original location and the deck area becomes a glass-walled dining area.

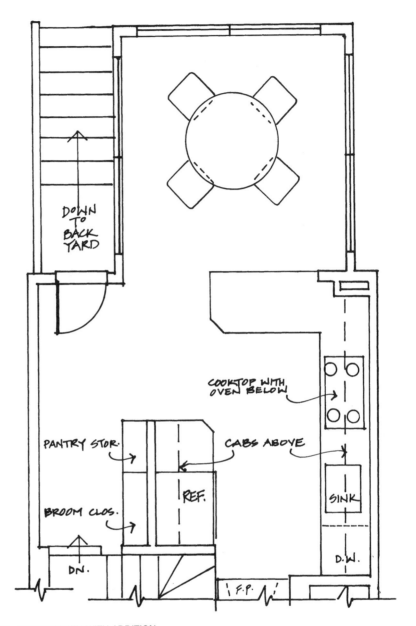

15. NEW KITCHEN WITH ADDITION

SCALE: ¼" = 1'0"

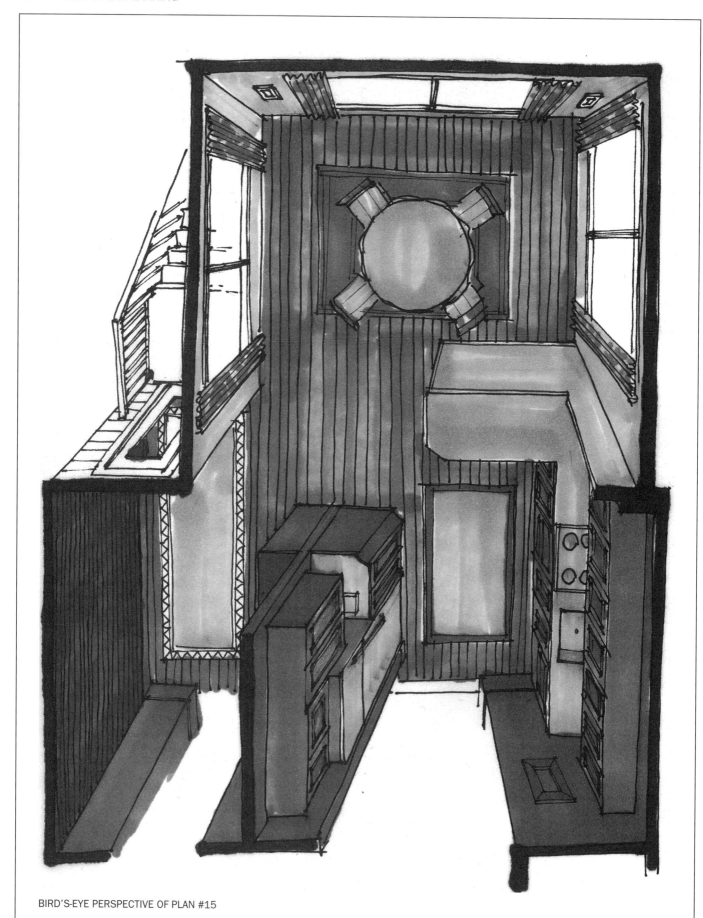

BIRD'S-EYE PERSPECTIVE OF PLAN #15

16 In another plan that encloses the deck, it is the kitchen which is located at the back, overlooking the backyard. Although this deprives the diners of their view and of natural light, it does permit the dining room to take a larger share of the space and is the best solution for providing the house with a formal dining room of acceptable size.

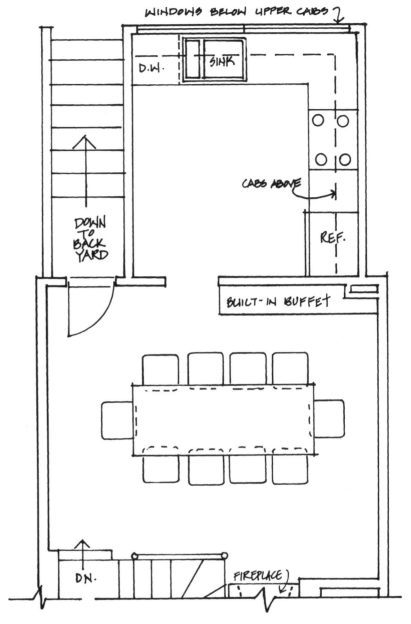

16. NEW KITCHEN WITH ADDITION
SCALE: ¼″ = 1′0″

PERSPECTIVE OF PLAN #16

Gable-Front Greek Revival House

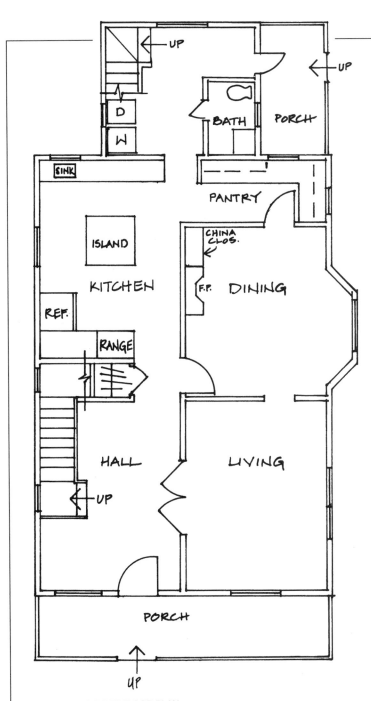

1. EXISTING FIRST-FLOOR PLAN
SCALE: ⅛″ = 1′0″

1 & 2

This two-story gable-front house was built in the early part of the twentieth century but was patterned after the Greek Revival houses of the mid-nineteenth century. It is one of a type whose form was widespread throughout the Northeast and the Midwest and was imitated to a lesser extent elsewhere in the country. In this example, the front door opens into a large hall with French doors into the living room. The stairs are attractive, with highly detailed balusters and railing, and are enhanced by leaded glass windows on both landings. The interior finishes in the dining room are also somewhat elaborate; there is ash wainscoting, a built-in china closet with leaded glass doors, glazed, colored tiles surrounding the fireplace, and a built-in decorative mirror above the mantle. The rest of the house is relatively plain, particularly the kitchen and the second floor.

The original kitchen contained a large porcelain sink, located where the sink is shown on the plan, a freestanding range and refrigerator, and no cabinets, since there was a long pantry for storage. The probability is that a large table in the center of the kitchen provided a surface for food preparation.

When this house was sold in 1980 to its third set of owners, a few cabinets had been added to the kitchen, as well as an enormous island made of plywood. The previous owners had installed a half-bath in the back hallway, with walls also constructed of plywood. The new owners know that they will be living in the house for five or six years, after which they plan to put it on the market and move further east. They therefore decide to renovate the house with its resale in mind. This renovation needs to be done inexpensively and efficiently. In addition, they feel they should preserve the pretty front hall and stairs and the detailed woodwork in the dining room.

The new owners' wish list includes making the kitchen layout more effective and attractive. The work triangle, consisting of movement between refrigerator, sink, and range, is seriously compromised by the presence of the big island, whose scale is too large for the overall size of the room. The fridge is too close to the range, so that when one person is cooking, another has difficulty getting the fridge door open! Also on the first floor, the half-bath has been placed in such a way that the path out the backdoor into the yard is awkward and less direct than it should be. On the second floor, the owners would like to have a master bedroom/bathroom suite, which means adding another, private, bathroom.

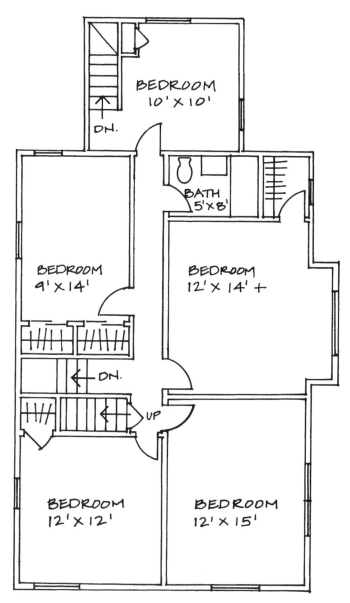

2. EXISTING SECOND-FLOOR PLAN
SCALE: ⅛" = 1'0"

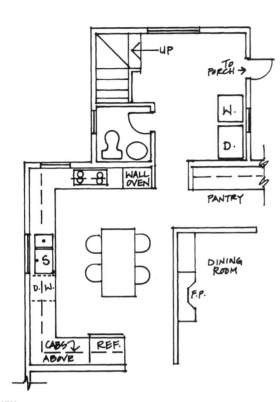

3. NEW KITCHEN
SCALE: ⅛″ = 1′0″

3 In this plan, the areas surrounding the kitchen—pantry, back hall, and dining room—remain intact, although the half-bath and laundry area have exchanged places. This alteration to the back hall makes the route through the backdoor to the yard more direct and more comfortable. Note that the washer and dryer could be enclosed by a closet, which would give a more finished look to the back hall but would eliminate the light coming from the window above the appliances. There is still plenty of room in this back hall to install a coat closet or hooks, if the area functions like a mud room.

The kitchen layout is very simple and is one of the least expensive modifications possible. The appliances have been located partly with an eye to the view into the kitchen. Since the kitchen can be seen from the front door of the house, its look is important. It is true that a door could be installed at the entrance to the kitchen; however, the reality is that it would surely be open most of the time. Thus, the refrigerator has been placed so that it is hidden from view. It could have a return wall built on the doorway side to give it a more finished look. Because most traffic moves directly from the fridge to the sink, the sink has been moved to the window on the long wall. The cooking center, which in this case is made up of a cooktop and wall ovens, is moved to the back wall. The room is large enough to accommodate a table for four or even six.

4 In a variation on Plan #3, the cooktop/wall oven combination has been replaced by a range, either freestanding or drop-in style, and the table is moved against the wall. This eliminates the view of the wall ovens from the front door, permits the use of a longer table (which could be built in and constructed of the same material as the counter top), and keeps the work triangle somewhat more separate from the eating area. This arrangement does, however, make movement through the kitchen from the front of the house to the back more awkward, because the table interrupts the flow of traffic.

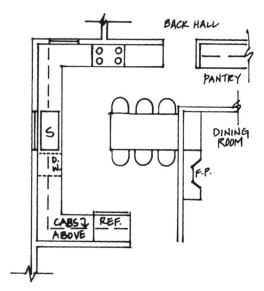

4. NEW KITCHEN
SCALE: ⅛″ = 1′0″

5 Here is an entirely different type of layout. The work triangle remains fairly separated from the eating area. On one short wall, storage cabinets are installed which could either include a counter or be floor-to-ceiling pantry cabinets. The angled counter to the right of the cooktop could abut a full wall, which would shield the kitchen from view. The main advantages of this plan are that the sink remains in its original location, eliminating the need to move the plumbing, and the table is now placed against the windows, where diners can enjoy the view to a stream outside. To enhance the view, the windows are enlarged. A disadvantage is that there is now less counter area for preparation. Circulation from the front of the house to the back is less difficult than in Plan #4, but is not as straightforward as it is in Plan #3, since traffic moves through the work triangle itself.

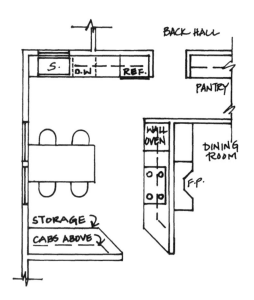

5. NEW KITCHEN
SCALE: ⅛″ = 1′0″

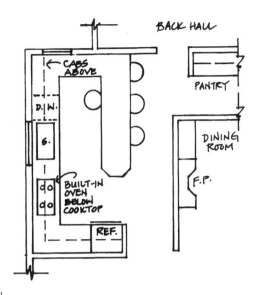

6. NEW KITCHEN
SCALE: ⅛" = 1'0"

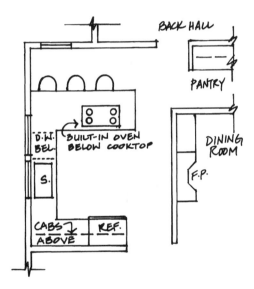

7. NEW KITCHEN
SCALE: ⅛" = 1'0"

6 This is one of seven redesigns which utilize a peninsula or island. Once again, the fridge is located so that it is hidden from view; here, the return wall is shown. In this plan, a built-in oven which fits below the counter is located beneath the cooktop; it could as easily be located elsewhere, with storage cabinetry below the cooktop. An attractive feature of this plan is the dead-end nature of the work triangle, with no cross-traffic, as well as the long peninsula with seating for at least four and a big surface for preparation. A drawback is the relatively small amount of counter space surrounding the sink and cooktop. These appliances could be placed at greater distance from one another but would become somewhat less accessible, since the peninsula would then be in the way.

7 Here, the peninsula is laid out differently. This permits the cooktop/oven combination to be placed farther from the sink, creates a better and more spacious work triangle, and maintains an area for informal eating. Both the work and eating areas are placed so that they cannot be seen from the front door and also do not hinder traffic flow to the back.

8 This plan uses an island rather than a peninsula, which creates a better circulation pattern than does Plan #6. The curved end of the island could be built at a height of 30 inches, like a dining table, or could be a continuation of the cooking surface, in which case stools would be used for seating. There are many variations possible here, depending on the appliances chosen. Once again, a built-in oven could be installed below the cooktop, which would permit the fridge to be moved against the wall, creating more counter space between it and the sink. (The area surrounding the sink is heavily used in food preparation.)

9 This is one of three plans in which the existing back porch is incorporated into the house; here, a new back porch is added, which could be the same size as or larger than the original. Since the existing porch is roofed, enclosing it and adding a source of heat is a relatively easy matter. This is also one of two designs in which the back stairs have been removed. When the house was first built, it is likely that the back stairs led to a bedroom used by a servant; thus, the link between back bedroom and kitchen/pantry area made sense. Today, however, the back stairs are not a necessity, although removing them significantly increases the expense of the renovation. Eliminating the back stairs allows the back hallway to function like a breakfast/family room, with enlarged windows. The original back porch now houses the laundry area and half-bath. The kitchen is laid out similar to Plan #8.

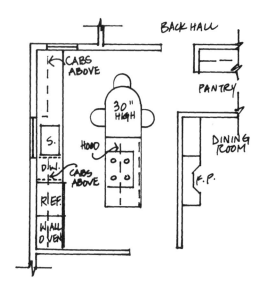

8. NEW KITCHEN
SCALE: ⅛″ = 1′0″

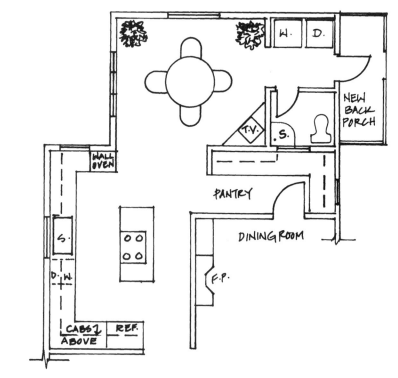

9. NEW KITCHEN AND BACK PORCH
SCALE: ⅛″ = 1′0″

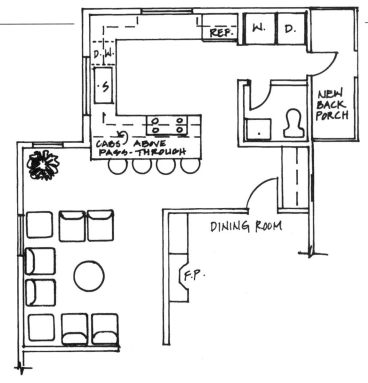

10. NEW KITCHEN AND FAMILY ROOM
SCALE: ⅛" = 1'0"

10 What happens if the essential structure shown in Plan #9 remains intact, but part of the pantry is removed and the kitchen and family room switch places? Taking out some of the pantry cabinetry enlarges the kitchen area. This spacious kitchen with a peninsula for informal eating overlooks the family room and is also accessible to the dining room.

11 Here is a design which, like Plan #10, puts the kitchen into the back of the house and creates a family room in the original kitchen. Here, the back stairs are left in place, and the original back porch becomes part of the new kitchen. If a back door is desired, which is likely, it is best located where noted on the plan. The pantry has now been entirely eliminated to make room for the new kitchen, with its central island. The layout of appliances is efficient, and the size of the kitchen is adequate.

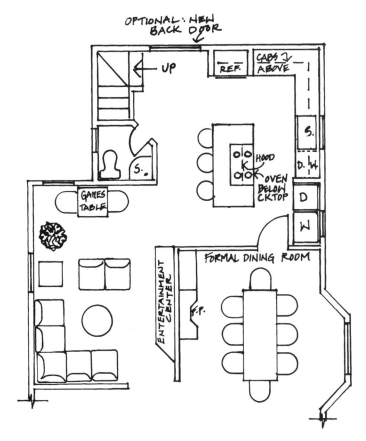

11. NEW KITCHEN AND FAMILY ROOM
SCALE: ⅛" = 1'0"

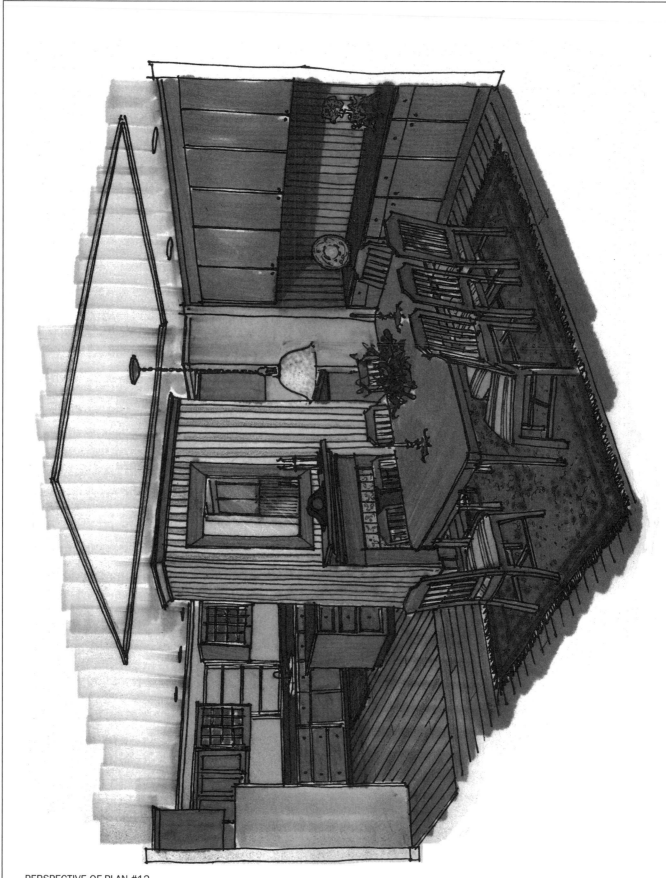

PERSPECTIVE OF PLAN #12

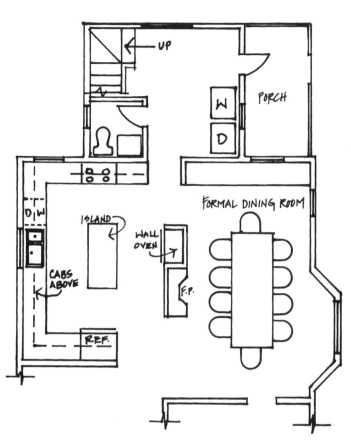

12. NEW KITCHEN AND DINING ROOM
SCALE: ⅛″ = 1′0″

12 All of the previous examples have maintained the separate character of the dining room. In this plan, the dining room is partially opened up to the kitchen. (Eliminating the fireplace would be undesirable, both because it is decorative and because its removal would be too expensive. In addition, the visual barrier created by fireplace and wall oven (facing the kitchen) acts to partially separate the dining area from the kitchen. Here, there is no distinction between formal and informal dining areas, though the center island could accommodate stools or could even be changed to a 30-inch-high table.

Opening the dining room to the kitchen and pantry changes the character of the house substantially; now, it is much more contemporary in feel. Removing the wall separating the dining room and pantry makes it possible to install a much larger table. It also requires that the cabinetry of both kitchen and pantry be attractive and of high quality, since they are so visible. The fact that the Victorian-style fireplace remains in place does not dictate cabinet style; an eclectic mix of antique and contemporary styles is possible, as shown in the sketch.

13 A variation on plans in which the original kitchen is made into a family/informal eating area, the back stairs are removed, and the back porch is incorporated into the house. Here, the introduction of angled walls creates a more dynamic and perhaps surprising interior. The corner of the dining room is angled as well, but the china cabinet is modified. An alternative to moveable furniture in the family room would be a built-in banquette with lots of pillows. It is possible that this design, which suggests more contemporary finishes and colors, is less in keeping with the character of the rest of the house, but this may not matter.

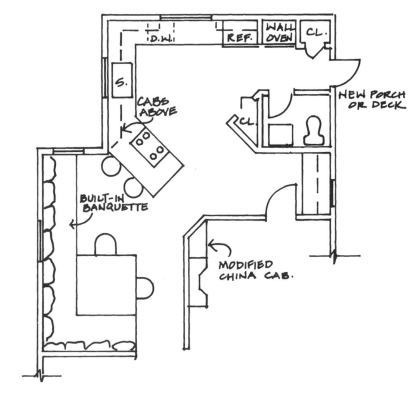

13. NEW KITCHEN
SCALE: ⅛" = 1'0"

PERSPECTIVE OF PLAN #13

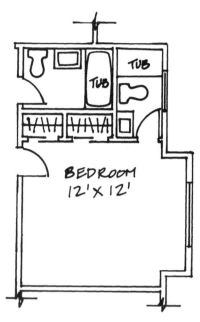

14. NEW BATHROOM AND CLOSETS
SCALE: ⅛″ = 1′0″

15. NEW BATHROOM AND CLOSETS
SCALE: ⅛″ = 1′0″

14 This is a simple and inexpensive solution to the problem of how to add a bath on the second floor which is directly accessible to the master bedroom. The walk-in closet has been fitted with a toilet and lavatory; new closets have therefore been installed within the bedroom. The main disadvantages of this scheme are that the new closets diminish the size of the bedroom and that only a half-bath is provided.

15 Here, through the simple measure of moving the bathroom door, a third fixture is able to be added. Because the original walk-in closet is not wide, only a short tub or shower can be installed.

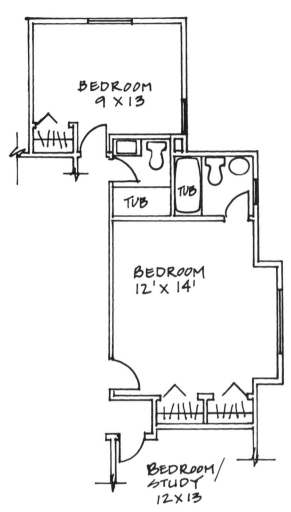

BEDROOM
9 X 13

TUB

TUB

BEDROOM
12' X 14'

BEDROOM/
STUDY
12 X 13

16. NEW BATHROOM AND CLOSETS
SCALE: ⅛″ = 1′0″

16 If a three-fixture master bath and new closets are desired without changing the size of the existing bedroom, space will have to be taken from both the front and back bedrooms. The entry and one wall of the front bedroom are changed in order to permit the installation of closets. Since the front bedroom is already fairly large, this seems a reasonable decision. The existing bathroom is reorganized in such a way that the back bedroom is made smaller; this plan works best when the back stairs are removed. (Otherwise, the back bedroom becomes quite small and might be used as a study or little guest room.) The changes in the layout of the existing bathroom allow the master bathroom to be made somewhat larger. This plan accomplishes more than previous plans without major renovation.

17 This is one of three designs in which at least one bedroom is given up in order to create a more spacious and elegant master bedroom suite. In this example, the larger front bedroom becomes the master, with the smaller front room converted into a large bathroom-cum-dressing room area. The specific layout of both bathroom and dressing room could be easily changed. For example, the sinks could be set up in a separate room from the toilet and tub (as is often done in hotels). The small closet behind the stairs to the attic could be made into a built-in dresser. While this plan does create a nice master bedroom suite, its principal disadvantage is that the new plumbing is remote from the existing, which adds to its expense.

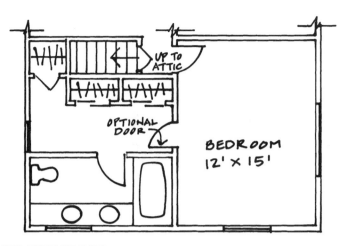

17. MASTER BEDROOM SUITE
SCALE: ⅛″ = 1′0″

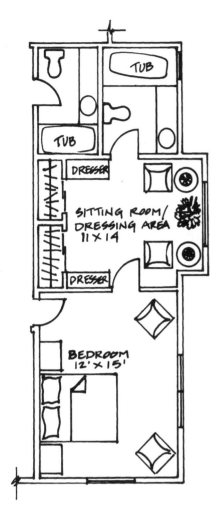

TUB

TUB

DRESSER

SITTING ROOM/
DRESSING AREA
11 × 14

DRESSER

BEDROOM
12' × 15'

18. MASTER BEDROOM/SITTING ROOM SUITE
SCALE: ⅛" = 1'0"

18 In this design, on the other hand, the plumbing remains consolidated. The master bedroom is here created from both the large front and adjacent bedroom, with the existing bathroom both enlarged and reorganized. This is a more elaborate plan, in which the master suite is made up of a sleeping area and a separate sitting or dressing room area. The new bathroom is also spacious.

19 A different bedroom is now designated the master, and the back room is fitted with a new bathroom and closets. The disadvantage to this solution, as to Plans #16 and #17, is that there are now fewer bedrooms; however, the plumbing costs are fairly conservative, since the existing bathroom is left intact and the new bathroom abuts it. Note that a new hallway is created which makes the master bedroom larger and another one smaller. This is done by relocating one wall only; the wall labeled "load-bearing" is left in place.

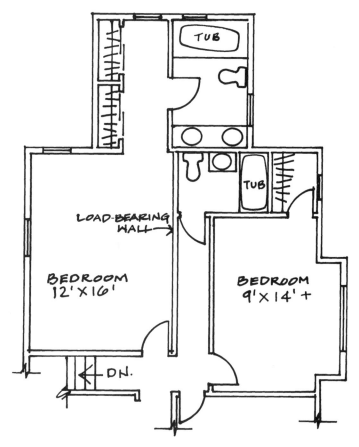

19. MASTER BEDROOM SUITE
SCALE: ⅛" = 1'0"

BIRD'S-EYE PERSPECTIVE OF PLAN #19

Peter and Sarah Cloyes House, 1693

This very old house located in Framingham, Massachusetts, has a fascinating history. In 1693, the original portion of the house was built by Peter and Sarah Cloyes. Sarah, née Towne, was the sister of Rebecca Nurse and Mary Esty, both of whom were condemned and executed following the Salem Witch Trials of 1692. Sarah was also accused and convicted of witchcraft, but she was lucky enough to escape execution. In 1693, her husband Peter rescued her from an Ipswich jail. Together, they fled to Framingham, known at that time as Danforth's Farms and located about 40 miles west of Salem. They settled in a part of town known as Salem End, due to the number of refugees who had left Salem following the trials.

Sarah lived only another few years at Salem End, but Peter remarried and raised another family and was also Framingham's first selectman and the founder of its first church.

There is another piece of important history attached to the house. On the second floor, abutting the stairs to the attic, there is a "closet" which is actually a brick-lined chute—like a chimney—leading to a finished portion of the attic where, it is said, slaves were hidden during the Civil War. Thus, the house has much historical significance beyond simply its age.

The house is presumed by architectural historians to have been built as a saltbox. It was greatly modified by subsequent owners in the eighteenth, nineteenth, and twentieth centuries. As the house existed in 1993, the interior of the oldest part remained substantially unchanged. The original painted, wide board floors, the stairs and beams, the shallow fireplaces, and locations of rooms, doors, and windows remained intact, although the room which contained the original kitchen, with its large fireplaces and ovens, had been converted into a living room. Bathrooms were added, and a simple kitchen was installed at the back of the house, probably during the mid-twentieth century. Some early, floral murals, believed to be the work of an itinerant painter, were uncovered during restoration work; a landscape painting on wood built into a parlor mantel was, however, sold to a museum.

At one time, the house was surrounded by farmland. Today, it possesses only an acre and sits in the middle of sparse suburban development. Its views are lovely: large, old maple trees at the front, rolling lawns and woods to the sides, and a babbling brook in the back.

1 & 2

The existing plans show the house in 1993. Its plan and character are that of a typical New England farmhouse which has grown over time in somewhat haphazard fashion, with a multitude of extensions. Two barns, one attached and one located a short distance to the house, are not shown on the plan. Many of the additions were built to accommodate earlier lifestyles: the woodshed, cold storage rooms, larders, and so on.

The house was recently sold by a childless couple, who had lived for some years in the house without making changes or improvements. The challenge to the new owners, a professional couple with two children and the need for a home office, is to preserve the antique character of the house while adapting it to their more contemporary lifestyle. Bill is a computer programmer; Maddy, a well-known children's book writer, needs an office at home. Their two children are seven and nine

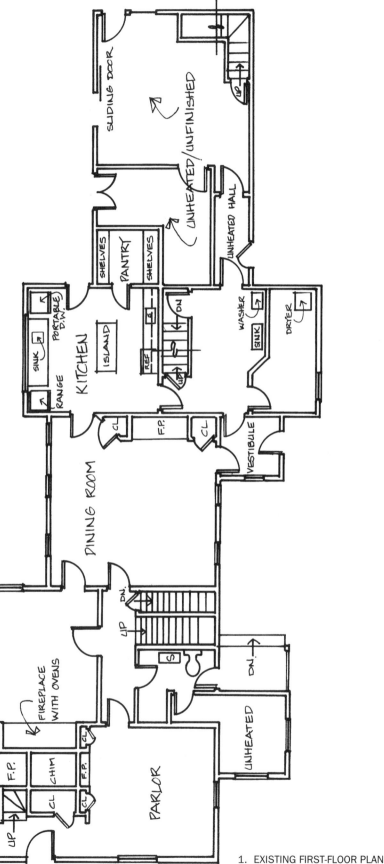

1. EXISTING FIRST-FLOOR PLAN

years old; they want separate bedrooms and have an immense number of toys for which they need storage. This family also wants space for guests, a kitchen with improved circulation and counter space, a family/TV room near the kitchen, storage for books, more closets in the master bedroom, and better-planned bathrooms on both levels.

These are some of the specific problems which the new owners face. On the main floor, there is a large and pleasant living room with an interesting fireplace, but there are also two square parlors, each 14′ × 14′, which seem difficult to utilize well. Each of these parlors, like the living room, has magnificent floor boards and detailing which the owners want to preserve. The existing kitchen is functional, but the appliances are poorly located and the layout is inefficient. The range, tucked into a corner, lacks counter space on one side; the sink is an old porcelain structure on legs, next to a portable dishwasher. On the other side of the room there is another,

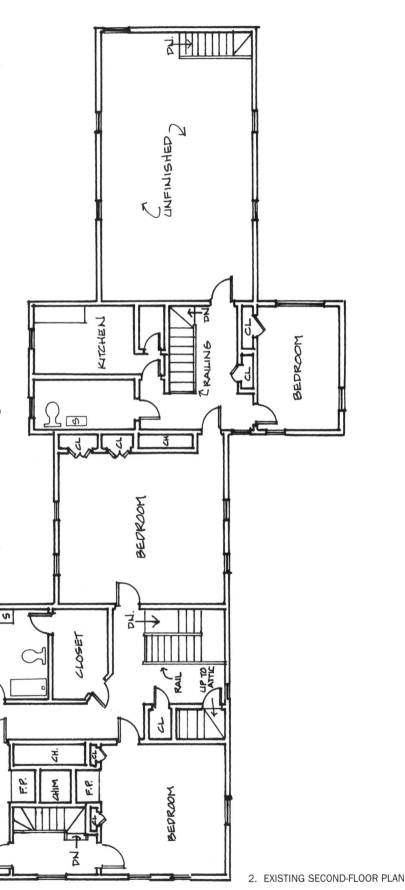

2. EXISTING SECOND-FLOOR PLAN

more modern sink and a refrigerator. If one thinks about the standard work triangle in a kitchen, and the typical progression from fridge to sink to range, it is easy to see how inefficient and cumbersome the existing layout would feel. On the same floor, there is a peculiar arrangement of laundry appliances, with the washing machine located in one room and the dryer in another. Behind the kitchen there are two large, unfinished spaces with a great deal of unrealized potential.

Upstairs, there are three bedrooms which were part of the original house. These rooms are sunny, with antique floors, fireplaces, and details similar to the rooms downstairs—but with no closets! For the childless couple, who occupied the large bedroom and who used a variety of spaces in the house for clothes storage, the absence of closets in the front rooms was not a problem, but for the family who wish to use all the bedrooms, storage space must be provided. The largest bedroom, which is located over the dining room, has very little closet storage and does not have direct access to a private bathroom. At some point, the three rooms located between the largest bedroom and the unfinished portion constituted a legal apartment: bedroom, bathroom, and kitchen. The existing bathrooms may be thirty years old, with small fixtures and inadequate storage.

3 This first-floor plan leaves the front of the house basically intact, makes small modifications to the existing bathroom and laundry areas, changes the kitchen, and creates a family room out of the unfinished room behind the kitchen.

The two parlors are furnished as a guest bedroom (with an armoire for closet storage) and a library, for the couple's many books. The living room is comfortably laid out with generous seating and a games table with two chairs by the window. A hutch against the wall near the fireplace is both decorative and functional.

The dining room, with windows on both sides, is flooded with sunlight and has wonderful views. It accommodates a hutch, a buffet for serving, and a large table.

This plan shows one of several possible kitchen layouts. Numbers of different plans are economical, since there is existing plumbing on two kitchen walls. Here, the exterior wall houses the refrigerator, dishwasher, and large sink. In addition, a floor-to-ceiling pantry cabinet has storage space which is not provided in this design by upper cabinets. A large island contains a drop-in range ventilated through the floor. The plan has plenty of space for circulation and an open, airy feeling. The existing pantry is removed, and the unfinished space beyond the kitchen can function as an informal dining and family room.

The small room which housed the dryer can be made into an efficient home office space for Maddy. The old soapstone sink next to the washer is removed to make room for a better laundry layout, with both appliances and a built-in linen closet. This space—essentially a passageway off which are located office, vestibule, kitchen, stairs and family room—is wide enough to accommodate additional closet or shelf space if needed.

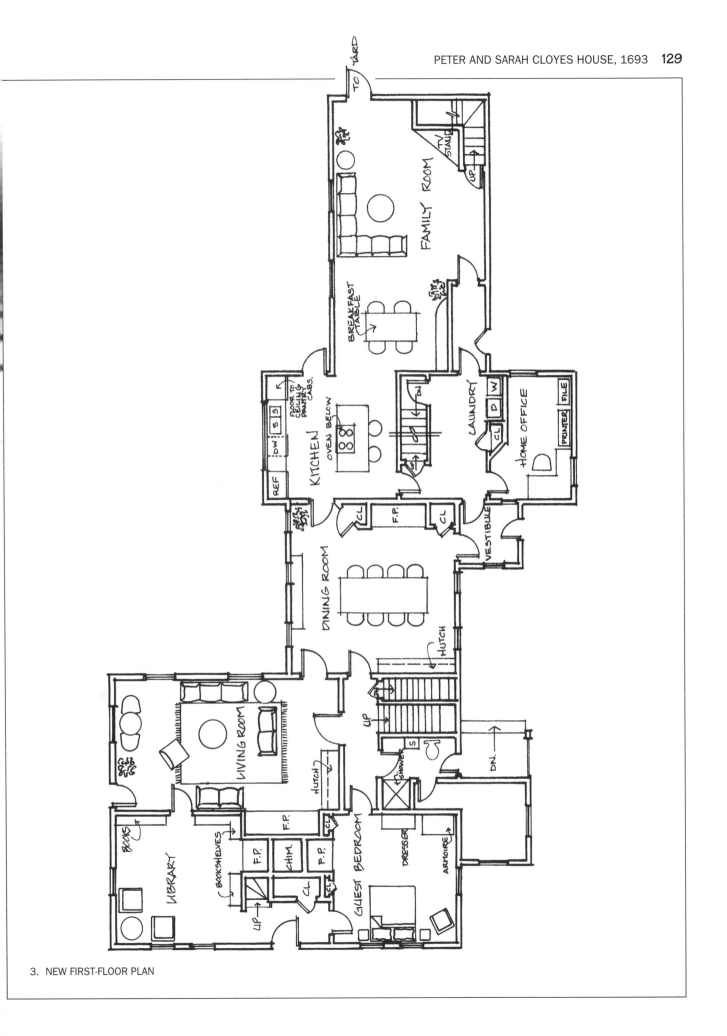

3. NEW FIRST-FLOOR PLAN

KITCHEN IN PLAN #3

CLOYES HOUSE LIVING ROOM

4 Here is a variation on the kitchen redesign shown in Plan #3. A conventional L-shaped layout is possible because the existing back entrance is closed off. (This entrance could be relocated into the new family room.) This eat-in kitchen can be provided with a freestanding table in the center or a built-in island with stools.

5 This plan duplicates the three-tiered arrangement of the existing kitchen but improves the layout of appliances for greater efficiency. The center island, for preparation and storage, is enlarged. The exterior wall houses refrigerator, wall ovens, clean-up sink, and dishwasher, while the interior wall has cooktop and vegetable sink. Although the existing backdoor does not need to be moved, it would be nice to create a spacious breakfast room (with door to family room beyond) and to install decorative French doors leading to the side yard.

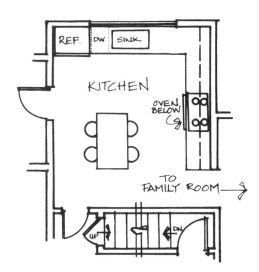

4. NEW KITCHEN WITH BACK ENTRY CLOSED OFF

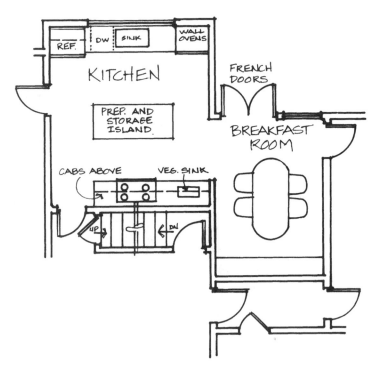

5. NEW KITCHEN WITH BREAKFAST ROOM

6 An alternative to the small home office shown in Plan #1 would be this larger office created when the laundry wall is taken down. This sizable office, with space for files and a conference table, could be a home office for a lawyer, psychotherapist, etc.

7 If the laundry is removed from the first floor as shown in Plan #6, then the laundry must be relocated. A reasonable place to put it would be in the large, central closet on the second floor, since it is then back to back with the bathroom plumbing. Note that now there need to be new closets provided for the master bedroom. The room is large enough that building a wall of closets leaves the room easy to furnish.

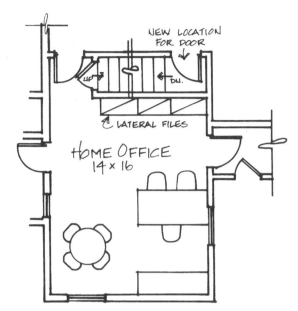

6. NEW HOME OFFICE ON FIRST FLOOR

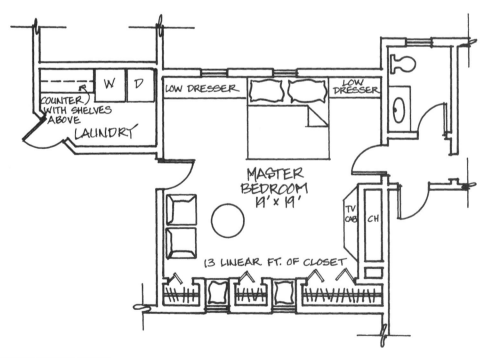

7. NEW LAUNDRY ON SECOND FLOOR

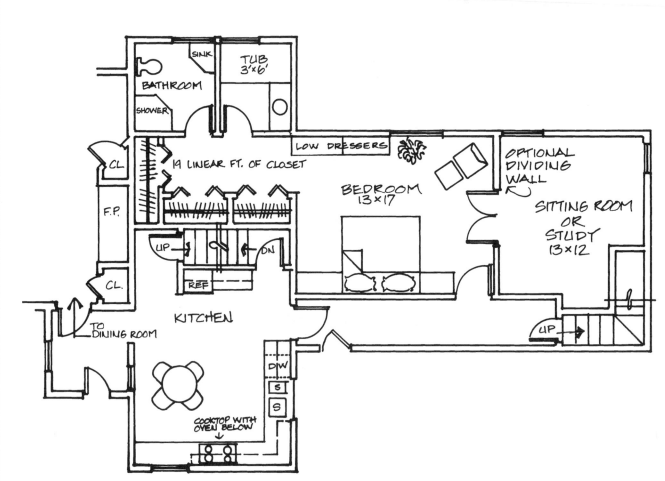

8. NEW KITCHEN AND MASTER BEDROOM SUITE ON FIRST FLOOR

8 This plan shows two variations on earlier layouts. First, the kitchen is now located where the original washing machine was installed. This is economically feasible, since the plumbing already exists. It is also a convenient location, since it remains close to the dining room. Many kitchen layouts are possible; here, an essentially L-shaped kitchen is provided with a breakfast table near the window.

This plan also shows how a master bedroom suite with large, private bath, sitting room or study, and plenty of closet storage could be built in the unfinished space. The sitting room could be separated from the sleeping area, as shown, or left open to it. The square footage for the bathroom(s) is great enough so that many fixture layouts could be accommodated.

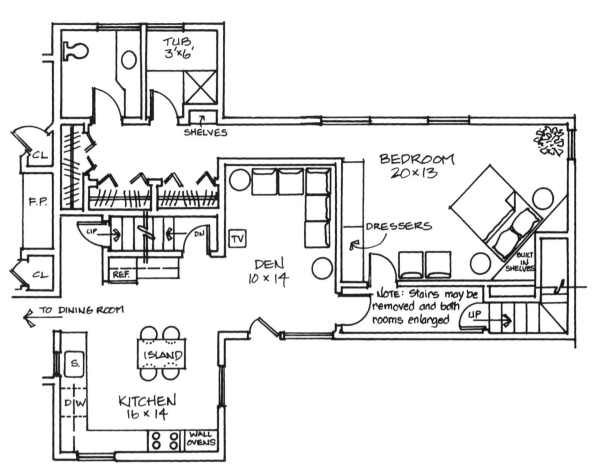

9. NEW KITCHEN, BEDROOM, AND DEN ON FIRST FLOOR

9 Plan #8 does not provide a family room or den off the kitchen, a room much in demand. This plan shows how a moderate-sized den could be built next to the bedroom. It is important to note that the back stairs abutting the bedroom could be removed, thereby making it possible to enlarge the bedroom, the den, or both. Note also that this drawing shows variations on both bathrooms and kitchen.

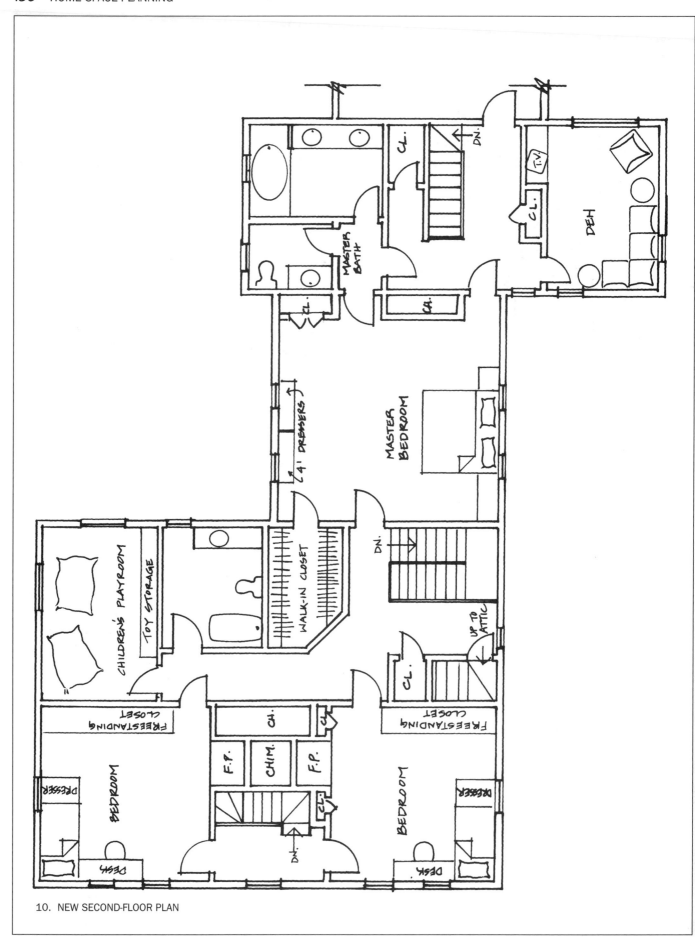

10. NEW SECOND-FLOOR PLAN

10 This plan shows one way that the second floor can be used; modifications are slight. The front bedrooms are left intact, preserving their antique character, and freestanding cabinets are provided for storage. These rooms are adequate in size (14′6″ × 14′6″) for children, with single or even bunk beds in place. The side bedroom could be furnished as another bedroom, as a playroom (shown here), or as a study. The common bathroom can be modernized as much as desired. Here, the closing of the door into the closet makes it possible to install a long vanity.

The master bedroom, like the dining room below, is large and sunny, but the existing closet space is inadequate. Simply changing the opening of the hallway closet provides more storage for the bedroom.

The fifth bedroom is another space which could continue to be used as a bedroom or could be used as a second home office. Here, however, it is shown furnished as a small den, a place to watch TV upstairs.

The changes to the second bathroom are economical and yet represent a substantial improvement. The location for plumbing remains unchanged. However, by removing the old bathtub, a door can be provided which gives direct access to the master bath from the bedroom. The old kitchen is large enough to accommodate both a 3′ × 6′ tub and a long vanity with double sinks. The separation of the fixtures into two rooms is an added convenience.

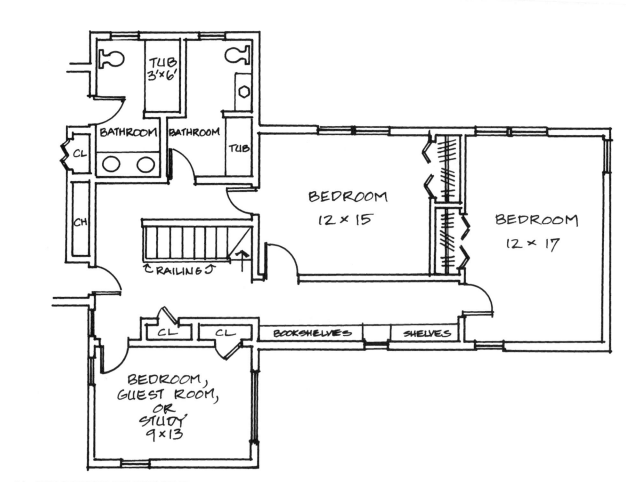

11. NEW SECOND-FLOOR BEDROOMS

11 This is the first plan to show how the unfinished space on the second floor might be laid out. Here, two bathrooms of moderate scale are shown, one attached to the master bedroom, the other open to the hall and available to three other bedrooms. One of those is existing, and two have been created out of the unfinished area. It would probably be desirable, though not absolutely necessary, to remove the back stairs, so that the back bedroom could be as large as possible. One of the new bedrooms has nearly direct access to the second bathroom, while the other is fairly removed.

If the second floor is built as shown, then the house has a master bedroom with private bath and another bath serving three bedrooms at the back of the house. What then becomes of the three smaller, antique bedrooms and bathroom at the front of the house? These could serve as adjunct spaces such as studies, computer rooms, playrooms, guest rooms, artist's studios, etc. They could also be wonderful, romantic bedrooms for a bed-and-breakfast operation, particularly since, on the first floor, one of the old parlors could be reserved for the use of guests.

Pacific Northwest Bungalow: Staying On

1 & 2

This Seattle house, built in the '40s, was originally a single-story bungalow with a one-car garage under an unfinished basement. In the '70s, it was purchased by a couple new to the city. At the time of their purchase, they were childless. Joshua, the husband, was about to establish a practice as a chiropractor; his wife, Camilla, was a weaver.

Within a few years, the couple had a young son and needed more space. They decided to expand the house on the first floor by opening up most of the space and installing a new kitchen, and they also added a second floor. The basement was partially finished with the addition of a bathroom and a bedroom. Plans #1 and #2 show the renovated first floor and the second floor. The large bedroom was used as the master, the medium-sized bedroom was for the first child, the small bedroom was used as Camilla's weaving studio, and the family room, with its large windows overlooking Seattle's harbor, was used for watching TV.

After a few more years, Josh and Camilla adopted two children: a boy almost the same age as their first child and an infant girl. They decided to let the boys share a bedroom and to give the studio

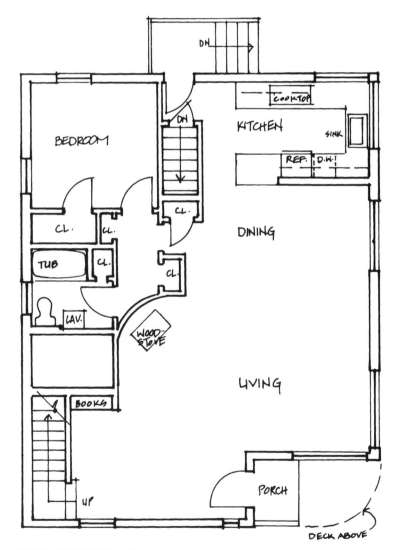

1. EXISTING FIRST-FLOOR PLAN
SCALE: ⅛" = 1'0"

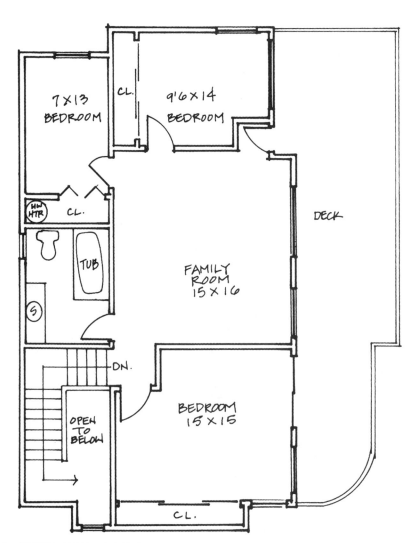

2. EXISTING SECOND-FLOOR PLAN
SCALE: ⅛″ = 1′0″

to the girl; the loom and yarns were moved into a corner of the family room.

Several years later, Josh and Camilla are looking forward to the boys' adolescence and would like to add a second bathroom on the upper floor. They have found that they rarely use the deck and are willing to enclose as much deck as possible to gain interior space. (It must be noted that the northern and southern corners of the deck could not be enclosed without additional support from below.)

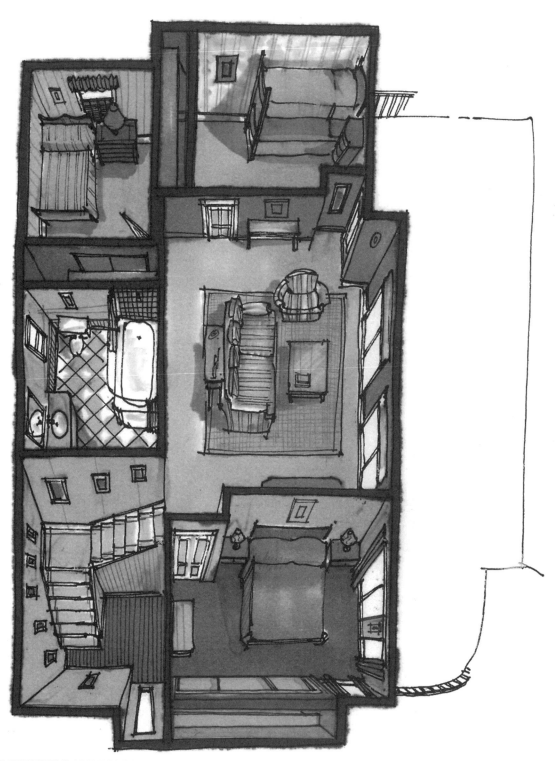

BIRD'S-EYE PERSPECTIVE OF EXISTING SECOND FLOOR

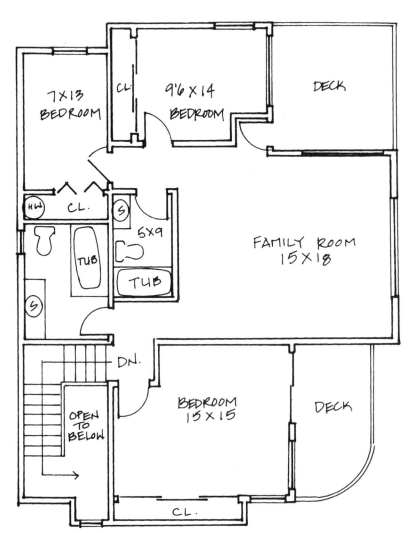

3. BATHROOM ADDITION
SCALE: ⅛" = 1'0"

3 Keeping in mind that it is cost-effective to install the new bathroom close to the existing one, this plan represents the simplest and most economical solution. The entrance to the new bathroom faces the children's rooms, while the original bathroom's entrance is nearer the master bedroom; the children are thus encouraged, through its proximity, to use the new facility. The family room is expanded onto the deck and is larger than it was before. This plan does not, however, give the master a private bath.

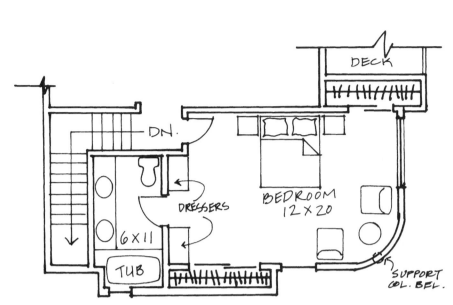

4. MASTER BEDROOM SUITE
SCALE: ⅛″ = 1′0″

4 Here, the area labeled "open to below" on Plan #2 is floored over; the added space is adequate to provide a generous private bath for the master bedroom. The bedroom has been expanded onto the deck and is larger than before. Extra closet space is shown, but a door from the bedroom onto the deck could be indicated instead. Plumbing costs are increased in this plan.

5 This is the first of several plans which show the bedrooms in new locations. Since these plans involve moving walls, there is some added expense. Here, the original bath serves the children, whose rooms occupy the space where the master and deck had been. The old kids' rooms are opened up to become a master with dressing area; the family room is expanded as in Plan #3. The new bath is contiguous to the old and, like the deck, is private to the master bedroom.

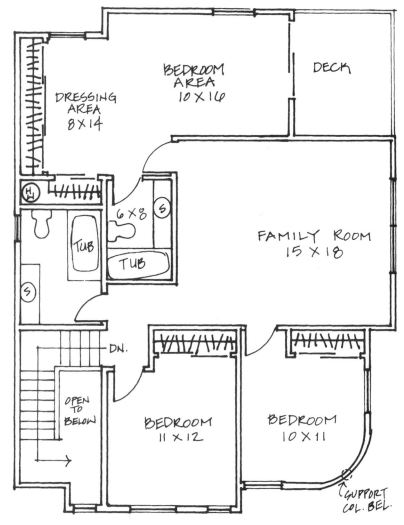

5. NEW SECOND-FLOOR LAYOUT
SCALE: ⅛″ = 1′0″

BIRD'S-EYE PERSPECTIVE OF PLAN #6

6 Here, the original bathroom is rearranged so that it is accessible only to the master. The family room has windows on the north side, which admit more light, though the deck is, in this case, less private.

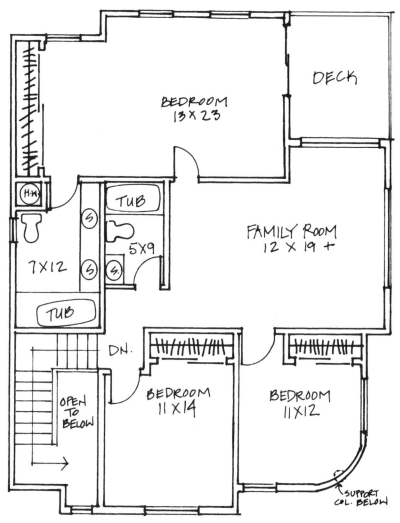

6. NEW SECOND-FLOOR LAYOUT

SCALE: ⅛″ = 1′0″

7 This is a slight variation on Plans #5 and #6. The kids' new bedrooms are carved from the space occupied by the master and the floored-over area. The new bath is very small. This plan requires less expansion onto the deck. The family room could be left in its existing state, but by pushing it out onto the deck, it is almost doubled in size.

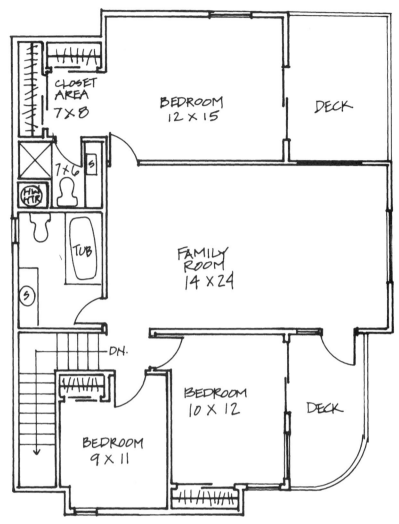

7. NEW SECOND-FLOOR PLAN

SCALE: ⅛" = 1'0"

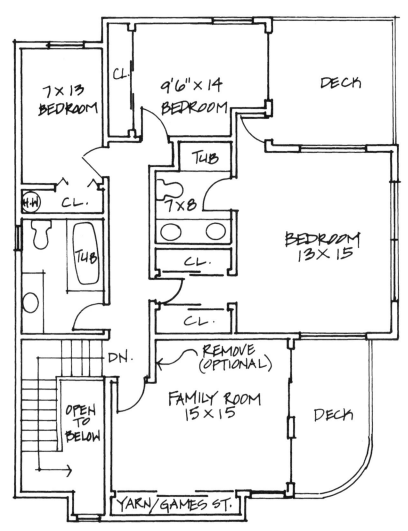

8. NEW SECOND-FLOOR PLAN
SCALE: ⅛" = 1′0″

8 This plan appears much more radical than it actually is. The children's rooms and master bedroom remain unchanged, except that the master becomes a family room. The original family room and adjacent deck become new bath, closets, and master bedroom. The organization of rooms here gives auditory privacy to everyone. The earlier plans, which, like the original layout, have bedrooms opening onto the family room, do not give bedrooms enough separation from TV noise. Here, the problem is solved with the creation of a hallway and complete separation of spaces. This plan effects a big change in the way the rooms are organized and experienced, with relatively few changes to the existing layout.

9 Here, an extensive rebuilding of the floor allows all the bedrooms to take advantage of the view of the harbor. The master has a private bath and walk-in closet. The family room is long enough that it can be functionally separated into a TV room and a weaving studio, divided by a games and puzzle table (or by freestanding or built-in storage units).

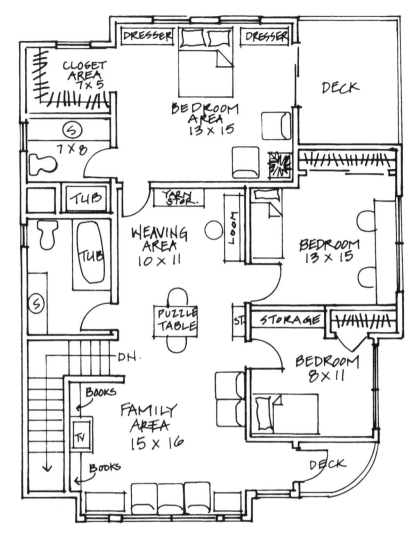

9. NEW SECOND-FLOOR PLAN

SCALE: ⅛″ = 1′0″

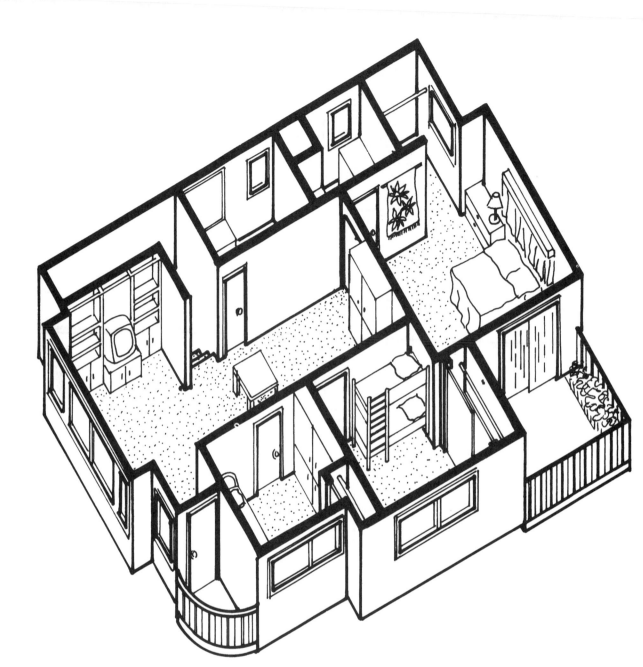

AXONOMETRIC VIEW OF PLAN #9

Pacific Northwest Bungalow: Moving Out

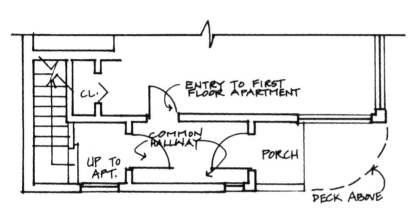

10. NEW FIRST-FLOOR VESTIBULE
SCALE: ⅛″ = 1′0″

Josh and Camilla have decided to get an au pair and to give the two boys separate bedrooms. After a prolonged house hunt and many discussions about lifestyle and commuting time, they have decided to buy a large house on Vachon Island, but instead of selling their two-story bungalow, they will create two apartments so that they can use one while renting the other. This will enable Josh to use the Seattle house during the week, since it is close to his business. In addition, Camilla will want to come into the city from time to time, with or without the children, and she can also use the apartment. Josh and Camilla would keep the downstairs apartment, since it has a bedroom and bath in the basement, and they would rent the upstairs, one-bedroom unit.

10 This is a reasonable approach to the separation of the upper and lower floors. A common hallway is created from which doors lead to either the lower or upper apartments. The stairs become part of the upstairs unit.

11 This plan leaves the bathroom intact and locates the kitchen next to it, thus keeping plumbing costs conservative. The rest of the space is largely rebuilt, with the new living room taking over part of the existing deck. The closets, which create a hallway to the kitchen/dining area, not only provide storage but also act to shield visitors from a direct view into the bathroom.

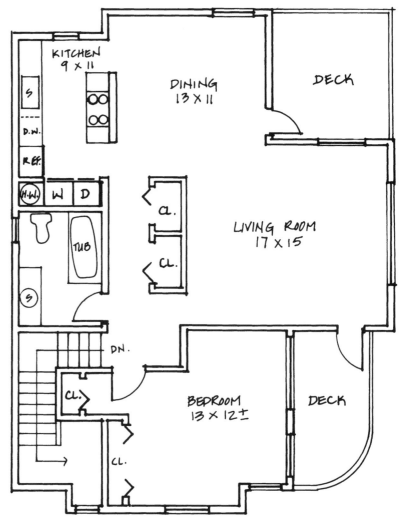

11. NEW SECOND-FLOOR APARTMENT
SCALE: ⅛" = 1'0"

12 This variation on Plan #11 places the kitchen in a location approximately above the downstairs kitchen. The bathroom is reorganized in order to move its door closer to the bedroom—with little difficulty, the bathroom could be made into a private master bath. A short partition separates dining room from bathroom and creates a hall. However, if the bathroom opened directly into the bedroom, this partition could be eliminated.

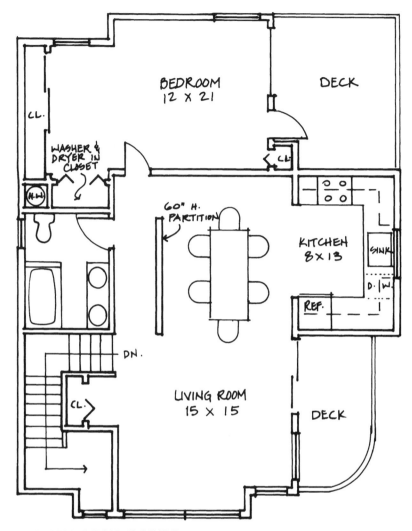

12. NEW SECOND-FLOOR APARTMENT
SCALE: ⅛″ = 1′0″

Attached Rowhouse

This is a London "terrace" or townhouse with party walls, one of a long row of identical houses. Many houses of this type were built during the eighteenth and nineteenth centuries in both European and American cities. The footprint of each house can be quite small, because they are narrow, but the house can be as tall as four or even five stories, so that the overall square footage is surprisingly large. Generally, such houses have little backyard space.

This house is owned by a professional couple with two boys, ages 9 and 11, and a baby girl. It needed a great deal of work when they bought it, and over a period of several years they have added modern bathrooms and kitchen as well as a master suite.

1 The first-floor plan clearly indicates how long and narrow this house is. The existing layout on the first floor is a standard one, with a long hallway which bypasses individual rooms: first, the living room, or parlor, with its single bay window, then the dining room, with a small window overlooking part of the tiny back patio, then a half-bath whose layout is not very efficient, and finally the kitchen. The kitchen has all modern appliances, including an under-counter washing machine (a

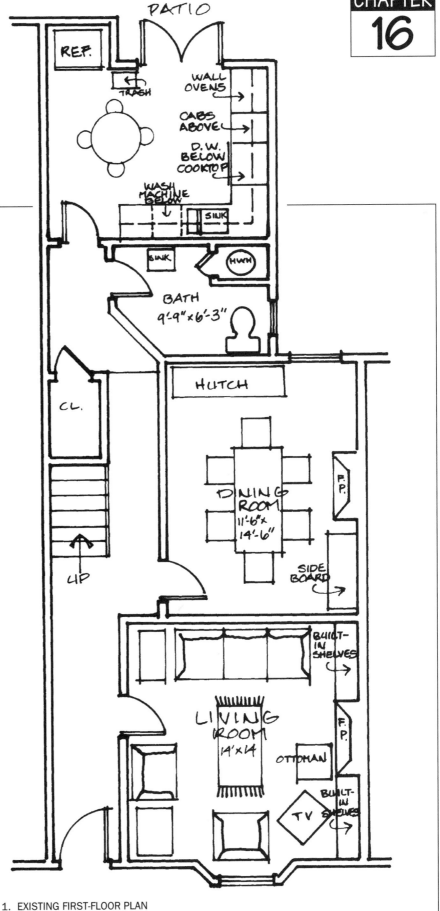

1. EXISTING FIRST-FLOOR PLAN

155

front-loading machine which is standard in Europe). The French doors at the back of the room open onto a concrete patio of about 120 square feet, at most, with a perimeter flower bed.

There are several problems with this plan, both functional and aesthetic. First of all, the space feels confining, due to the small size and the separation of rooms and lack of natural light. Another factor is the height of the ceiling (about 11 feet), which makes the hall seem even narrower than it is.

The house needs more closets and other places for storing such things as old papers, suitcases, off-season clothing, toys, books, and so on. Note that on the ground floor there is no coat closet; the storage space beneath the stairs is filled with electrical panels, vacuum cleaners, and other cleaning supplies.

The kitchen is poorly designed. The refrigerator is tucked into an out-of-the-way alcove, in spite of the fact that the fridge is the appliance most frequently used and should be easily accessible. The placement of the breakfast table in front of the fridge and, incidentally, blocking the wastebasket, makes access even more difficult. Locating the washing machine in the kitchen, a commonplace in European kitchens, deprives the room of needed storage for food and utensils.

A quick look at the plans for the upper floors (#10 and #11) shows that all the upstairs rooms are used as bedrooms and furnished with beds. When they first bought the house, the parents occupied the largest of the second-floor bedrooms and the boys shared another; the attic was unfinished. After the birth of the baby, three bedrooms were really not enough, particularly because in-laws often come to visit and one bedroom was needed as a guest room. The couple then finished off the attic space to make a master suite, with its own bathroom and adequate closet space. It is worth noting that there are no built-in closets in the second-floor bedrooms.

The TV, VCR, Nintendo, and stereo are all located in the living room. As a result, if children are watching a video or playing video games, adults have no quiet, comfortable place in which to read; on the other hand, if adults are entertaining in the living room, the children cannot at the same time watch TV.

Thus, the requirements are for a greater feeling of spaciousness, especially in the first-floor rooms, more closet and other storage space, a better-designed kitchen, with good access to all appliances, and a TV/games room which is separate from the living room.

2 Here is the first of several suggested redesigns for the townhouse. In the living room, a better-organized furniture layout is possible because the door is moved to the corner of the room. An opening between living and dining rooms means that it is not necessary to go out into the hall to move between rooms; also, the light from the small window in each room can penetrate to the other room, making both seem brighter. The hutch has been removed from the end of the dining room, and instead two servers—sideboards or hutches—have been placed next to the fireplace; this facilitates movement around the table.

The kitchen layout has been somewhat changed, although it is an L-shape with the eating area in the corner. The little alcove which housed the fridge now opens to the patio and functions as a toolshed. The fridge is now located where the wall ovens were; instead of wall ovens, there is a range. (There could be a cooktop with under-counter oven below.) The sink and range are separated here to provide as much counter space as possible between the two, but it would also be reasonable to switch the locations of sink and dishwasher, so that there could be some counter next to the fridge for unloading. The eating area shown here is a built-in banquette with table, and the available space for the banquette is extended because one of the French doors is removed. Storage in the kitchen is improved, too, because the washing machine (as well as a new dryer) is now placed in the newly organized half-bath.

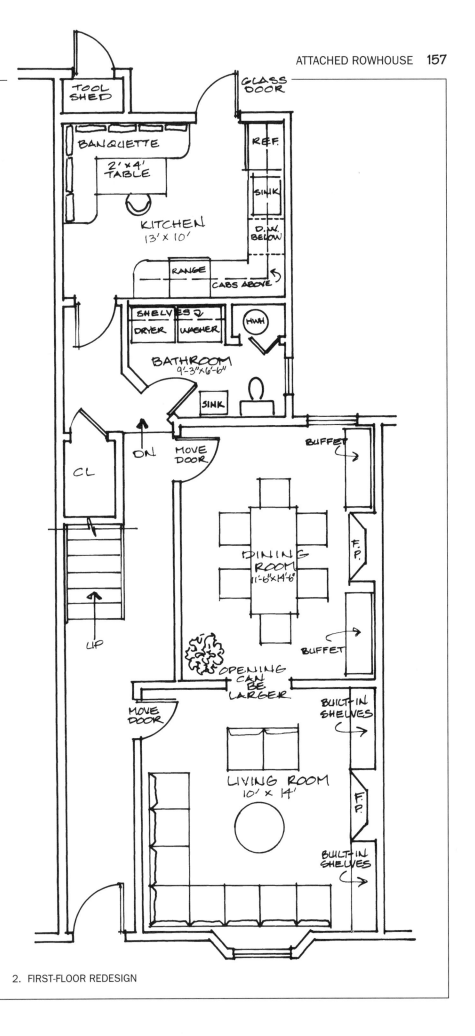

2. FIRST-FLOOR REDESIGN

3 A key to the organization of this plan is the relocation of the bathroom to the back of the house. Among other things, this makes service to the dining room much easier, because it is now adjacent to the kitchen.

The kitchen is laid out in a new way, and its entrance has been moved, so that passage to the patio does not interrupt the work flow. Windows have been added along the exterior, non-party wall to bring in natural light. A small vestibule or mud room has been created at the backdoor, where the laundry is located. Note that cabinets could be mounted over the washer and dryer. A closet beneath the stairs could be used as a coat closet for visitors, as a broom closet, or both.

The living and dining rooms are now completely open to one another, and the hallway has also been removed. This makes all spaces seem much larger. In the plan drawing, as well as the accompanying perspective, the remnants of the original separating wall can be seen in the columnar supports.

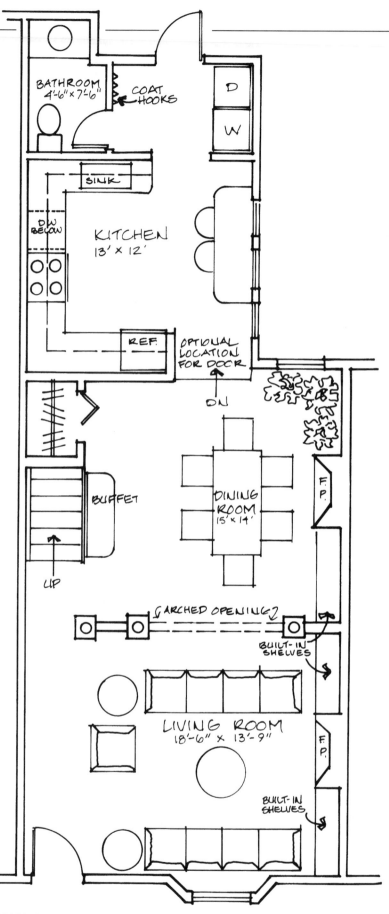

3. FIRST-FLOOR REDESIGN

PERSPECTIVE VIEW OF PLAN #3

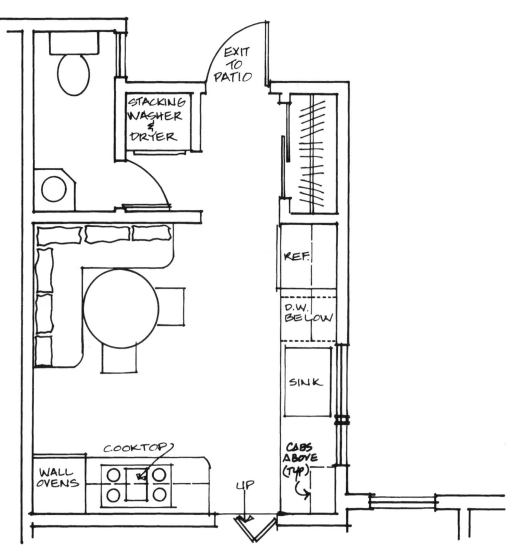

4. NEW KITCHEN
SCALE: ¼" = 1'0"

4 Here is a variation on the layout for kitchen, mudroom/laundry, and bath. Instead of a U-shaped kitchen, the appliances are located on two discontinuous walls. This plan is made possible by moving the entrance from dining room into kitchen slightly to the left. The plan has the advantage of leaving a remote corner for use as a more substantial breakfast area than the previous plan, which had only a counter and stools. On the other hand, cooking activities will now be interrupted by traffic to the back of the house. Installation of a stacking washer/dryer unit permits the location of a large coat/broom closet. This would allow the closet under the stairs to be used for visitors' coats.

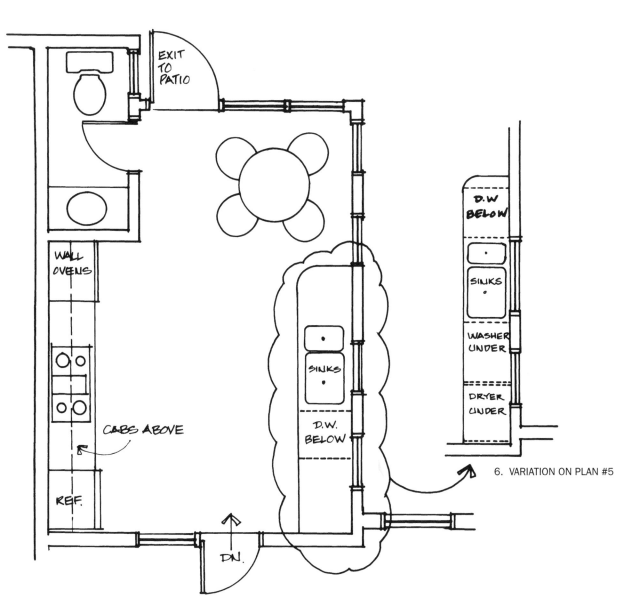

EXIT TO PATIO

WALL OVENS

CABS ABOVE

REF.

SINKS

D.W. BELOW

DN.

D.W BELOW

SINKS

WASHER UNDER

DRYER UNDER

6. VARIATION ON PLAN #5

5. NEW KITCHEN
SCALE: ¼″ = 1′0″

5 Many more windows have been installed here! The eat-in, galley-style kitchen is now a sunny space with a good view of the garden in back. Note that in this plan, the washer and dryer are assumed to have been moved to the upstairs bathroom (see Plan #13).

6 In a slight variation on Plan #5, the washer and dryer are installed below the counter, and the placement of sink and dishwasher are adjusted to accommodate them.

7 Once again, the washer and dryer are under the counter, but this time, they are located towards the back of the kitchen near a new linen closet. The counter over the laundry appliances is useful preparation space abutting the range. This kitchen is big enough for a breakfast table and a wall of pantry storage cabinets, yet it is generous in both counter and floor space.

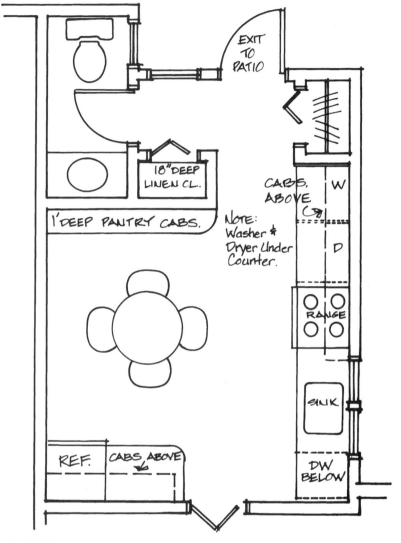

7. NEW KITCHEN
SCALE: ¼″ = 1′0″

8 Here the kitchen is very open, bright, and contemporary in feel. The laundry area and bathroom are divided from the kitchen by a large peninsula which serves also as a breakfast counter. There is plenty of counter space, as well as upper cabinets for storage. The main drawback to this plan is the absence of a closet. However, if the washer and dryer were located in the upstairs bathroom (see Plan #13), there would be space for a closet like that in Plan #7.

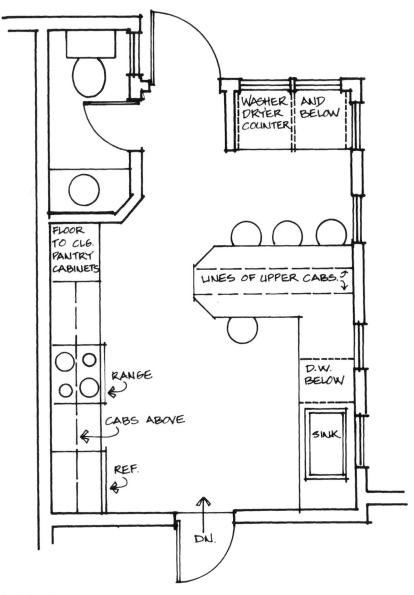

8. NEW KITCHEN
SCALE: ¼" = 1'0"

9 This is a more radical redesign. Here, the kitchen is located between the living and dining rooms. There is only one eating area, and this is at the back of the house, in a sunny room overlooking the garden. The living room here is larger, because it borrows some of the square footage originally assigned to the dining room. The leftover space—between living room and new dining room—is perfect for a kitchen which is compact, self-contained, and efficiently laid out. The fireplace in the kitchen could be treated as a decorative asset.

Two disadvantages to this plan are the lack of bathroom and breakfast area. However, this is compensated for by the fact that the existing spaces are larger. The perspective shows how the living room would look if furnished in what might be called "Eurostyle contemporary."

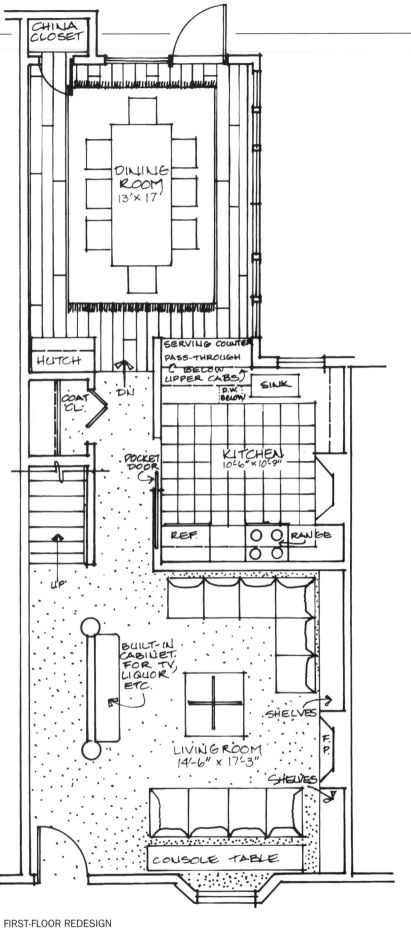

9. FIRST-FLOOR REDESIGN

PERSPECTIVE VIEW OF PLAN #9

10 Here is the second floor of the house as it was laid out and furnished after the renovation of the attic. The boys share the big front room, with two twin beds and two wardrobes, as well as a dresser and many toys both under the beds and scattered about. The second bedroom is the guest room; it has a double bed, as well as wardrobe, dresser, nightstands, and a fireplace. The three-fixture bathroom separates the guest room and the baby's room, which is small and is furnished with a crib, dresser, and toy box.

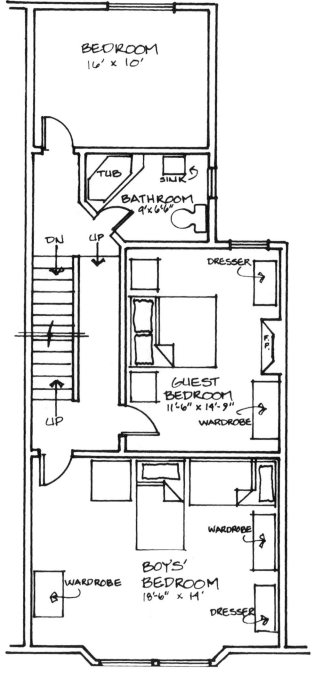

10. EXISTING SECOND FLOOR

11 Space for a third-floor master suite was created by lifting the back half of the roof. The roof pitch towards the front of the house remains steep. This is why there is plenty of room for storage in the eaves. It is also why skylights rather than windows were installed at the front of the house. This layout functions well, with good closet space and a large window overlooking the garden. Another occupant might have chosen a different bathroom configuration, with a tub instead of shower; this change would be easy to accommodate, even within the given layout.

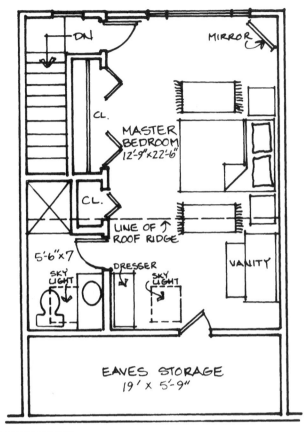

11. EXISTING THIRD FLOOR

12 In this slightly redesigned second floor, the boys' front room has been improved with a more orderly layout and the installation of built-in closets and dresser. Each child has a bed with storage drawers beneath and a long desk which doubles as a nightstand. The guest room is furnished with a sectional which has a fold-out bed, and a TV sits on the dresser. This room now does double duty, so that the TV does not have to be located in the more formal living room. The bathroom is reorganized so that it has two sinks.

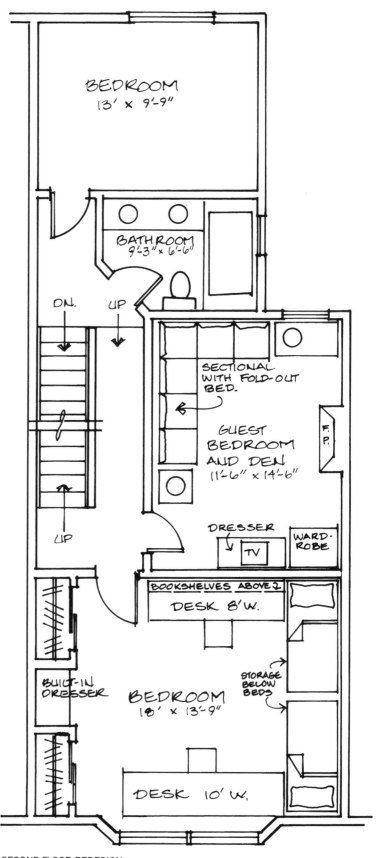

BEDROOM
13' × 9'-9"

BATHROOM
9'-3" × 6'-6"

DN. UP

SECTIONAL WITH FOLD-OUT BED.

GUEST BEDROOM AND DEN
11'-6" × 14'-6"

F.P.

UP

DRESSER TV WARD-ROBE

BOOKSHELVES ABOVE 2
DESK 8'W.

STORAGE BELOW BEDS

BUILT-IN DRESSER

BEDROOM
18' × 13'-9"

DESK 10'W.

12. SECOND-FLOOR REDESIGN

13 The square footage in the bathroom is actually large enough to accommodate the laundry appliances as well as three main fixtures. Stacking washer and dryer could be built in, which would make the bathroom less crowded.

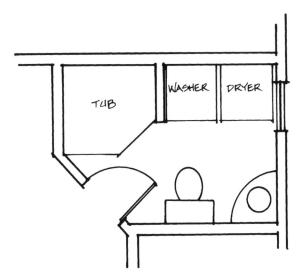

13. SECOND-FLOOR BATHROOM REDESIGN
SCALE: ¼″ = 1′0″

Ranch House on Slab: New Second Story

1 This little house, built in the '50s, is one of a large number of such houses which were partially modeled after the Levittown houses in New York. Behind the house there is a walking path connecting to others which thread through the development; the builders' notion was that children would be able to visit one another's homes without having to cross streets. Like the other houses in the neighborhood, this house has a minimum number of spaces: no foyer or dining room, and small bathroom and closets. Since it is built on slab, it lacks storage space and must accommodate a mechanical room with furnace and hot water heater. There is no washer or dryer or space to install them.

The second owner of the house was an architect who added a long, narrow room with cathedral ceilings which open into the living room and the kitchen. (This new room is shown on Plan #2, which also illustrates changes made by later owners.) He used the space as a small dining room at one end and an expansion to the living room at the other; between the two areas he installed a wood-

stove. It was in this form that the third owners, a family of four, purchased the house.

This active family consisted of a working couple, Dick and Mary, and their two small children, Lynn and Matt. They bought the house because they liked the neighborhood and the large garden surrounding the house. Before long, they—like many of their neighbors—decided they had outgrown the house and needed to build an addition.

Dick and Mary called me to discuss their needs. It quickly became apparent that an entire second story would have to be built. They needed a family room for toys, TV, and piano, a master bedroom with its own bathroom, and two good-sized bedrooms for the children, with another bathroom for them to share. Dick needed a small study, and Mary wanted both a sewing room (which might double as a guest room) and a laundry room with side-by-side appliances, storage shelves, and room for ironing and for a rod on which to hang shirts. It would also be necessary to locate stairs leading to the second story.

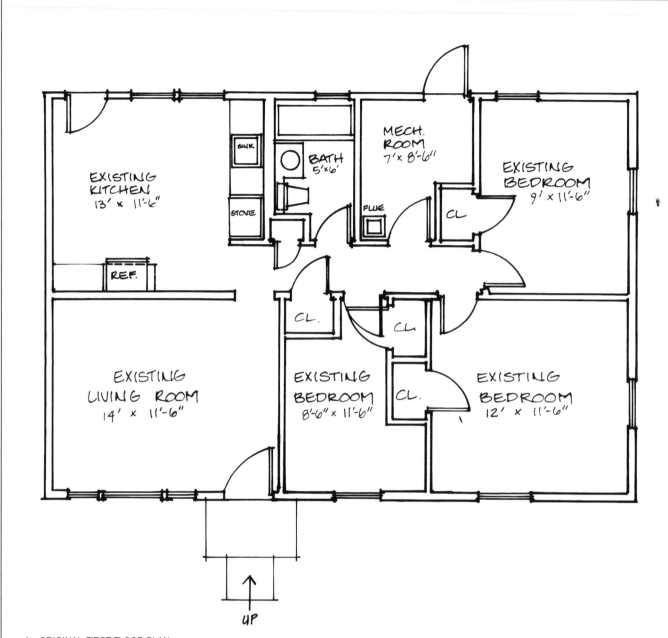

EXISTING
KITCHEN
13' × 11'-6"

SINK

STOVE

BATH
5'×6'

MECH.
ROOM
7'× 8'-6"

EXISTING
BEDROOM
9' × 11'-6"

CL

REF.

FLUE

EXISTING
LIVING ROOM
14' × 11'-6"

CL.

CL.

EXISTING
BEDROOM
8'-6" × 11'-6"

CL.

EXISTING
BEDROOM
12' × 11'-6"

UP

1. ORIGINAL FIRST-FLOOR PLAN

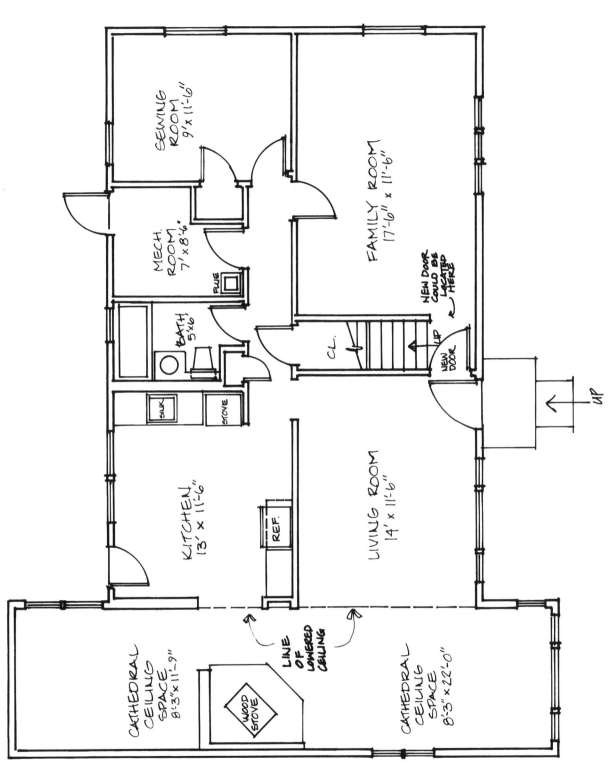

SEWING ROOM
9' x 11'-6"

MECH. ROOM
7' x 8'-6"

FLUE

BATH
5 x 6'

SINK

STOVE

FAMILY ROOM
17'-6" x 11'-6"

NEW DOOR COULD BE LOCATED HERE

CL.

UP

NEW DOOR

UP

KITCHEN
13' x 11'-6"

REF.

LIVING ROOM
14' x 11'-6"

CATHEDRAL CEILING SPACE
8'-3" x 11'-9"

WOOD STOVE

LINE OF LOWERED CEILING

CATHEDRAL CEILING SPACE
8'-3" x 22'-0"

2. REVISED FIRST-FLOOR PLAN

2 Here is the revised first floor, with the smallest of the original bedrooms eliminated in order to build stairs and create a large family room. The other small bedroom has been made into the sewing/guest room.

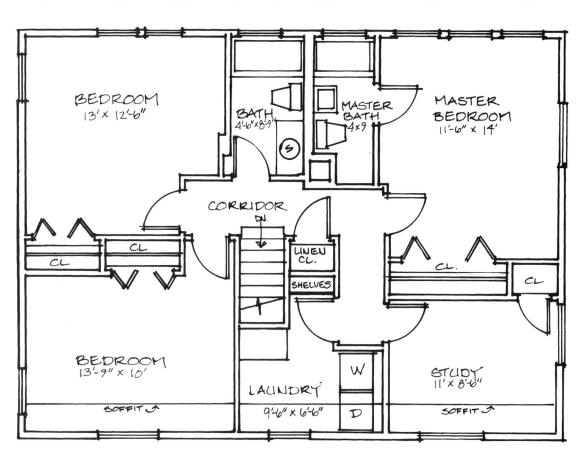

3. NEW SECOND-FLOOR PLAN

3 Planning the second floor was an exercise in conservation of space, but after some discussions, Dick and Mary approved this layout. The study is small, and the laundry area and bathrooms are only as large as they must be in order to accommodate the required fixtures; in this way, most of the available space is given to the bedrooms.

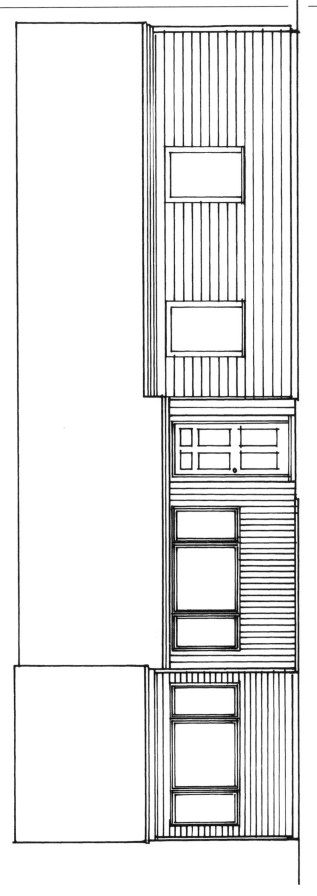

4 & 5

Elevations showing the house with its first addition, before the upper story was added.

4. ORIGINAL FRONT ELEVATION

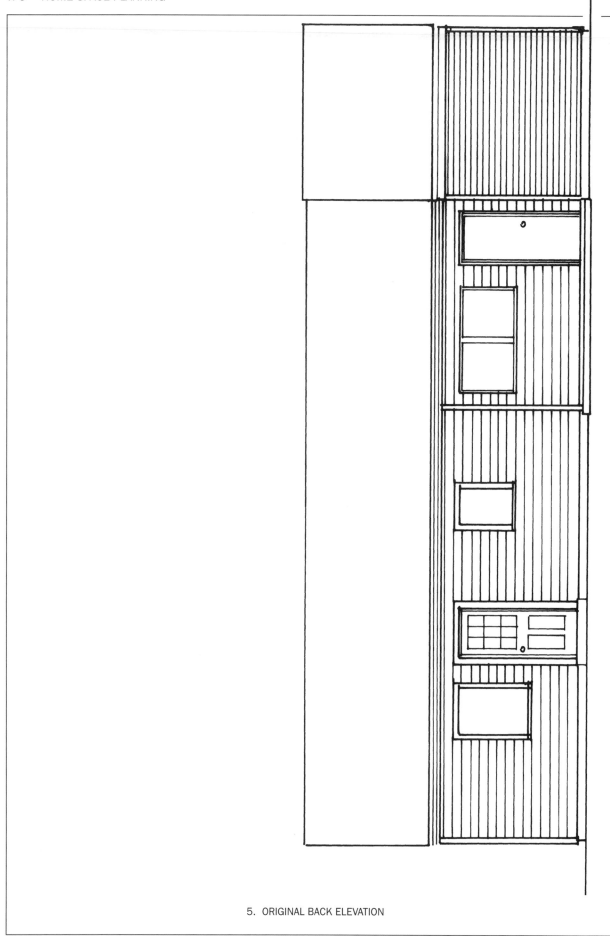

5. ORIGINAL BACK ELEVATION

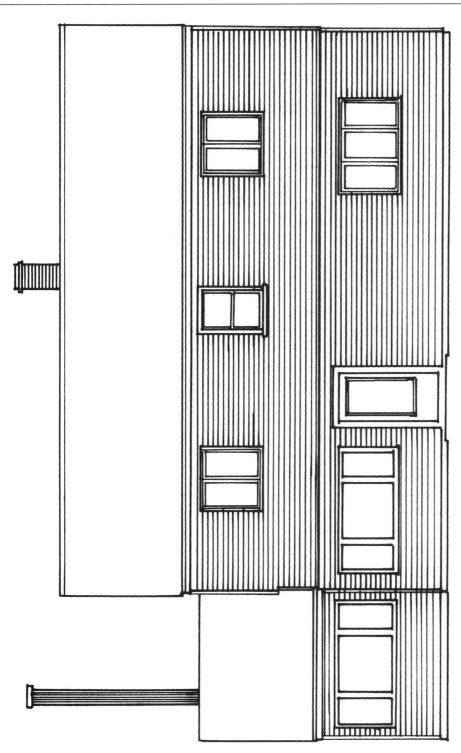

6. NEW FRONT ELEVATION

6-9

Elevations showing the house with its second story.

Shortly after the addition was completed, Dick and Mary sold the house and moved to another part of town. This decision was based in part on their dissatisfaction with the neighborhood school and in part because the house, lacking a basement, was chroni-

7. NEW BACK ELEVATION

cally short of needed storage space. Before they decided to sell, however, they were discussing with me the possibilities for making improvements to the original kitchen. Mary wanted more counter and storage space and a dishwasher; in addition, she noted that the kitchen functioned as a hallway or bridge between other spaces, so that her work was constantly interrupted by children going out to the backyard or passing from the long room to the rest of the house. The following plans explore the options for a kitchen redesign.

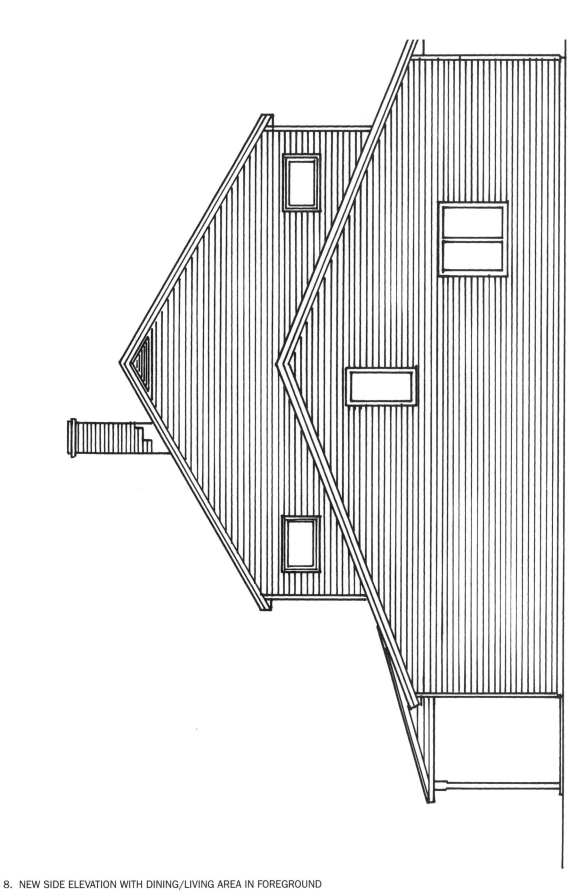

8. NEW SIDE ELEVATION WITH DINING/LIVING AREA IN FOREGROUND

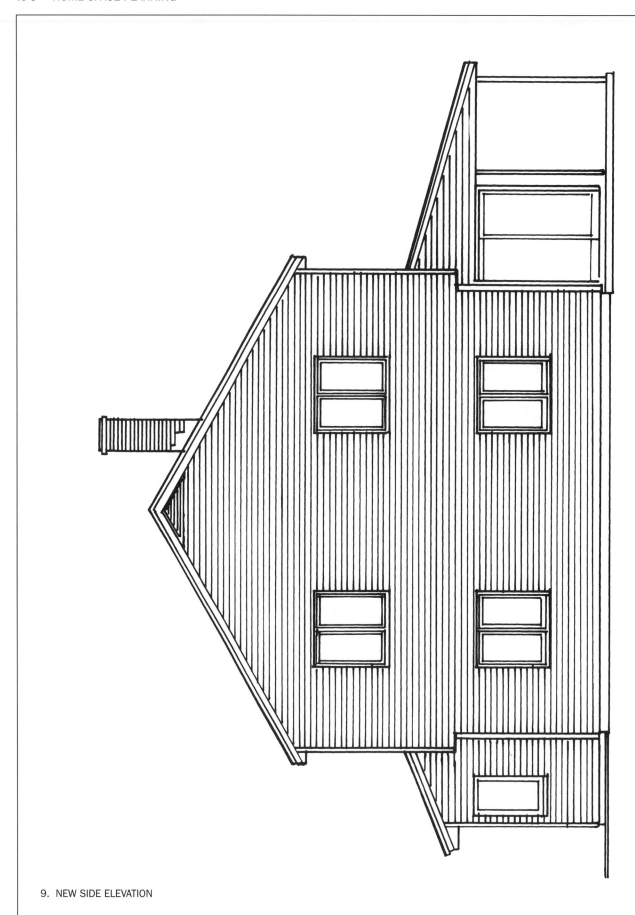

9. NEW SIDE ELEVATION

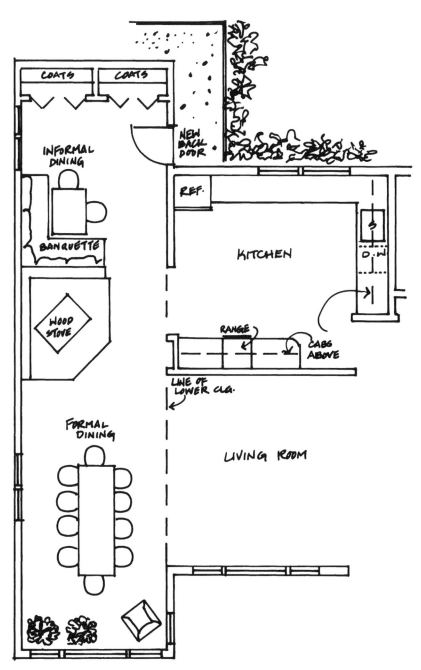

10. NEW KITCHEN

10 By moving the backdoor, valuable space is gained in the kitchen. The area behind the woodstove is made into a combination entry with coat closets and informal dining room. Now there is enough room in the kitchen for storage cabinets, work counters, and a dishwasher. This design would be economical, because demolition and new construction are kept to a minimum, and because the plumbing remains intact. Windows are installed near the built-in banquette.

11 This is a similar solution, except that the kitchen has a different organization, which permits family members to bypass the work triangle when going towards the bathroom or guest room. A large peninsula functions as a cooking center and also as a breakfast bar.

12 Here, the existing back-door is left in place, but since the plumbing is moved to the window wall, there is room for the appliances to be efficiently arranged. There is also lots of counter space next to each appliance.

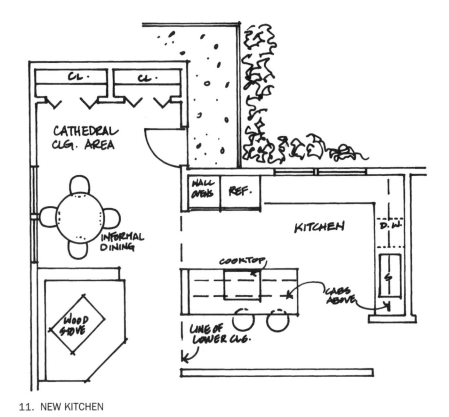

11. NEW KITCHEN

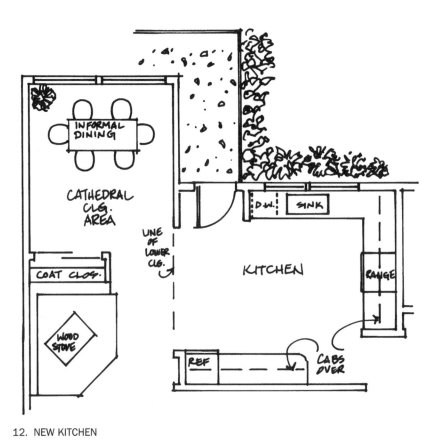

12. NEW KITCHEN

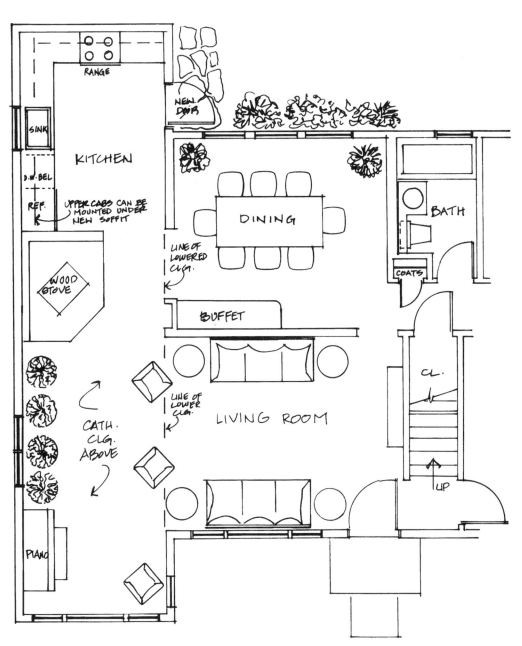

13. KITCHEN IN NEW LOCATION

13 There would be additional expense to moving the plumbing in this house built on slab, but it is an option which gives the house a bigger living room and spacious dining room. In this redesign, an L-shaped kitchen is located behind the woodstove; though small, it is efficient and could be quite attractive.

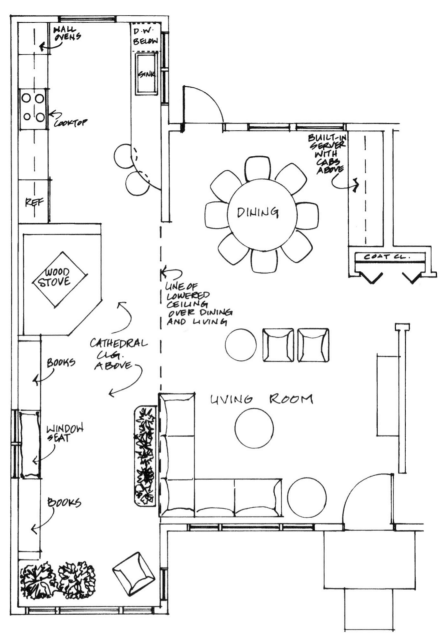

Labels within the floor plan:

WALL OVENS

D.W. BELOW

SINK

COOKTOP

REF

BUILT-IN SERVER WITH CABS ABOVE

DINING

COAT CL.

WOOD STOVE

LINE OF LOWERED CEILING OVER DINING AND LIVING

CATHEDRAL CLG. ABOVE

BOOKS

WINDOW SEAT

BOOKS

LIVING ROOM

14. KITCHEN IN NEW LOCATION

14 Here, the living and dining rooms are combined into one great room. Once again, the kitchen is behind the woodstove; this time it is a galley-style layout. On the other side of the wood-stove, a library is set up, with window seat, comfortable chair for reading, and plenty of book-shelves.

VIEW OF KITCHEN/DINING IN PLAN #14

Updating and Enlarging a Raised Ranch

1 Here is a fairly typical plan for a single-story house built in the '50s. The public areas, consisting of living room, dining room, kitchen, and, in this case, a library, are located on one side of the house, while the bathrooms and bedrooms are somewhat removed and separated from the public spaces by a hallway. This house has some very attractive features, including a number of glassed-in porches, a spacious and sunny living room, and good closets. On the other hand, it is outdated by today's standards. The kitchen has relatively little counter space and a small area for an eat-in table. (The dining room is quite small, as well.) The master bath is very small, and the powder room is a later addition with barely enough room for a sink. Most newer houses will have a more substantial master bathroom; many will have three family bedrooms in addition to the master; most will have a family room directly off the kitchen; most will also have a better half-bath.

This plan also has two aesthetic drawbacks. One is the very common problem which arises when the kitchen opens directly into the entry hall: unless the family remembers to shut the door, the kitchen is the first thing seen on entering. Similarly, from the entry (and the living room), one has a direct view down the hallway into the bathroom. What we might call "sense of entry"—one's first impression on entering—could be improved.

The redesigns which follow include kitchen renovations, bathroom and bedroom additions, as well as the creation of an improved master bedroom suite.

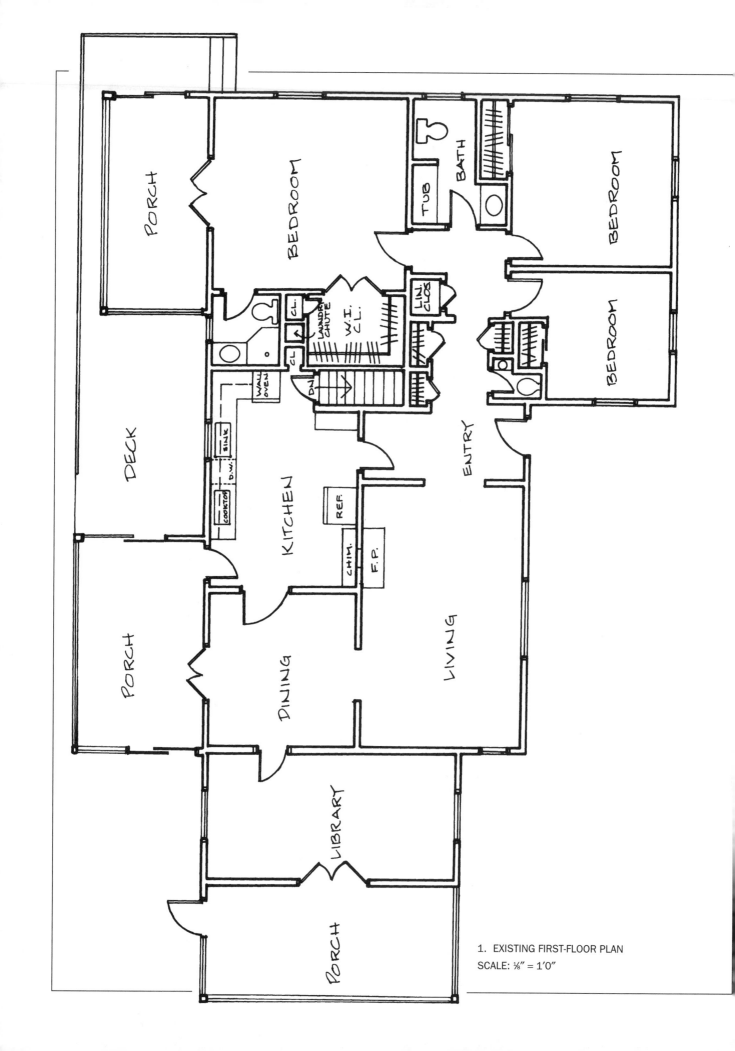

PORCH

BEDROOM

BATH

TUB

BEDROOM

DECK

CL.

LAUNDRY CHUTE

W.I. CL.

LIN. CLOS

CL.

WALL OVEN

DN

BEDROOM

SINK

ENTRY

D.W.

KITCHEN

COOKTOP

REF.

PORCH

CHIM.

F.P.

LIVING

DINING

LIBRARY

PORCH

1. EXISTING FIRST-FLOOR PLAN
SCALE: ⅛″ = 1′0″

2 This very simple renovation creates a better eat-in space by moving the refrigerator. The fridge takes the place of the old wall ovens, and in place of the cabinetry below the cooktop, an under-counter oven is installed. The sink and dishwasher remain in place, which makes this rehab very economical. The built-in table can be manufactured out of the same material as the countertop, if desired, and can be cut to fit around the chimney.

3 This kitchen plan duplicates Plan #2 in part, but instead of the built-in table it has a counter-height island which can be used for food preparation as well as informal eating. A small section of cabinets is moved, which makes traffic flow around the island more efficient.

4 In a variation which combines elements of both previous plans, a peninsula houses a cooktop and some space for eating. Here, wall ovens are installed in the space previously occupied by the cooktop. Many alternative specifications for appliances exist; the cooktop could be replaced by a drop-in range, or an under-counter oven could be placed in the peninsula.

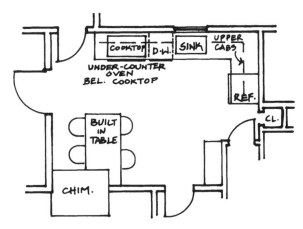

2. NEW KITCHEN
SCALE: ⅛" = 1'0"

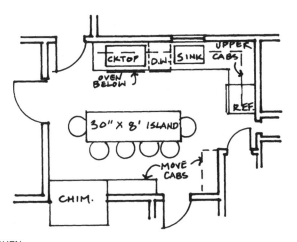

3. NEW KITCHEN
SCALE: ⅛" = 1'0"

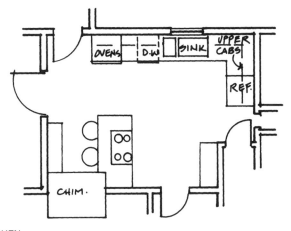

4. NEW KITCHEN
SCALE: ⅛" = 1'0"

PERSPECTIVE VIEW OF PLAN #4

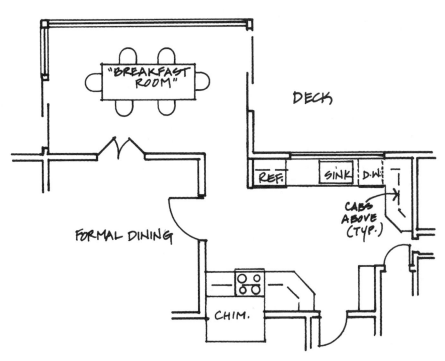

5. NEW KITCHEN AND BREAKFAST ROOM
SCALE: ⅛" = 1'0"

5 When the informal eating area is moved out of the kitchen and into the porch, the kitchen becomes a much more spacious place for preparation, with good counter space. The work triangle, consisting of fridge, sink, and stove, is well organized here. There is ample space for unloading next to the fridge, counter space for preparation adjacent to the sink, and counter space on both sides of the stove. Note that the window over the sink is enlarged, bringing light into what was a fairly dark space.

6. PERSPECTIVE VIEW OF PLAN #5

6 & 7

Two perspective sketches show how finishes and cabinet selections alter the character of the same layout. In Drawing #6, the overall look is traditional, with paneled cabinets, wood flooring, wood wainscoting, decorative tile counters, and a pendant lamp over the sink. In Drawing #7, the look is more contemporary, without being high tech. Flush wood or laminate cabinets have a clean, European look. The counter and walls are simply finished. The only real decorative note is in the pattern of floor tiles.

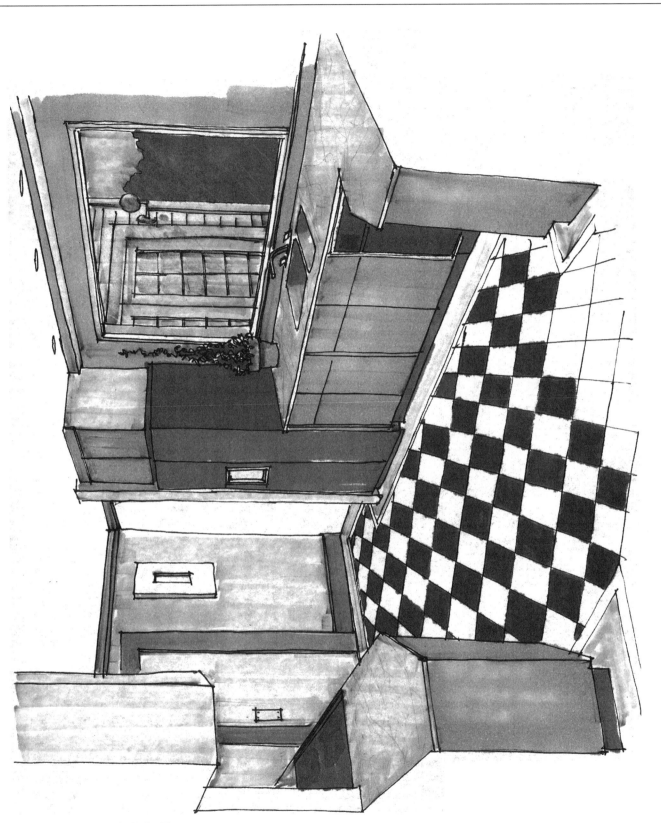

7. PERSPECTIVE VIEW OF PLAN #5

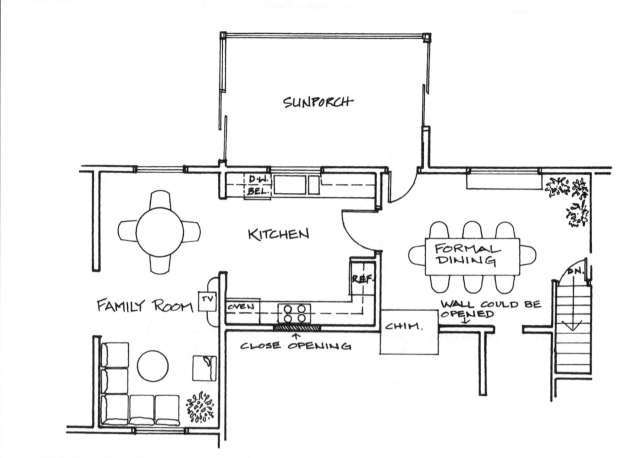

8. KITCHEN IN NEW LOCATION
SCALE: ⅛" = 1'0"

8 Two disadvantages to the original plan were the fact that the kitchen was visible upon entry and the small size of the dining room. In addition, it was mentioned that the house had no family room off the kitchen. The layout shown here accomplishes a great deal by switching the locations of kitchen and dining room. The dining room (which could be isolated from the entry hall by a door if desired) is now visible upon entry, and the room now accommodates a larger table. As in Plan #5, this room is shown with a large window, and it will also receive light from the sun-porch beyond. The kitchen in its new location is convenient to the dining room but is also adjacent to the original "library" space, which can be used for informal dining and TV viewing. The sun-porch next to the library (not shown in this drawing) could be a wonderful place for children's playthings. The opening between original dining room and living room is closed, in order to isolate the new kitchen. The new dining room could be opened up to the living room by removing a section of wall next to the chimney.

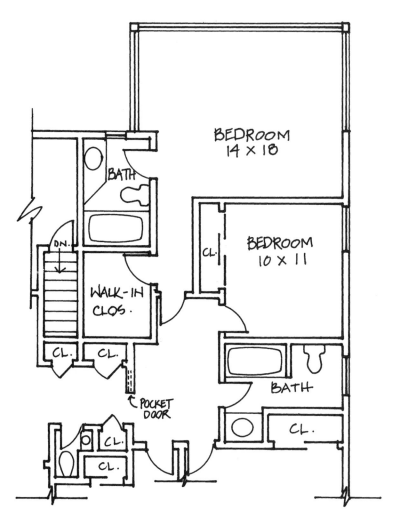

9. ADDING A BEDROOM
SCALE: ⅛″ = 1′0″

9 If a new master bathroom is desired, as well as a fourth bedroom, this plan shows a simple solution which does not involve any additions to the house. The glassed-in porch off the original master bedroom has been combined with the master, and this larger space has been subdivided into a new, sunny, and spacious master as well as a second, smaller bedroom. The original walk-in closet has been modified so that the master bath could be enlarged enough to install a big tub and larger vanity. The bathroom which is shown could be organized in a number of different ways, but the fact that this plan uses the existing plumbing makes the renovation less radical. On the whole, this is a plan which accomplishes a lot with relatively little expense. Note the addition of a pocket door which can shield the view of the bathroom from the entryway.

10 There are a number of ways in which additions can be put onto this house. One way is by extending a portion of the house towards the front. (The location for an addition depends on several factors, among them the desired interior layout, the placement of the house on its lot, and zoning regulations which determine setbacks. In addition, there are important structural and aesthetic architectural concerns such as roof lines, foundation support, window placement, and so on, which must be considered.) This plan shows an addition of 18′ × 30′. Two bedrooms are added, and the original small bedroom is eliminated in order to create, first, a hallway into the new bedrooms; second, a laundry alcove and linen closet; and, third, a larger bathroom taking the place of the powder room. Note that this new bathroom connects to both hallways, making it accessible to guests as well as family. In this plan, the original second, or family, bath is now made private to a second bedroom, so that this layout has two master suites. Once again, as in Plan #9, the walk-in closet is made slightly smaller in order to enlarge the master bath. An enlargement to a house like this one would be likely to include a full basement as well, so that more space is also added to the lower level.

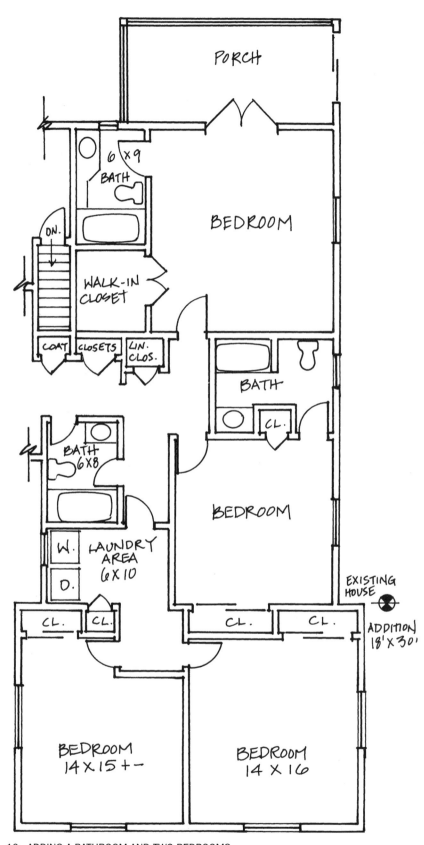

10. ADDING A BATHROOM AND TWO BEDROOMS
SCALE: ⅛″ = 1′0″

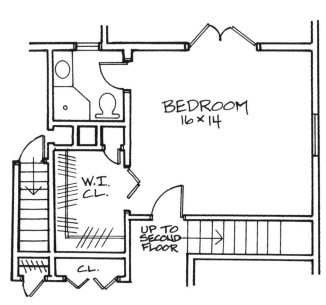

BEDROOM
16 × 14

W.I.
CL.

UP TO
SECOND
FLOOR

CL.

11. STAIRS TO SECOND STORY
SCALE: ⅛″ = 1′0″

11 So far, two plans have been shown which, in different ways, provide four bedrooms on the main level of the house. What if, however, a second story is added to part of the house? The most likely location for an addition is over the existing bedrooms, since this maintains the division of the house into private and public areas. There are several places where a staircase leading to an upper floor can be located. The one shown in this plan takes a 3-foot-wide piece out of the original master bedroom for building a staircase. Remember that a new master suite can now be located on the second floor, so that even though the original master bedroom is now made smaller, it is still, at 14′ × 16′, quite ample. In addition, if a new master bathroom is built upstairs, there is less need to alter the original bathroom. The original master might be used for a teen, for an au pair, or as a family room/den with a fold-out couch or futon, which could double as a guest room. This would be an especially nice use for this room, since it connects to the sunny porch and has direct access to the backyard.

12 In a variation on Plan #11, we see that the original bathroom is left intact, a small closet adequate for guests is installed beneath the stairs, and the original walk-in closet has been converted into a spacious laundry room. Plumbing is simple, since it abuts the bathroom. Although not shown in the drawing, there is enough space in the laundry room to accommodate either some counters or an ironing board, or both.

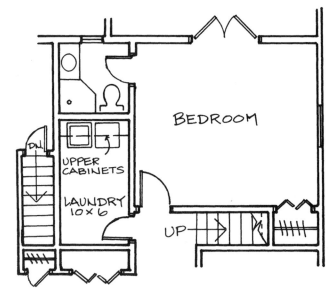

BEDROOM

UPPER CABINETS

LAUNDRY 10 × 6

DN

UP

12. NEW LAUNDRY AND STAIRS TO SECOND STORY

SCALE: ⅛″ = 1′0″

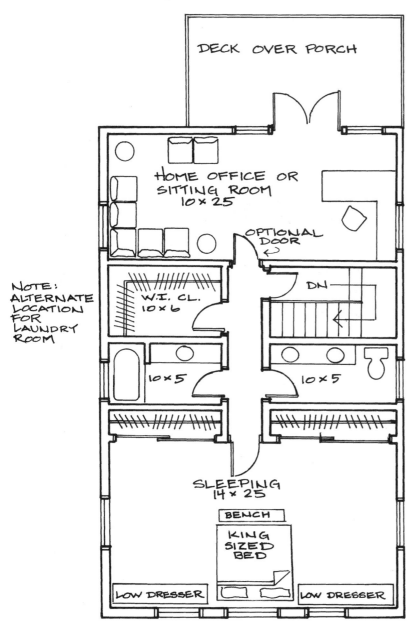

DECK OVER PORCH

HOME OFFICE OR SITTING ROOM
10 × 25

OPTIONAL DOOR

NOTE: ALTERNATE LOCATION FOR LAUNDRY ROOM

W.I. CL. 10 × 6

DN

10 × 5

10 × 5

SLEEPING 14 × 25

BENCH

KING SIZED BED

LOW DRESSER

LOW DRESSER

13. SECOND-STORY ADDITION
SCALE: ⅛″ = 1′0″

13 Here is the first of the second-story plans, which assumes that the stairs are located as in Plan #11. There is almost an infinite number of possibilities in the size of the upper story, from a single room to an entire second floor covering the whole house! Here, the second-story addition covers slightly more than the space occupied by the lower-level bedrooms and baths. This generous addition includes a spacious bedroom with over 20 linear feet of closet space, as well as a second, walk-in closet. There is another space, which is shown here as a combination home office/sitting room; this opens onto a deck situated on top of the porch. The bathroom is divided, for greater flexibility of use; the toilet and tub can be used simultaneously by different persons. Note, too, that the walk-in closet could be an alternate location for a laundry room. However, most laundry is generated by children, so that it makes most sense to install these appliances nearer to the children's rooms below.

14 Here is a second-story addition with the same set of stairs as in Plan #13 and which is the same size, although it does not have a deck. This plan provides two spacious bedrooms with generous closet space, and another divided bathroom with both tub and shower.

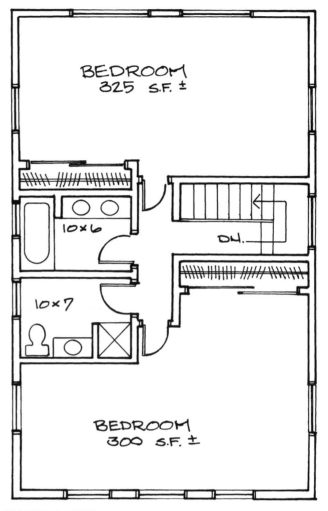

14. SECOND-STORY ADDITION
SCALE: ⅛" = 1'0"

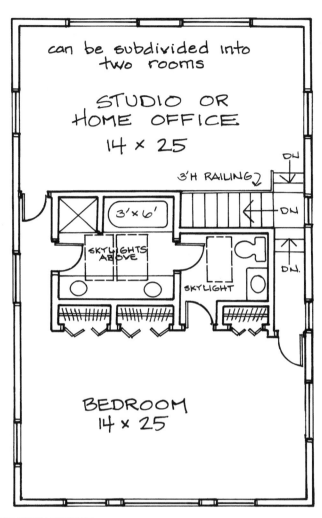

can be subdivided into two rooms

STUDIO OR HOME OFFICE 14 × 25

3'H RAILING

DN

DN

DN.

3' × 6'

SKYLIGHTS ABOVE

SKYLIGHT

BEDROOM 14 × 25

15. SECOND-STORY ADDITION
SCALE: ⅛" = 1'0"

15 Yet another addition with the same stair location as in Plans #13 and #14 creates a more unexpected and lively circulation pattern. Here the bathroom is once again subdivided into two rooms, with the toilet opening onto both bedroom and tub room. As in both of the previous plans, the toilet can be accessed without going through the tub/shower room, which is a nice detail in planning that is often overlooked. Because this bathroom is an interior space, hallways are created on both sides. Skylights bring light into the space; they could be operable if desired. Note that as the stairs approach the second floor, one may turn right and go into the bedroom or make a left turn into what could be a studio, office, or second bedroom. Since there are two entrances into this studio/office space, it could easily be subdivided into two rooms. In that case, it might be furnished as a den, with TV, which is entered from the stairs and as a studio or office which is entered through the bedroom. There are many possibilities for using this flexible layout.

16 This plan shows an alternative location for the stairway leading from first to second floor. The walk-in closet as well as a first-floor hall closet have been removed. A more traditional 2-foot-deep closet now faces the bedroom, and the stairs are built in the remainder of the space. Note also that the original master bath is enlarged and configured in a new way.

17 This is the first of two plans related to the new stairway location. In both of these plans, a master suite with a single bedroom is shown. Here, the stairs lead to a hallway from which one can enter a standard, three-fixture bathroom or the bedroom. Two walk-in closets are provided. The bedroom is very large and could accommodate a sitting area furnished with comfortable, soft seating, or it could be provided with additional closets.

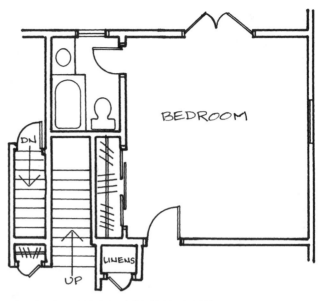

16. ALTERNATE LOCATION FOR STAIRS TO SECOND STORY
SCALE: ⅛″ = 1′0″

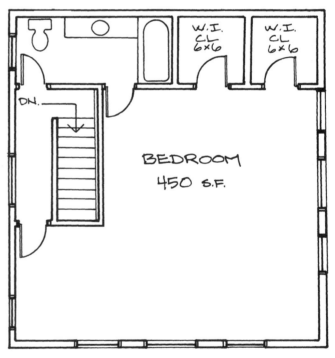

17. SECOND-STORY MASTER BEDROOM SUITE
SCALE: ⅛″ = 1′0″

18 Here is a variation on Plan #17. The bathroom is subdivided, two walk-in closets are provided, and the bedroom has a view of the backyard. In practice, many more variations could be created with this upper-story block of space.

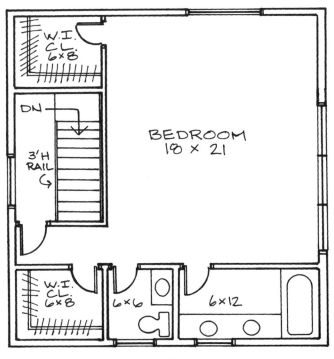

18. SECOND-STORY MASTER BEDROOM SUITE

SCALE: ⅛″ = 1′0″

Lake House with a View

Before he married Cynthia, Rob bought a bungalow with a wonderful view, built on a small hill with a lawn spreading down to the edge of a long lake.

1 Rob made some changes to the house soon after he bought it; Plan #1 includes his alterations. First, he updated the kitchen, installing a large commercial range and refrigerator and making the room open to the dining area. He also added a half-bath behind the coat closet. Next, he built a tile-floored sunspace, an informal living area with a small bar, from which he could see the lake. Finally, he added a deck, with steps to a path leading to the water and his sundry boats.

After Rob married Cynthia and they had lived in the house for a few years, they realized that the layout did not fully serve their needs. Rob found that he was constantly drawn to the view of the lake and spent most of his time in the sunspace during the day. However, as a committed cook, he also spent a lot of time in the kitchen, where he had no view of the lake and not enough natural light. His grown children began to have babies, and both his and Cynthia's family came often to visit and to enjoy swimming and boating. Often there were twenty people who gathered at the house, for weekend visits as well as Thanksgiving and Christmas holidays, but the dining area had a table that seated only six.

It became clear that the two guest bedrooms were not enough to house the growing number of visitors. In addition, Cynthia used both the full guest bath and the closets in the extra bedrooms; she resented having to give up her bathroom when guests came. Rob, a diabetic, needed to rearrange his bathroom so that it could accommodate a refrigerator for his insulin, as well as a locked cabinet to keep his syringes away from curious small children. Rob and Cynthia decided that they need a new kitchen, located within view of the lake, a large dining room (big enough to seat twenty), more bedrooms for guests, and more closets for Cynthia. They want to keep the sunspace (or build another one), and build a large deck with a hot tub. Rob also wants to install a complete security system with camera surveillance; he wants his video screens in the kitchen area. Finally, Cynthia needs space for a small home office with desk, computer, and some storage. The basement area, with garage, laundry, storage, and exercise rooms, is to be left undisturbed.

There are two basic ways in which Rob and Cynthia's requirements can be met. One is by enlarging the house on its existing level—that is, by adding bedrooms and bathrooms and moving the kitchen. Another approach is to relocate the kitchen but to use the first-floor bedrooms for guests; a new second floor would then be built for a master suite.

Whichever of these two approaches is taken, the new location for the kitchen is basically a given; it will need to be placed where the sunspace is, in order for the lake to be seen. With the

AREA FOR LARGER DECK

12'-0"

17'-0"

DECK

27'-6"

SUNSPACE

22'-0"

WALK-IN CLOSET

6'-0"

BEDROOM

12'-6"

BEDROOM

10'-0"

24'-0"

LIVING ROOM

RAISED HEARTH

1'-0"

10'-0"

BEDROOM

BEDROOM

SHOWER

BATHROOM

BATHROOM

TUB

PANTRY

5'-0"

COATS

REF.

ENTRY

UP

23'-0"

14'-0"

6 BURNER RANGE

S

DW

KITCHEN

DINING AREA

1. EXISTING FLOOR PLAN

kitchen here, it is clear that one obvious and inexpensive solution to the dining room problem is to locate it in the existing living room. The room is large enough, abuts the new kitchen, also has some view of the lake, and its fireplace adds a festive ambience to holiday meals. Since Rob and Cynthia only use the living room to watch TV at night, that room could be moved to a part of the house without the view. Thus, the original kitchen/dining space is an ideal place for the living room. Note that since the kitchen has no windows along one wall, the new plans show some kind of added fenestration. In all but one of the redesigns which follow, the reorganization described above is a constant.

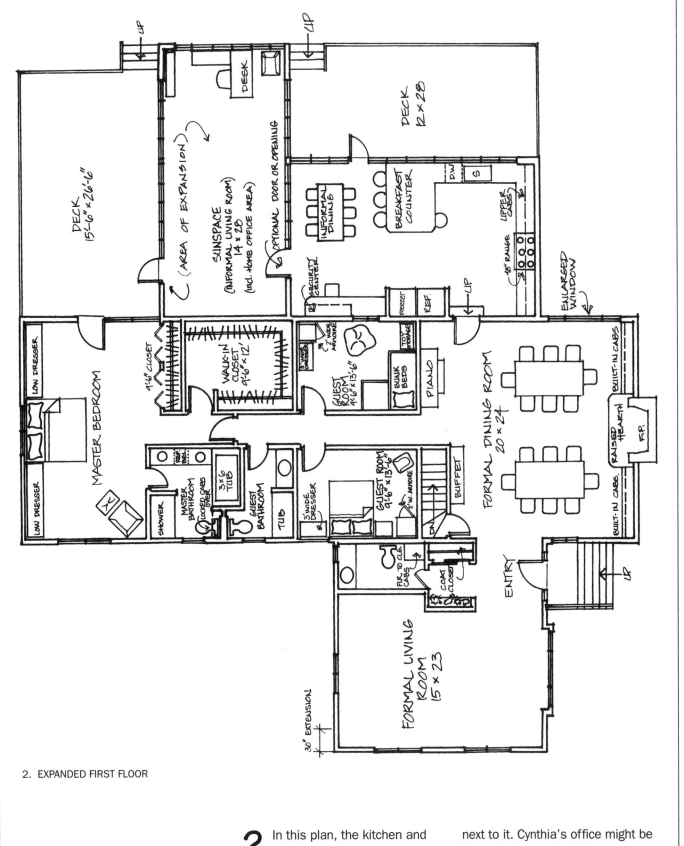

UP

UP

DECK

DECK 12 × 28

DECK 15'-6" × 26'-6"

(AREA OF EXPANSION)

SUNSPACE
(INFORMAL LIVING ROOM)
14 × 28
(Incl. HOME OFFICE AREA)

OPTIONAL DOOR OR OPENING

INFORMAL DINING

BREAKFAST COUNTER

D.W.

UPPER CABS

45" RANGE

ENLARGED WINDOW

SECURITY CENTER

FREEZER

REF.

UP

LOW DRESSER

MASTER BEDROOM

LOW DRESSER

9'-6" CLOSET

WALK-IN CLOSET
9'-6" × 12'

5' WIDE DRESSER

3' WIDE ARMOIRE

GUEST ROOM
9'-6" × 15'-6"

TOY STORAGE

BUNK BEDS

PIANO

FORMAL DINING ROOM
20 × 24

BUILT-IN CABS

RAISED HEARTH

F.P.

BUILT-IN CABS

SHOWER

MASTER BATHROOM
(CLOSED CABS OVER)

3 × 6 TUB

GUEST BATHROOM

TUB

3' WIDE DRESSER

GUEST ROOM
9'-6" × 13'-6"

3' W. ARMOIRE

BUFFET

DN

FIX. TO CLG.

FIX. TO CLG. CABS

COAT CLOSET

ENTRY

UP

30" EXTENSION

FORMAL LIVING ROOM
15 × 23

2. EXPANDED FIRST FLOOR

2 In this plan, the kitchen and informal dining area are moved into the existing sunspace area, and a new sunspace is built next to it. Cynthia's office might be located at the end of this sunspace, so that she enjoys the view while working at home. The original deck is maintained and another is added next to the master bedroom.

Cynthia acquires additional closet space because the walk-in closet now incorporates a guest room closet. (The guest room is served by an armoire or wardrobe.) With the door to the walk-in closet moved to the hallway, a new closet can be built facing into the bedroom.

Rob's bathroom is slightly altered and enlarged by removing closets which were in both bathrooms as well as the closet in the other guest room, and by moving its entrance. Now, it has a shower, a tub, and a long counter with double sinks and an under-counter fridge; his locked cabinet is over the toilet. This bathroom serves both Rob and Cynthia, leaving the second bathroom for guests.

The new living room is in the space occupied by the old kitchen, and it is expanded by 30 inches. An expansion of this size can be accomplished by cantilevering the room out over the driveway. The entry to the half-bath is changed, so that the bathroom does not open into the formal living room. Other changes include the coat closet and the installation of a full or partial wall which creates a hallway leading to the half-bath.

3 This plan shows an expansion of a different kind on the lake side. Here, the kitchen, informal dining, and sunspace become one big, open room, full of light and flowers. The kitchen is large, with a refrigerator, a separate freezer, a six-burner range, and a great deal of counter space and upper cabinetry for storage. There are two places for informal eating: stools at the counter and a round table near the security center. The rest of the room is given over to comfortable seating—a casual living room overlooking the water, in which Rob, Cynthia, and their guests will probably spend most of their time. The sunspace opens onto a large deck with hot tub and stairs leading to the lake path.

An 11-foot-wide addition on the other side of the house makes it possible to add a home office, extra closets, a new guest room with closet, and a hallway. This hallway was created by using space carved out of one of the guest rooms. The rest of the original bedroom has become a laundry room, large enough for cabinets, folding counter, and ironing board.

The hallway is a key to several changes in design. It permits access to the new guest bedroom, as well as to the original half-bath, which has become a three-fixture bath. (Note that the bathroom also opens into the living room, but that door could be omitted.) Since the half-bath is now a complete guest bath, the two separate, original bathrooms have been combined into one and redesigned. The new master bath is luxurious, with a separate toilet room, double sinks, large tub, and a room for Rob which contains shower, sink, and small fridge. Cynthia's closets are modified as they were in Plan #2. The drawback to this plan is that there are only two guest rooms. If more were required, they could be located in the basement. With new and attractive finishes—pretty carpet and wallpaper—these lower-level rooms could be quite nice.

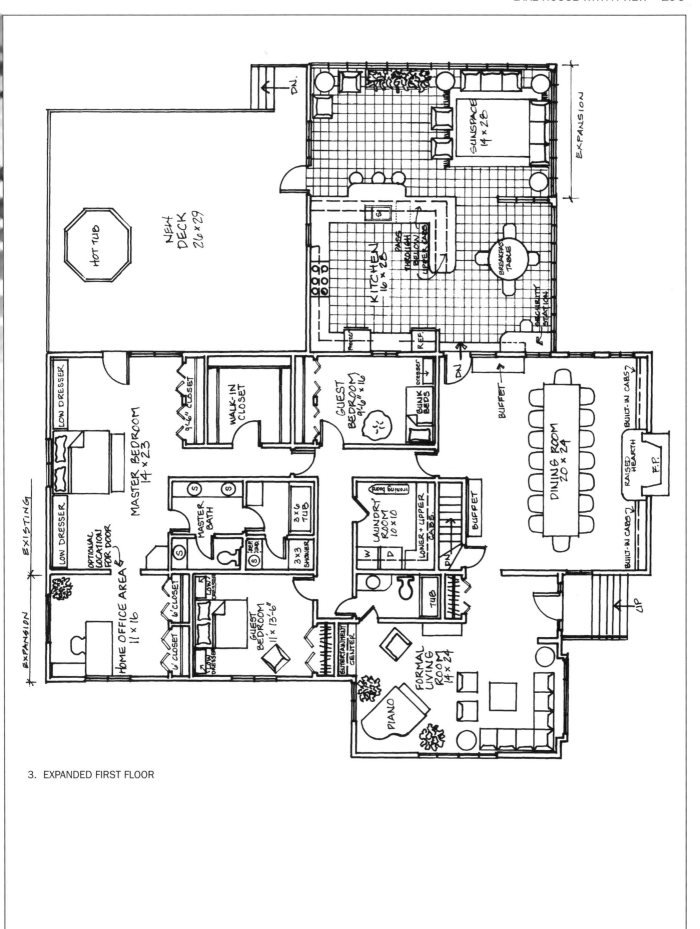

3. EXPANDED FIRST FLOOR

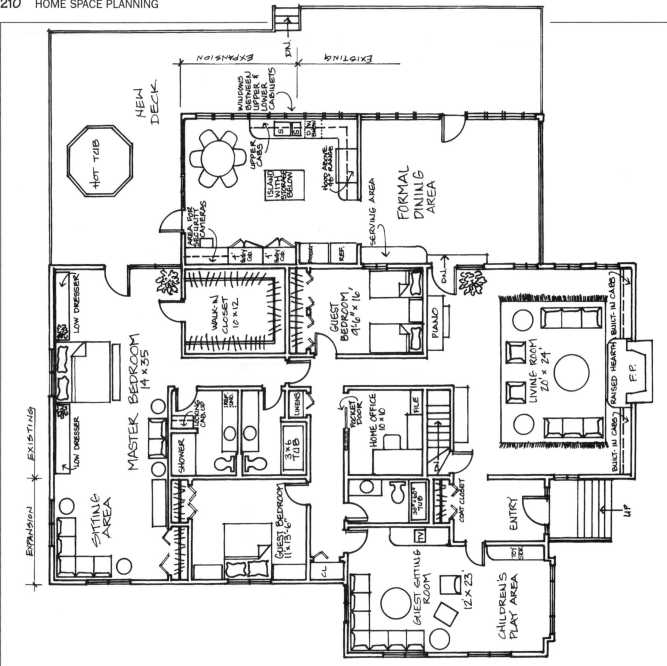

4. EXPANDED FIRST FLOOR

4 This is the only plan in which the original living room is left unchanged. Here, the sunspace is enlarged to create a kitchen and formal dining area. The room which had been the kitchen is a sitting and play room for guests. The same hallway seen in Plan #3 is shown here; the room shown as a laundry before is now a separate home office. The expanded portion of the master bedroom is furnished on the plan as a sitting room, but it could be a big dressing room with plenty of closet space. Rob and Cynthia's bathrooms are left essentially intact, but a new door in the hall makes both bathrooms a part of the master suite.

Although this plan fulfills many of Rob and Cynthia's requests, there are some problems. The dining room is not as large a space as the living room, although it is probably large enough for most of their dinner parties. There is no sunspace here, but the existing living room does have a view of the lake.

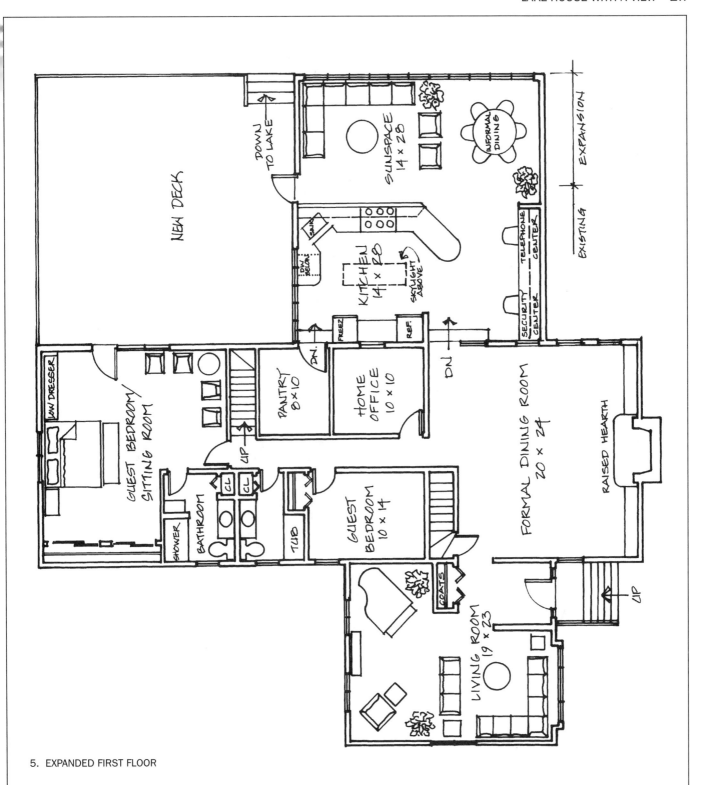

5. EXPANDED FIRST FLOOR

5 Here is the first plan which assumes the existence of a new, partial second story consisting of the master suite. The staircase is located in the walk-in closet. One of the guest rooms has been subdivided into a home office and a pantry. The master bedroom is now a combined guest and sitting room, with a private bathroom.

Once again, the sunspace area has been expanded to create a large room for the kitchen as well as informal dining and living rooms. The layout for the kitchen is different from before, and it is separated from the sunspace by a full-height wall. An angled portion of the counter acts as a serving counter for both the formal and informal dining areas. Note that this is the first plan in which the half-bath is removed, which makes the living room larger and permits the installation of another window in the back.

6 Here is one possible layout for the master suite on the second floor. Again, there are two bathrooms; they are located over the bathrooms below, which makes plumbing more economical. The bedroom space is approximately the same size it was downstairs. There are two standard closets and a walk-in closet. A wall of windows gives a good view of the lake.

7 In this plan, there is only one bathroom, and the bedroom is larger. It is furnished so that one end is a sleeping area and the other has a sofa with a water view. This plan shows plenty of windows on three sides of the room.

8 This perspective sketch gives a sense of the interior of the bedroom in Plan #7 and its view.

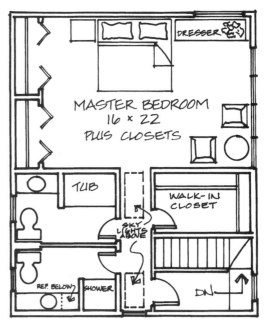

6. NEW SECOND FLOOR

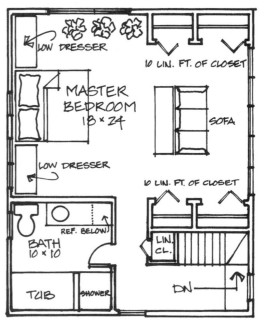

7. NEW SECOND FLOOR

8. INTERIOR VIEW OF BEDROOM IN PLAN #7

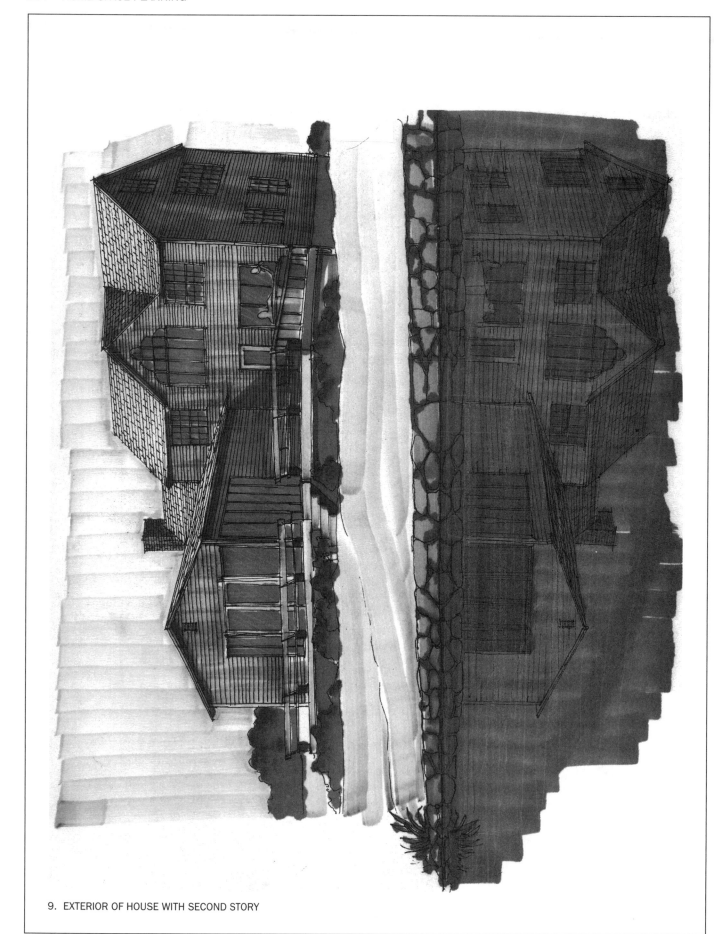

9. EXTERIOR OF HOUSE WITH SECOND STORY

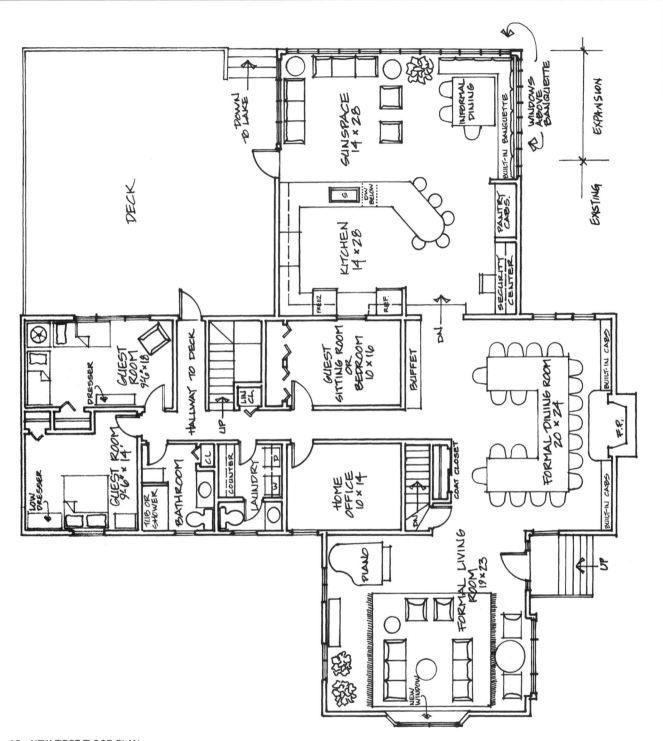

DECK

DOWN TO LAKE

SUNSPACE 14 x 28

INFORMAL DINING

WINDOWS ABOVE BANQUETTE

EXPANSION

EXISTING

BUILT-IN BANQUETTE

KITCHEN 14 x 28

DW BELOW

PANTRY CABS.

SECURITY CENTER

FREEZ

REF.

DN

BUFFET

GUEST SITTING ROOM OR BEDROOM 10 x 16

GUEST ROOM 9'6" x 18

DRESSER

HALLWAY TO DECK

UP

LIN CL.

FORMAL DINING ROOM 20 x 24

BUILT-IN CABS

F.P.

BUILT-IN CABS

LOW DRESSER

GUEST ROOM 9'6" x 14'

TUB OR SHOWER

BATHROOM

CL

COUNTER

LAUNDRY

W

D

HOME OFFICE 10 x 14

COAT CLOSET

DN

UP

PIANO

FORMAL LIVING ROOM 19 x 23

NEW WINDOW

10. NEW FIRST-FLOOR PLAN

9 A sketch of the exterior suggests one way that the house might be designed if a second story were added.

10 This plan makes significant changes in the organization of the bedroom wing on the main level. The original master bedroom is subdivided into two smaller, but perfectly adequate, guest rooms. Where the walk-in closet was, there are stairs and a hallway leading to the deck; this hallway eliminates the need to go through the kitchen (a long walk) or a bedroom (an invasion of pri-

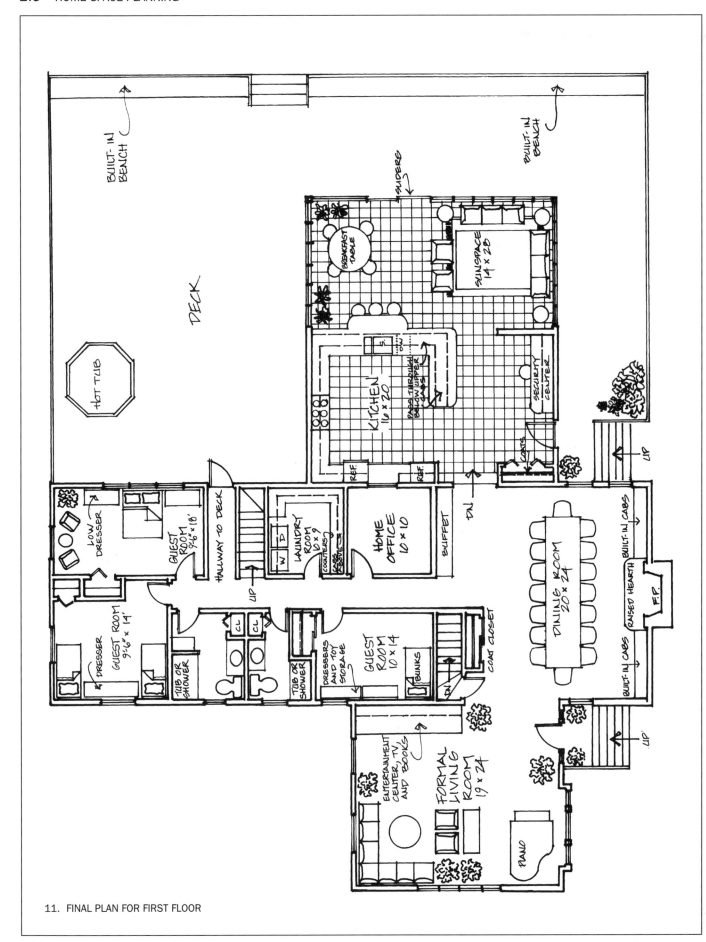

BUILT-IN BENCH

BUILT-IN BENCH

DECK

HOT TUB

BREAKFAST TABLE

SLIDERS

SUNSPACE 14 × 28

KITCHEN 16 × 20

PASS THROUGH BELOW UPPER CABS

SECURITY CENTER

COATS

REF.

REF.

DV

BUFFET

HOME OFFICE 10 × 10

LAUNDRY ROOM 10 × 9

COUNTERS

UP

HALLWAY TO DECK

GUEST ROOM 9'6" × 18'

LOW DRESSER

GUEST ROOM 9'6" × 14'

DRESSER

TUB OR SHOWER

CL CL

TUB OR SHOWER

DRESSERS AND TOY STORAGE

GUEST ROOM 10 × 14

BUNKS

COAT CLOSET

DINING ROOM 20 × 24

BUILT-IN CABS

RAISED HEARTH

BUILT-IN CABS

F.P.

UP

UP

ENTERTAINMENT CENTER, TV, AND BOOKS

FORMAL LIVING ROOM 19 × 24

PIANO

11. FINAL PLAN FOR FIRST FLOOR

vacy) to get outside. Since only one full bathroom is needed for guests, the second bathroom has borrowed space from an abutting bedroom closet and is now a half-bath and laundry room. One guest room is made into a home office. This efficient layout thus has an office, laundry center, and three guest rooms all on one level.

The kitchen is once again part of a big room. It is much like the layout in Plan #5 but is more open and has a built-in banquette as part of the informal dining space.

11 The first nine plans were brought to Rob and Cynthia for their feedback and suggestions. They liked different parts of the various plans. They voted in favor of the kitchen/sunspace in Plan #3, and they also liked the subdivision of the master bedroom into two rooms and the new hallway leading to the deck. They commented that the guest sitting or bedroom in Plan #10, abutting the kitchen, was a room which tended to get hot and stuffy, so they thought that it and the Plan #10 office should switch places. Rob also wants a direct entrance from the side of the house into the kitchen, with a deck which would wrap around the entire sunspace.

As the main level was redesigned to accommodate their suggestions, it became clear that, with the home office in its new location, a comfortable laundry room could also be installed; this leaves the original bathrooms intact.

Rob and Cynthia also felt that the new master suite on the second floor was too small, with insufficient closet space, so in the following plans it is enlarged. The designer suggested that room could be made for a small upstairs den where they could watch TV at night, and Rob said that he would like to put a computer in that room. These additions are shown in the next two plans.

VIEW OF LIVING ROOM IN PLAN #11

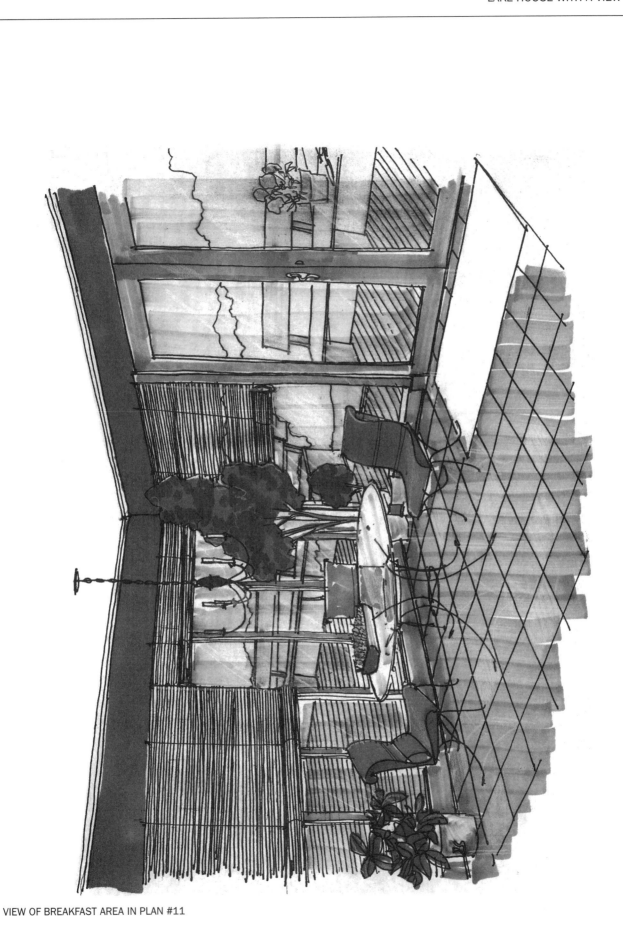

VIEW OF BREAKFAST AREA IN PLAN #11

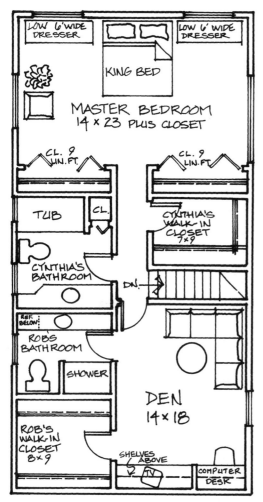

12. NEW SECOND STORY

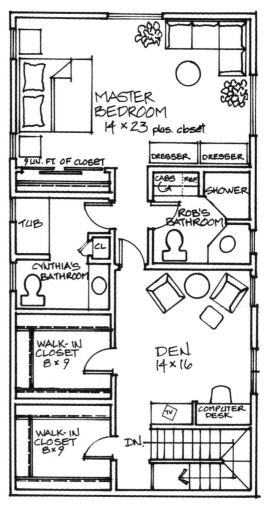

13. NEW SECOND STORY

12 This plan assumes that the stairs are in the same place as in Plan #11. The bathrooms are back to back and located above those on the first floor. The master bedroom is spacious; there are two standard and two walk-in closets, as well as a den.

13 Here, an effort is made to keep both bathrooms near the bedroom; this requires moving the stairs. (They could be located on the main level near the formal dining room.) In other respects, this plan is essentially like the other, although it is shown with a different furniture layout.

14–16

These elevations show the Lake House in its existing, one-story state.

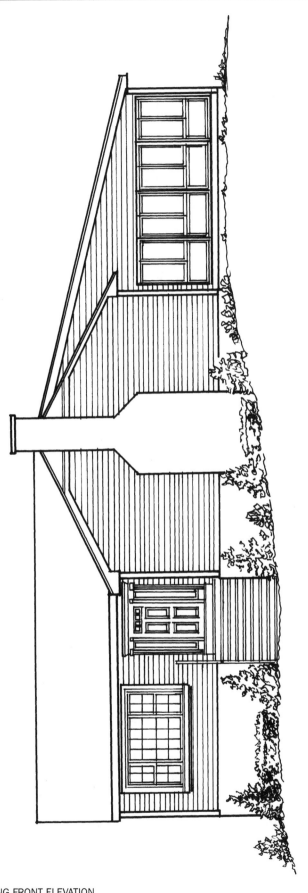

14. EXISTING FRONT ELEVATION

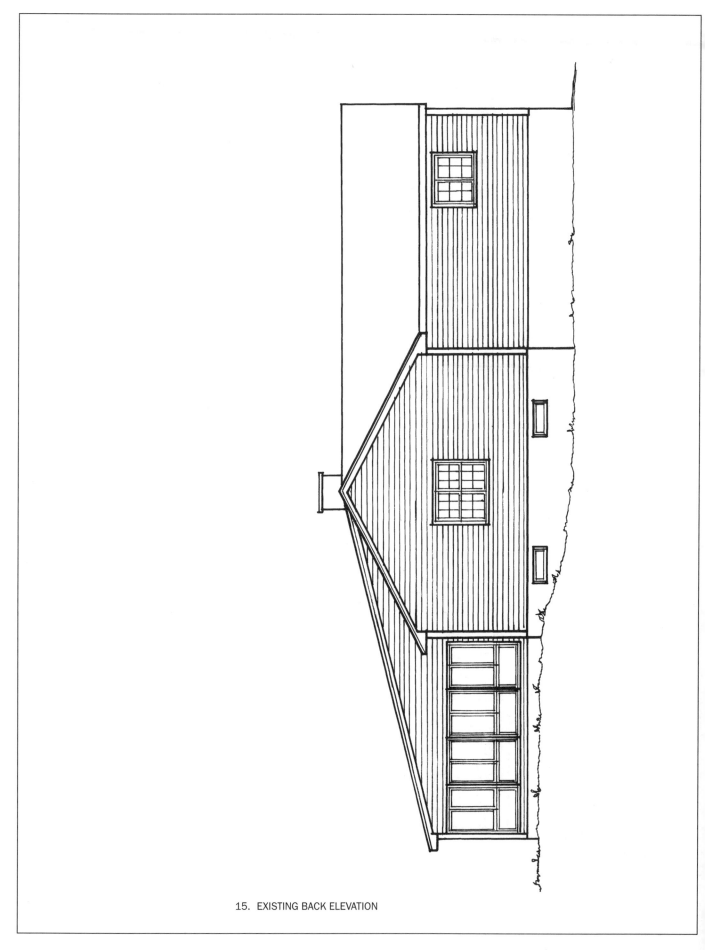

15. EXISTING BACK ELEVATION

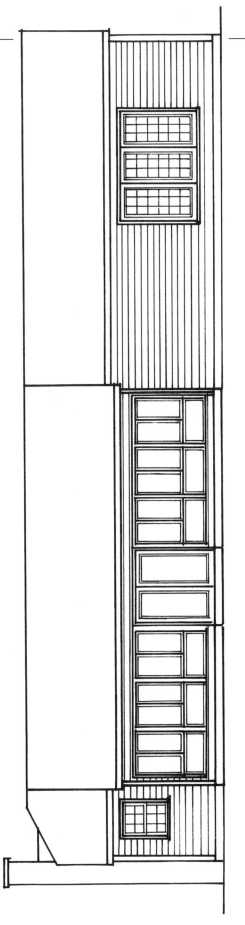

16. EXISTING SUNSPACE ELEVATION

17–19

These elevations show how the Lake House might look if a partial second story were added. Each of these pictures has the same elevation but shows how different fenestration affects the look of the house.

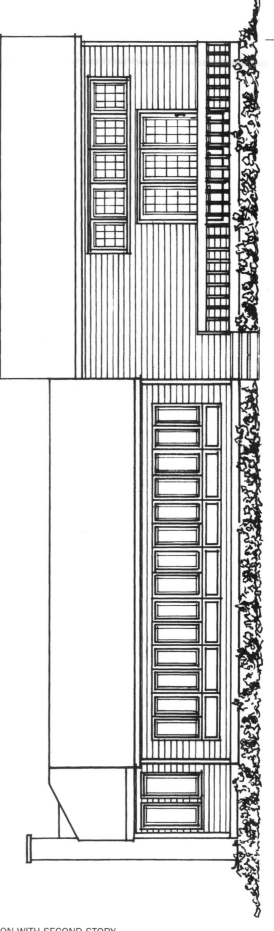

17. NEW ELEVATION WITH SECOND STORY

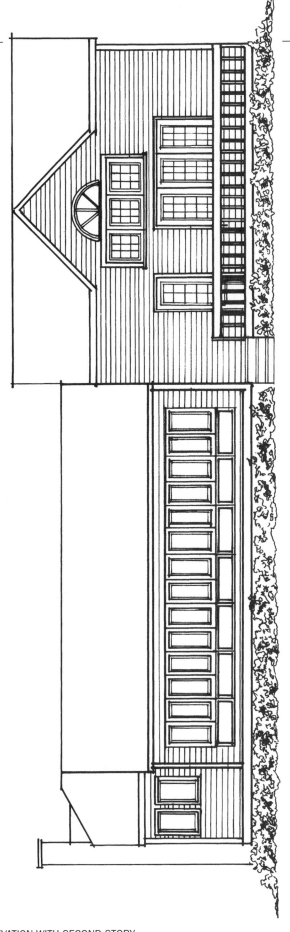

18. NEW ELEVATION WITH SECOND STORY

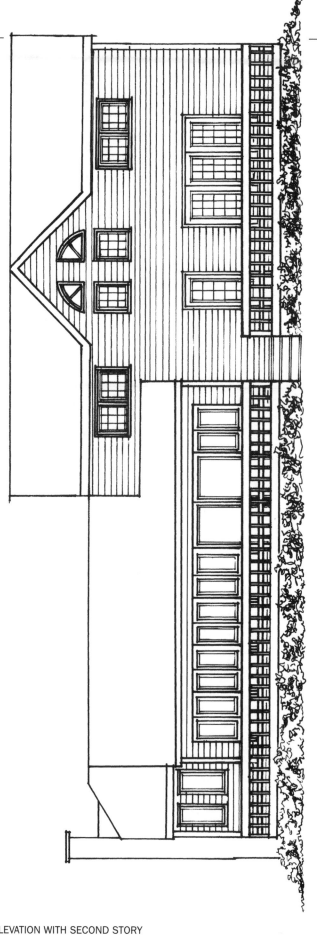

19. NEW ELEVATION WITH SECOND STORY

Lifting the Roof and Adding On

1 The Massachusetts Cape Cod which is pictured in Plan #1 was purchased in the 1970s by an architect who made extensive renovations and additions over a number of years. This plan shows the house as it was when he bought it—a very common layout for a small house of this type— with two rather small bedrooms, a small living room, no formal dining room, and a very compact kitchen. The unfinished basement contained hookups for washer and dryer; the attic was unfinished as well. The roof ridge ran parallel to the front of the house, and the roof pitch was steep on both sides. There were two little dormers in the attic overlooking the front yard.

This house was built on a steep hill, with the land falling away towards the back of the property. Thus, when the architect began to expand the house, his lowest level (the basement level) could be equipped with sliding glass doors which opened into the backyard. These sliders can be seen, on Plan #28, in the lower-level family room and in the workshop.

The following plans and other drawings show how this house evolved over time, under the ownership of two families, in response to their changing needs.

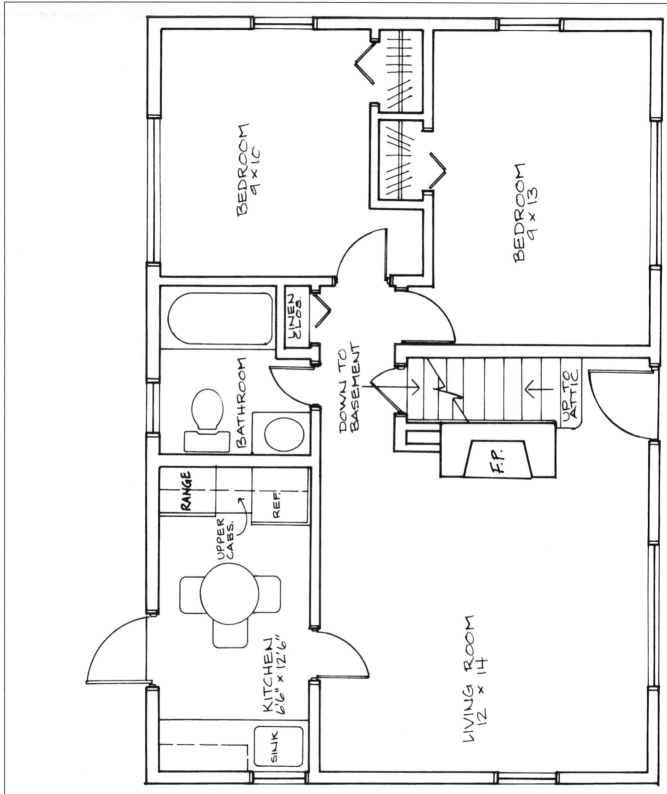

1. ORIGINAL FIRST-FLOOR PLAN
SCALE: ¼″ = 1′0″

2 A look at Plan #2 reveals the first steps taken by the architect in revamping and enlarging the house. On the right-hand side of the plan, the shape of the original Cape, with its central stair-

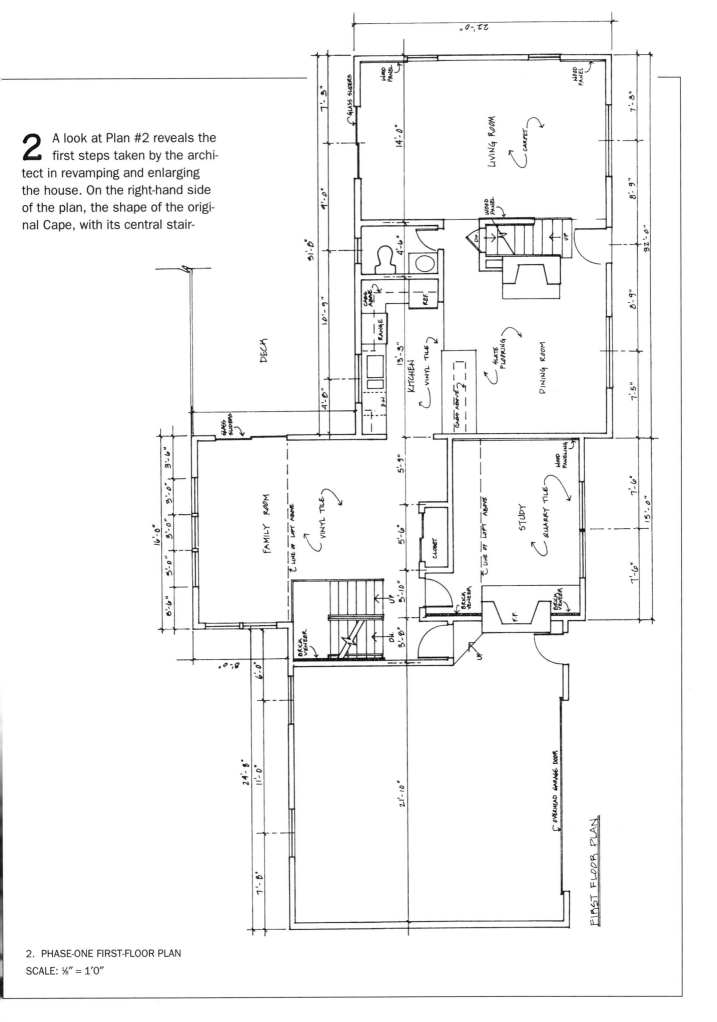

2. PHASE-ONE FIRST-FLOOR PLAN
SCALE: ⅛" = 1'0"

case, is clear. The two first-floor bedrooms have been removed to create a spacious living room, and the wall separating the original kitchen from the living room was removed, making it possible to create another spacious first-floor room which functions as an open kitchen/dining room. The three-fixture bath has been reduced to a half-bath.

Plan #3 shows the changes made to the upper floor (the unfinished attic). By altering the pitch of the back part of the roof to make it less steep, the architect gained floor space and head room. His planning for this upper floor was somewhat inhibited by the existence of the central staircase and chimney, which divide the space into two sections. He and his wife disagreed on the design for this floor. While he wanted to build a single, large master suite, she insisted on providing a second bedroom with its own bathroom, to be used as a guest suite. Keep in mind that, at this stage of the planning, the additional spaces shown on the plans (family room and study on the first floor, loft area on the second) did not yet exist and were not even anticipated. Thus, decisions needed to be made on the assumption that the house might not be enlarged. In the end, the architect's wife prevailed.

Some years later, the architect began to add on to the house. By this time, his wife had left him, so he was free to make his own decisions concerning the expansion. A study of Plan #2 (the first-floor

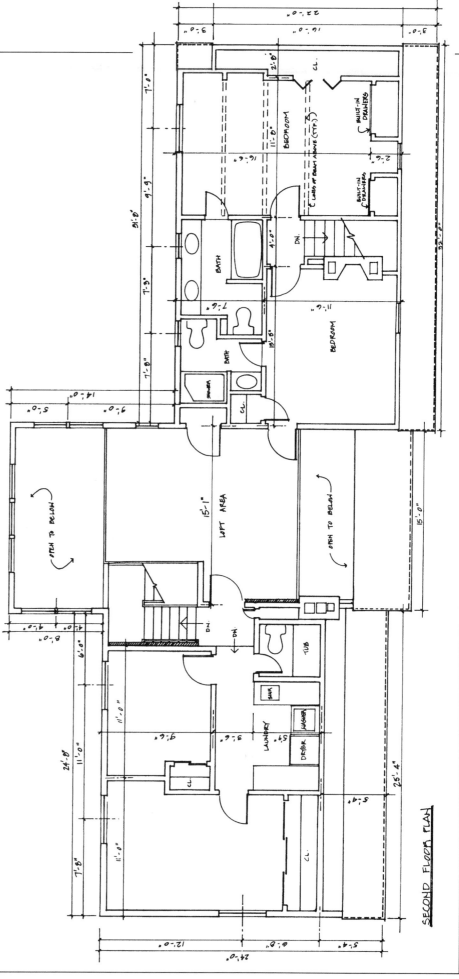

3. PHASE-ONE SECOND-STORY PLAN
SCALE: ⅛" = 1'0"

plan) shows how he added two more sections to the house: a central section, consisting of family room, study, coat closet, and staircase, and another section consisting of a two-car garage. Looking at Plan #3 (the second-floor plan), one sees that he located two bedrooms, bath fixtures, and a laundry center over the garage; he bridged the original bedroom wing and the new bedrooms (presumably, bedrooms for children) with a loft which was visually open to both the study on one side and the family room on the other.

The relationships between these lower- and upper-level rooms is clarified by Drawing #4, a section through the center of the house. Here, too, the differences in roof pitch can be easily seen.

Finally, the architect finished off part of the basement level, creating a finished playroom beneath the family room/study and a workshop room below the garage. He installed two additional bathrooms on this lowest level, left the original basement area unfinished and then decided to sell the house. For many years, this idiosyncratic house remained unsold. Finally, Michael and Nina, a couple with two young children and many interests—for whom the workshop and loft were attractive spaces for hobbies and office—bought the house. Michael used the workshop for woodworking tools, and Nina took over the loft as an office and studio space. The space on the first floor labeled "study" became a den/library/reading room—a quiet room for adults to read or watch TV when the children were playing downstairs. Over the next few years, they became increasingly aware of the house's shortcomings.

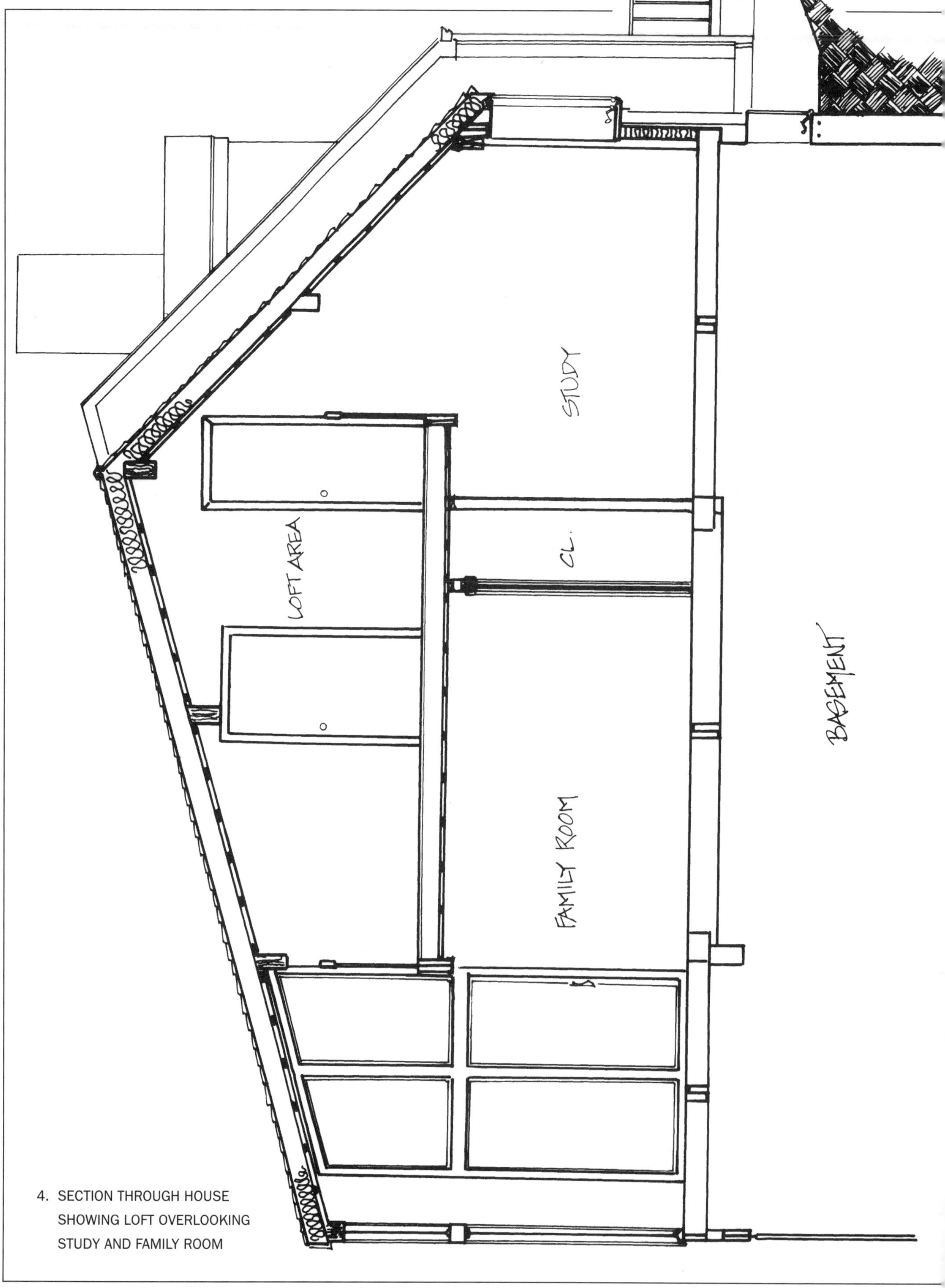

STUDY

LOFT AREA

CL.

BASEMENT

FAMILY ROOM

4. SECTION THROUGH HOUSE
   SHOWING LOFT OVERLOOKING
   STUDY AND FAMILY ROOM

A New Kitchen

Nina found that there were five major problems with the existing kitchen (as shown in Plan #2). First, the enormous peninsula, intended to serve as a breakfast bar as well as preparation counter, took up so much of the room that only a small, round table could be fit into the dining room. Second, the kitchen was essentially the first thing seen by visitors coming in the front door; thus, whenever Nina knew that someone was stopping by, she rushed to clean up the kitchen! Third, the actual space available for appliances was tight, so that they were placed close together, creating bottlenecks and diminishing counter space; the close proximity of sink and range made preparation especially difficult. Fourth, there was little visual or functional relationship between the kitchen and the area labeled "family room" on the plan. If a breakfast table was located in that family room, which seemed logical since it had tall glass walls and overlooked the forest behind the house, serving from the kitchen was difficult. Fifth, the kitchen was aesthetically outdated, with dark-stained oak cabinets and a pseudo-Scandinavian tile backsplash of brilliant orange poppies. All of these problems needed to be addressed.

Nina wanted to find a solution which would be as economical as possible, while successfully meeting all of her needs. The first step was to consider whether the new kitchen with an informal eating area could be installed in the "family room," so that demolition and construction costs could be minimized. Nine layouts follow which explore this possibility.

5 Here is a very simple and economical design which requires that a floor-to-ceiling wall be built abutting the stairway, so that cabinets can be installed. A galley-style kitchen results, with sink and dishwasher on one side of the room, cooking center on the opposite wall, and refrigerator located in the existing alcove next to the closet. A reasonable work triangle is created. The space next to the large windows is a pleasant breakfast nook. The dining room is now a very large space, and a new door to the deck could be installed; if so, the sliders might be removed to minimize traffic through the kitchen. The plan shows a pocket door between kitchen and formal dining room.

Nina was not satisfied with this design, however, because a traffic corridor exists between the backdoor, study door, and back stairway, and the front door and front staircase; this hallway cuts across the kitchen triangle. More important, the counter and storage space are insufficient; in fact, the scale of this kitchen is out of keeping with the rest of the house.

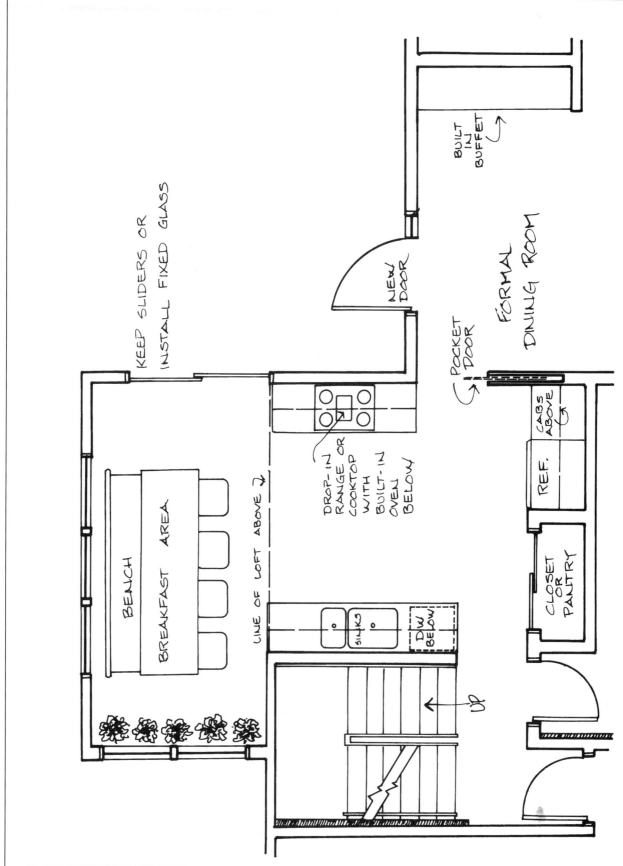

KEEP SLIDERS OR INSTALL FIXED GLASS

BUILT IN BUFFET

NEW DOOR

POCKET DOOR

FORMAL DINING ROOM

DROP-IN RANGE OR COOKTOP WITH BUILT-IN OVEN BELOW

LINE OF LOFT ABOVE

BENCH

BREAKFAST AREA

SINKS

DW BELOW

UP

CABS ABOVE

REF.

CLOSET OR PANTRY

5. NEW KITCHEN IN FAMILY ROOM; WINDOWS AND SLIDING DOORS LEFT INTACT

SCALE: ¼" = 1'0"

PERSPECTIVE OF PLAN #5, LOOKING OUT

PERSPECTIVE OF PLAN #5, LOOKING IN

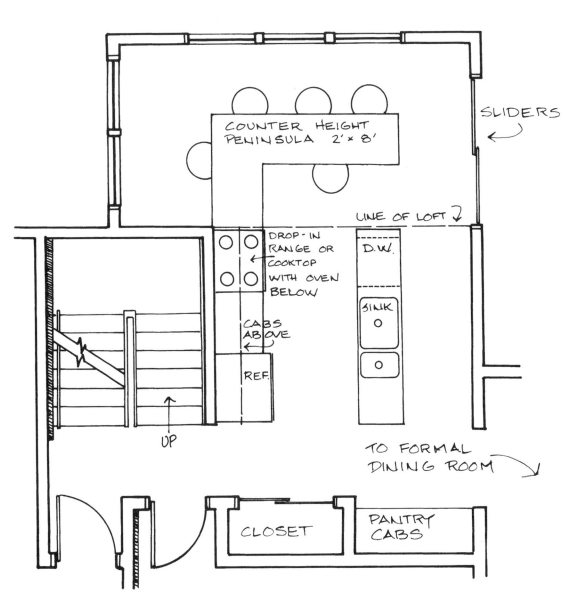

SLIDERS

COUNTER HEIGHT PENINSULA 2' × 8'

LINE OF LOFT

DROP-IN RANGE OR COOKTOP WITH OVEN BELOW

D.W.

SINK

CABS ABOVE

REF.

UP

TO FORMAL DINING ROOM

CLOSET

PANTRY CABS

6. NEW KITCHEN WITH ISLAND IN FAMILY ROOM; WINDOWS AND SLIDING DOORS LEFT INTACT
SCALE: ¼" = 1'0"

6 In an effort to solve the two problems identified in the discussion of Plan #5, this layout was created. Here, the refrigerator is moved to the wall abutting the stairs. The sink and dishwasher are now located in an island. The island accomplishes two things. First, it moves the appliances closer together, so that the work triangle is more efficient. Second, it permits traffic to the sliders and deck to bypass the kitchen. The alcove next to the closet is now fitted with floor-to-ceiling pantry cabinets, so that storage capacity is increased. Finally, the breakfast area becomes part of a counter-height peninsula which can be used as a surface for preparation. In this way, counter space has also been improved.

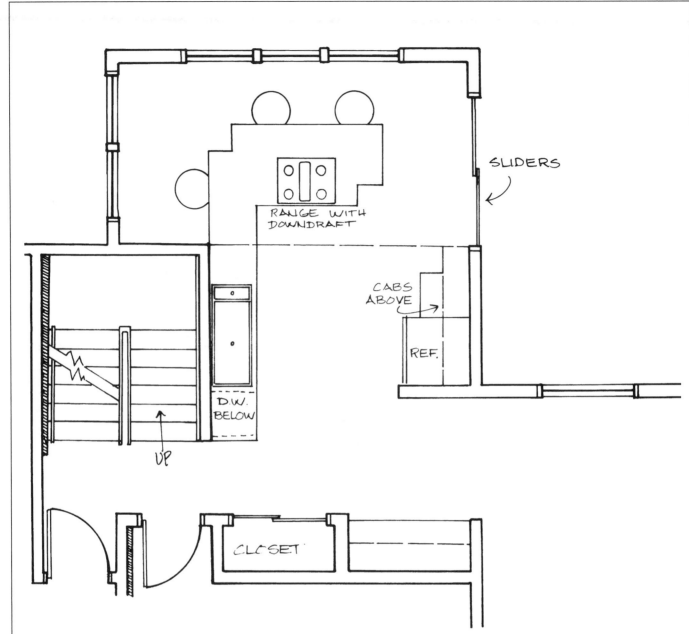

SLIDERS

RANGE WITH
DOWNDRAFT

CABS
ABOVE

REF.

D.W.
BELOW

UP

CLOSET

7. NEW KITCHEN IN FAMILY ROOM; SLIDING DOORS LEFT INTACT
SCALE: ¼″ = 1′0″

7 In a variation on Plan #6, the breakfast peninsula is made deep enough to install a range with downdraft, and the fridge and sink are located on opposite walls. Note that in the alcove, floor-to-ceiling cabinets are replaced with lower and upper cabinets, which means that there is additional counter space—probably an area where the mail gets dropped as occupants of the house enter from the garage.

Although Plans #5, #6, and #7 are fairly economical, in that they do not disturb existing windows or require an addition, all of them are short on counter space. In response to this problem, Nina did some designs which put the kitchen into the "breakfast nook" area. These plans follow.

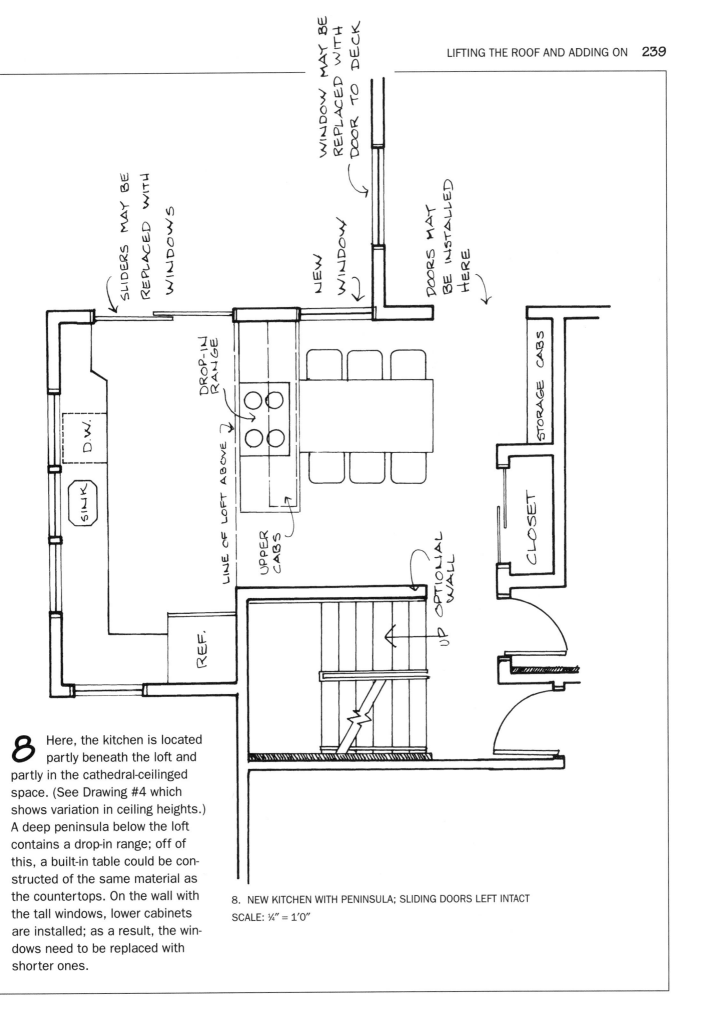

SLIDERS MAY BE REPLACED WITH WINDOWS

WINDOW MAY BE REPLACED WITH DOOR TO DECK

NEW WINDOW

DOORS MAT BE INSTALLED HERE

STORAGE CABS

DROP-IN RANGE

D.W.

SINK

LINE OF LOFT ABOVE

UPPER CABS

CLOSET

REF.

UP OPTIOIIAL WALL

8 Here, the kitchen is located partly beneath the loft and partly in the cathedral-ceilinged space. (See Drawing #4 which shows variation in ceiling heights.) A deep peninsula below the loft contains a drop-in range; off of this, a built-in table could be constructed of the same material as the countertops. On the wall with the tall windows, lower cabinets are installed; as a result, the windows need to be replaced with shorter ones.

8. NEW KITCHEN WITH PENINSULA; SLIDING DOORS LEFT INTACT
SCALE: ¼″ = 1′0″

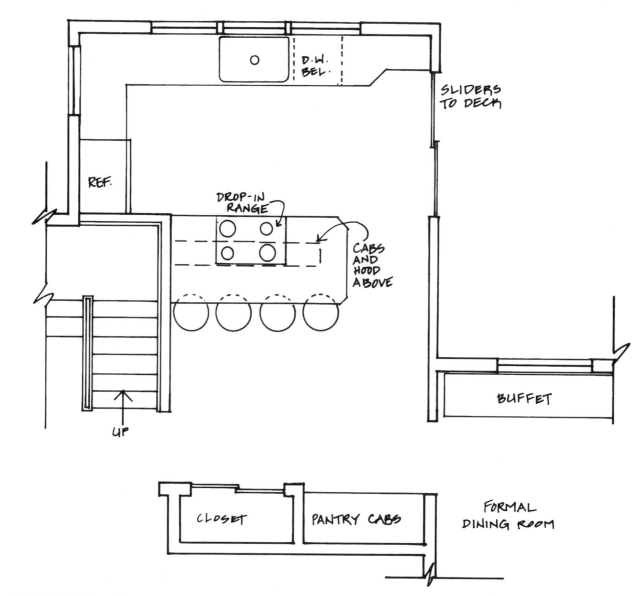

9. NEW KITCHEN WITH PENINSULA; SLIDING DOORS LEFT INTACT
SCALE: ¼″ = 1′0″

Note a variety of options with respect to windows and doors which are noted on the plan. The sliders to the deck may be replaced with windows, to eliminate traffic through the kitchen. The sliders, or a swinging door, could be relocated to the end of the dining room. A new window next to the breakfast table permits a view to the deck.

9 In a modification of Plan #8, the peninsula is located on the opposite wall, with stools provided for informal eating. Moving the peninsula means that people going out the sliders to the deck do not interfere with the kitchen work triangle.

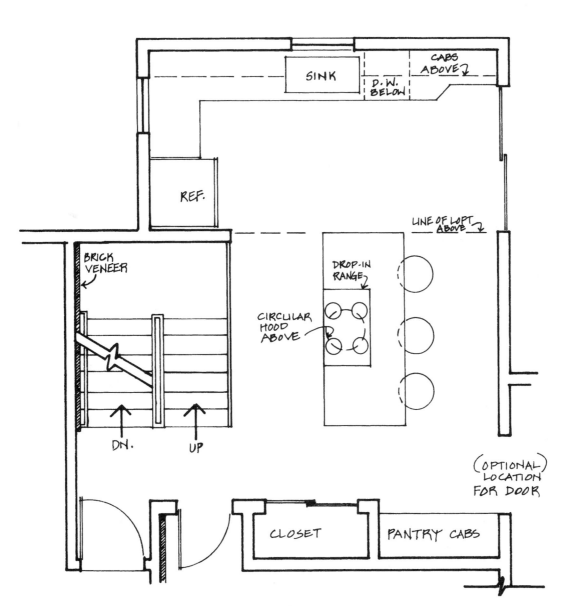

SINK

D.W. BELOW

CABS ABOVE

REF.

BRICK VENEER

LINE OF LOFT ABOVE

DROP-IN RANGE

CIRCULAR HOOD ABOVE

DN.   UP

(OPTIONAL) LOCATION FOR DOOR

CLOSET   PANTRY CABS

10. NEW KITCHEN WITH ISLAND IN FAMILY ROOM; SLIDERS LEFT INTACT
SCALE: ¼″ = 1′0″

10 Another modification shows the range in an island rather than a peninsula, once again with breakfast stools on the other side of the island. The improved traffic pattern, which bypasses the work triangle, is maintained here. A significant difference in this design is that the staircase remains open to the kitchen, with no intervening wall.

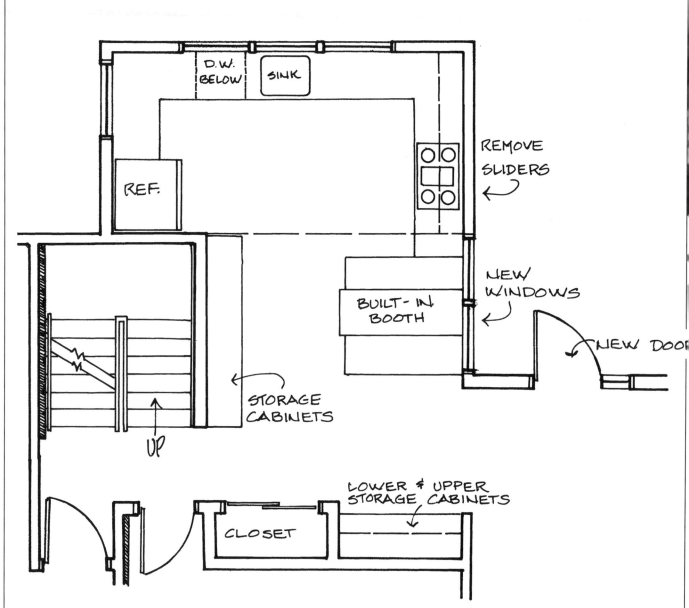

11. NEW KITCHEN IN FAMILY ROOM
SCALE: ¼″ = 1′0″

11 In this design, the sliders are removed so that additional cabinetry and the range can be installed. The bulk of the kitchen is in the cathedral-ceilinged space, and the area below the loft accommodates a built-in booth and a long wall of storage cabinets. This layout provides a lot of storage, both on the wall opposite the booth as well as in the alcove next to the closet, and it also gives an adequate amount of counter.

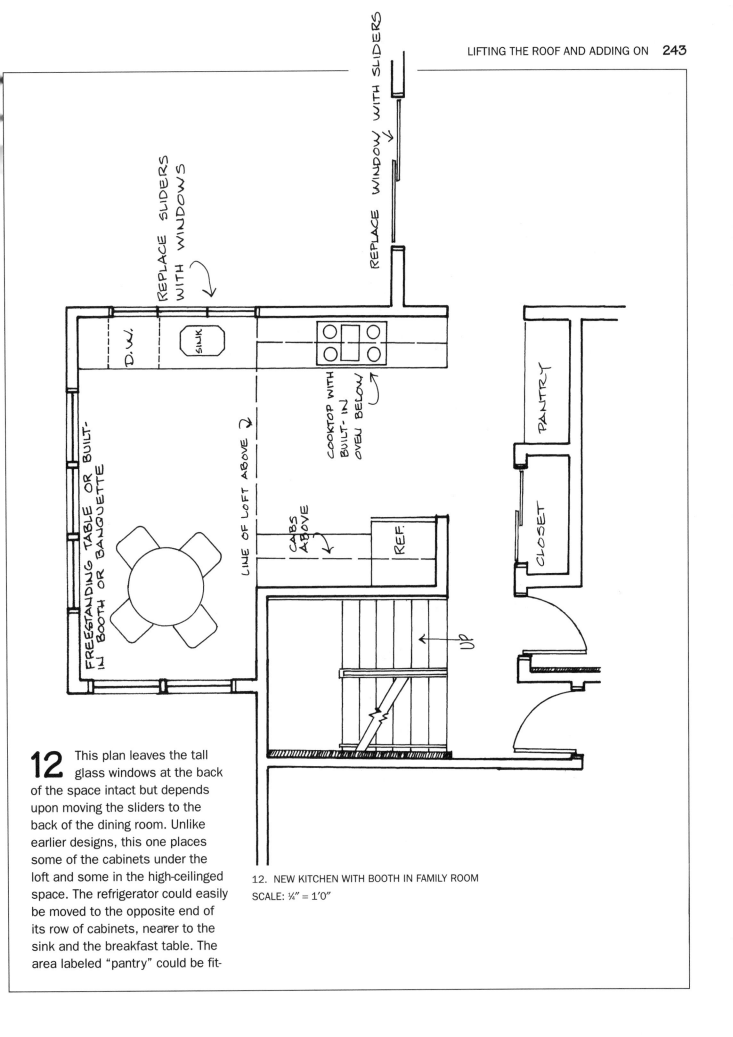

REPLACE WINDOW WITH SLIDERS

REPLACE SLIDERS WITH WINDOWS

D.W.

SINK

COOKTOP WITH BUILT-IN OVEN BELOW

LINE OF LOFT ABOVE

FREESTANDING TABLE OR BUILT-IN BOOTH OR BANQUETTE

CABS ABOVE

REF.

UP

PANTRY

CLOSET

12 This plan leaves the tall glass windows at the back of the space intact but depends upon moving the sliders to the back of the dining room. Unlike earlier designs, this one places some of the cabinets under the loft and some in the high-ceilinged space. The refrigerator could easily be moved to the opposite end of its row of cabinets, nearer to the sink and the breakfast table. The area labeled "pantry" could be fit-

12. NEW KITCHEN WITH BOOTH IN FAMILY ROOM
SCALE: ¼" = 1'0"

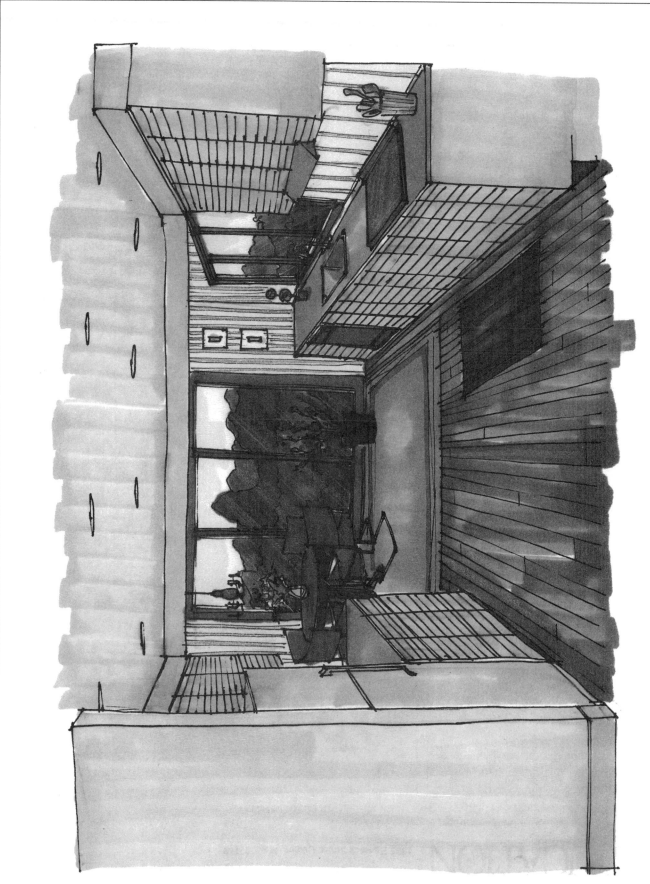

PERSPECTIVE OF PLAN #12

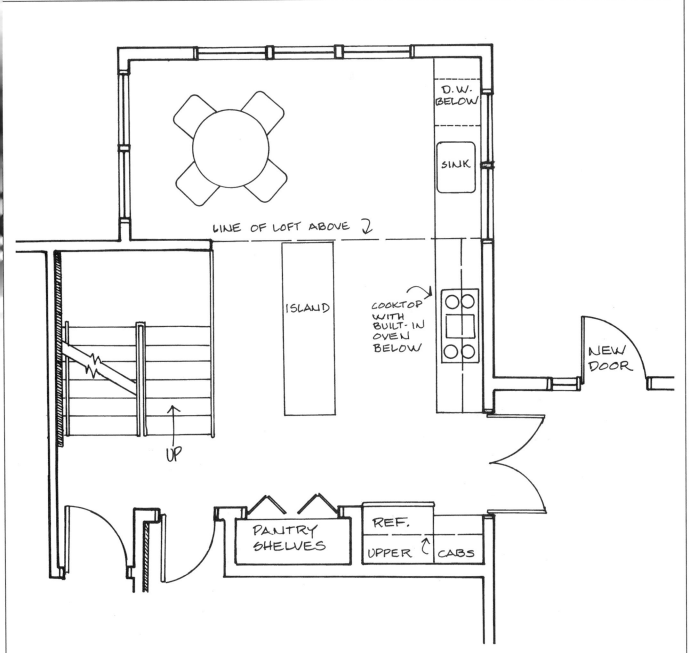

D.W.
BELOW

SINK

LINE OF LOFT ABOVE

ISLAND

COOKTOP
WITH
BUILT-IN
OVEN
BELOW

NEW
DOOR

UP

PANTRY
SHELVES

REF.

UPPER   CABS

13. NEW KITCHEN WITH ISLAND IN FAMILY ROOM
SCALE: ¼″ = 1′0″

ted with floor-to-ceiling or with lower and upper cabinets; if the latter, it would make a good surface for serving the dining room.

It is in some ways functionally and aesthetically preferable to lay out the kitchen so that it bridges the dining room and the breakfast area, rather than having both eating areas adjacent to each other.

13 This variation on Plan #12 moves the fridge into the alcove and shows an island in the center of the space which can be used for preparation. If desired, the locations for cooktop and sink could be switched, so that the fridge and sink are closer together; in that case, there would

have to be changes in window locations as well.

This plan shows how a pair of doors could isolate the kitchen from the dining room.

Ultimately, Nina was not completely happy with any of the kitchen plans described above. For one thing, she wanted to keep the cathedral-ceilinged area over-

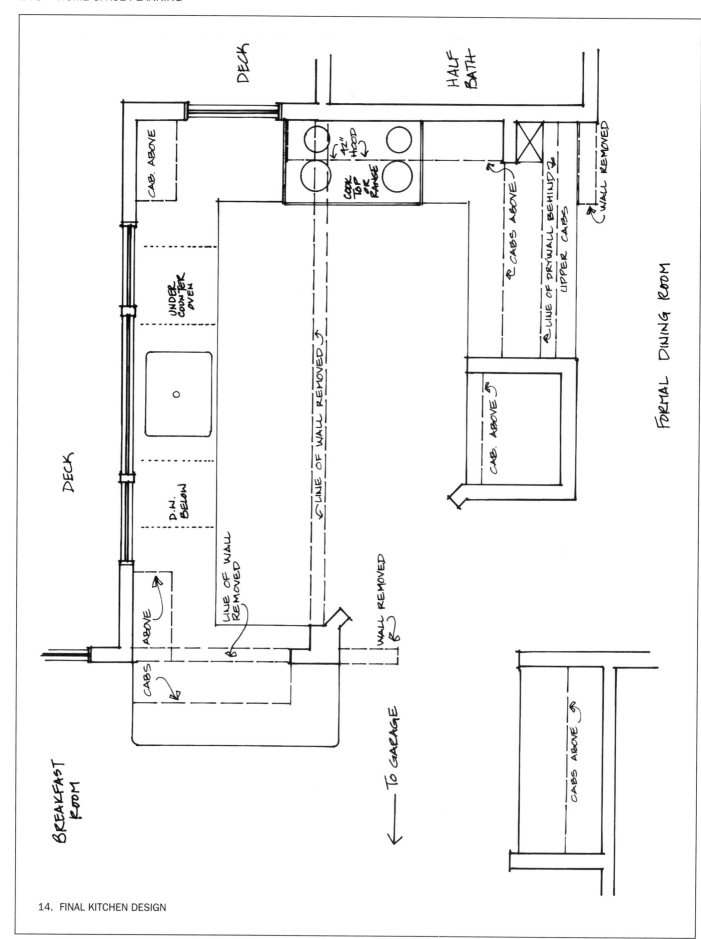

DECK

HALF
BATH

CAB. ABOVE

42" HOOD

COOK
TOP
OR
RANGE

CABS ABOVE

LINE OF DRYWALL BEHIND
UPPER CABS

WALL REMOVED

UNDER
COUNTER
OVEN

DECK

D.W.
BELOW

LINE OF WALL REMOVED

CAB. ABOVE

FORMAL DINING ROOM

CABS ABOVE

LINE OF WALL
REMOVED

WALL REMOVED

← TO GARAGE

BREAKFAST
ROOM

CABS ABOVE

14. FINAL KITCHEN DESIGN

looking the woods as a breakfast room; this decision eliminated some of the layouts. In addition, she really wanted a larger kitchen, with more counter space, than she could build in the "family room" area, and she wanted the kitchen to be close to the dining room. For some time, she experimented with the idea of building a substantial addition for a kitchen at the back of the dining room, but the expense was too great. Thus, she needed a modified version of the idea, with a smaller extension. Her ultimate solution is shown in Plan #14.

14 All of Nina's requirements are met in this design. The expense, first of all, was moderate, since the extension to the house measured merely 5′ × 13′. The decision to extend only 5 feet onto the deck was made in order to keep the sliders, and the clerestory windows above them, intact. By enlarging the house a little, and by gutting the original kitchen and reorganizing the layout, everything was finally accomplished—Nina's list of five major problems, which created her demand for a new kitchen, were all solved.

First, by changing the layout—specifically, by removing the peninsula and pushing the kitchen out onto the deck—the dining room is enlarged. The new dining room dimensions are 11′ × 17′, long enough to serve twelve people comfortably.

Second, the new configuration, with a wall behind the fridge and behind the upper cabinets adjacent to the fridge, means that the view of the kitchen is shielded from visitors entering at the front

door. The view of the kitchen could have been completely eliminated had Nina decided against building the pass-through to the dining room. However, she decided that the pass-through had some advantages which made it worth keeping, partly to expedite serving and partly to allow light from the large windows to penetrate into the dining area.

Third, because in this plan the counters make almost a complete circle, there is ample space to lay out appliances with plenty of counter space beside them. Note that Nina's choice of appliances was partly determined by issues other than function. Because Nina wanted to maximize the view into the forest—the relationship between indoors and out—she installed a 9-foot-wide window at the back of the kitchen. One result of this decision, in conjunction with the building of two pass-throughs, was that there was no room for wall ovens; therefore, an under-counter oven (looking much like a wide dishwasher) was installed.

Fourth, this plan creates a wonderful flow between the three spaces: dining, kitchen, and breakfast. The kitchen, shielded slightly from view as mentioned before, is nevertheless open to both eating areas (with a pass-through in each direction). At the same time, it is a dead-end workspace, which can be easily bypassed; its entrance faces both towards the dining room and towards the backdoor. The visitor arriving at the front door looks through the dining room into the breakfast area beyond, with its tall glass windows and view of the forest. Thus, the sense of entry into

the house has been greatly improved, with the first impression now one of an open and airy, light-filled interior.

Finally, in redoing the kitchen, Nina was able to make materials selections which seemed more in keeping with the rest of the house. Note that on Plan #2, the flooring in the original kitchen and the family room was a tacky, flowery-patterned vinyl. The rest of the house emphasized natural materials: slate floor in the dining room, quarry tile floor in the study, wood detailing everywhere, including a wood, coffered ceiling beneath the loft area. The choices made by the architect were decidedly contemporary (though dating back to the '70s) and somewhat institutional in style. Nina's challenge, then, was to integrate these directions, to select styles and materials which were contemporary and natural, but which were still economical (no granite countertops here!).

The solution lay in choosing oak cabinets with a light stain and in replacing the vinyl flooring with an irregular sand-colored ceramic tile throughout. The backsplash was also ceramic tile, but of an irregular off-white, and the countertop chosen was a deep brown laminate with a very subtle pattern suggesting brushstrokes of tan and gold, edged with oak which was stained to match the cabinets. The rest of the kitchen was black (appliances' fronts) and stainless steel (sink, cooktop, and large, industrial hood). The materials and colors, therefore, tied the kitchen into the adjacent spaces, an important consideration with spaces so open to each other.

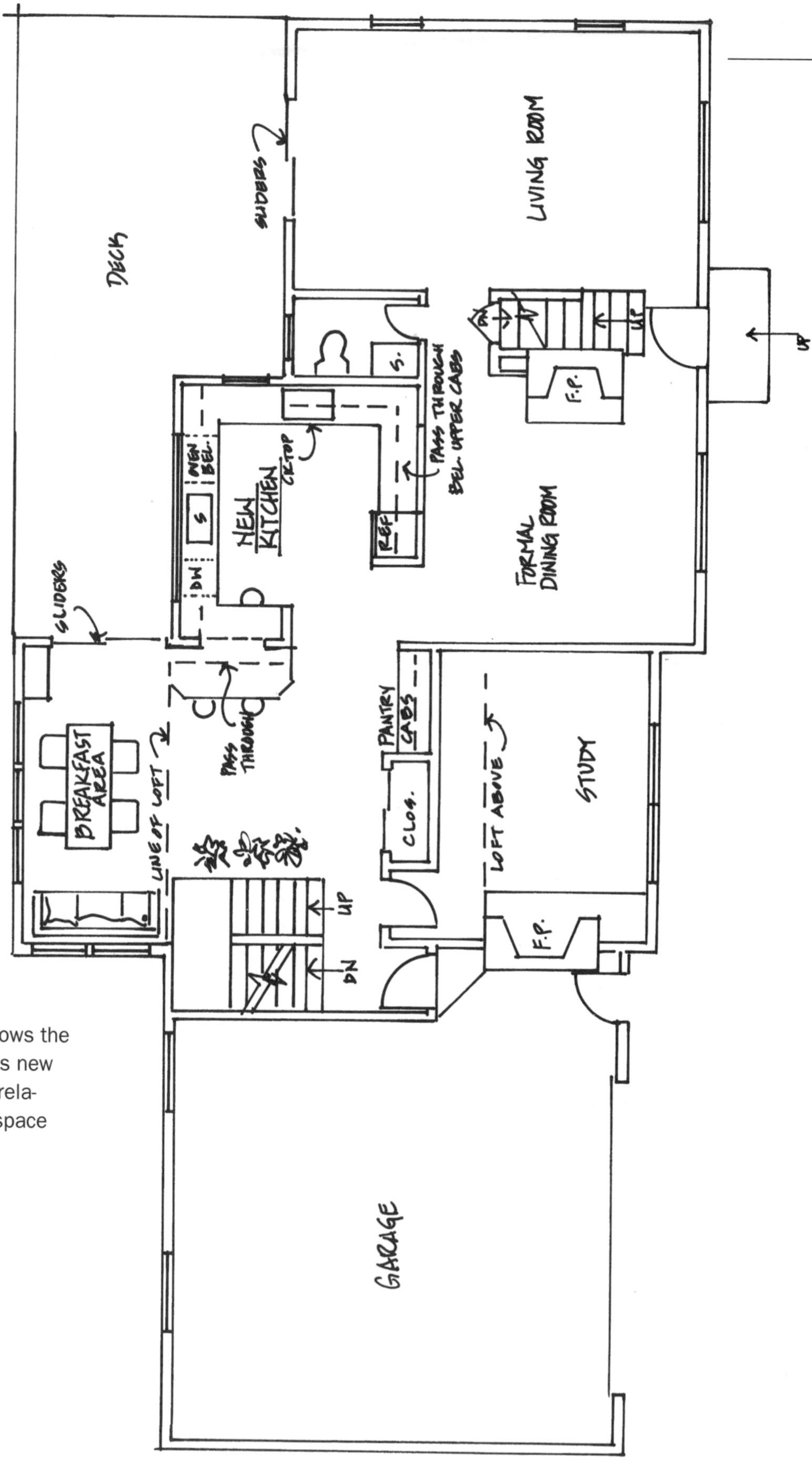

DECK

SBEAMS

LIVING ROOM

NEW KITCHEN

NEW BBL.

C'TOP

PASS THROUGH
BBL. UPPER CABS

S.

F.P.

DN

UP

REF

FORMAL DINING ROOM

DW

SLIDERS

LINE OF LOFT

PASS THROUGH

BREAKFAST AREA

PANTRY CABS

CLO.

LOFT ABOVE

STUDY

F.P.

UP

DN

GARAGE

14a This drawing shows the first floor with its new kitchen and illustrates the relationship between the new space and adjacent rooms.

14A. PLAN OF FIRST FLOOR WITH NEW KITCHEN

FINAL KITCHEN

FINAL KITCHEN DESIGN

New Master Bedroom Suite

Nina felt that the second story above the living and dining rooms also had some problems. The guest room (labeled "bedroom" on Plan #3), like the loft, was a bridge between the master bedroom and the children's rooms. Although the children could be told to go down one staircase and up another to avoid walking through the guest room, they usually forgot. Nina decided to finish off some basement space to create a new guest bedroom and to reorganize the second-story area to create a single master suite. Other concerns were insufficient clothing storage and a rather small master bedroom with too many openings into it, making it hard to find space for even a chair. Once again, Nina wanted to make changes without extensive structural changes; this meant leaving the central stairway and chimney in place, and keeping the plumbing approximately in its existing location. The next two drawings demonstrate two options for this upper-story space.

15 The two most important changes to the organization of space here are the removal of the long closet in the master bedroom and the consolidation of two bathrooms into one. Here, the new bathroom is shown opening off of the sitting room, where low bookshelves have been installed beneath the steep pitch of the roof. Part of the original bathroom space has been converted into a large walk-in closet. It is clear that simply removing the long closet accomplishes a lot. The extra floor space in the bedroom makes it possible to add a chair or some other piece of furniture in the corner of the room, and there is also room for a bench at the foot of the bed. Note that another set of drawers built into the eaves can also be accommodated. If desired, the closet and bathroom could change places, so that the bathroom opened directly into the bedroom. Two perspective sketches show the sitting room and bedroom in Plan #15 and show how the roof pitch affects the layout of furniture.

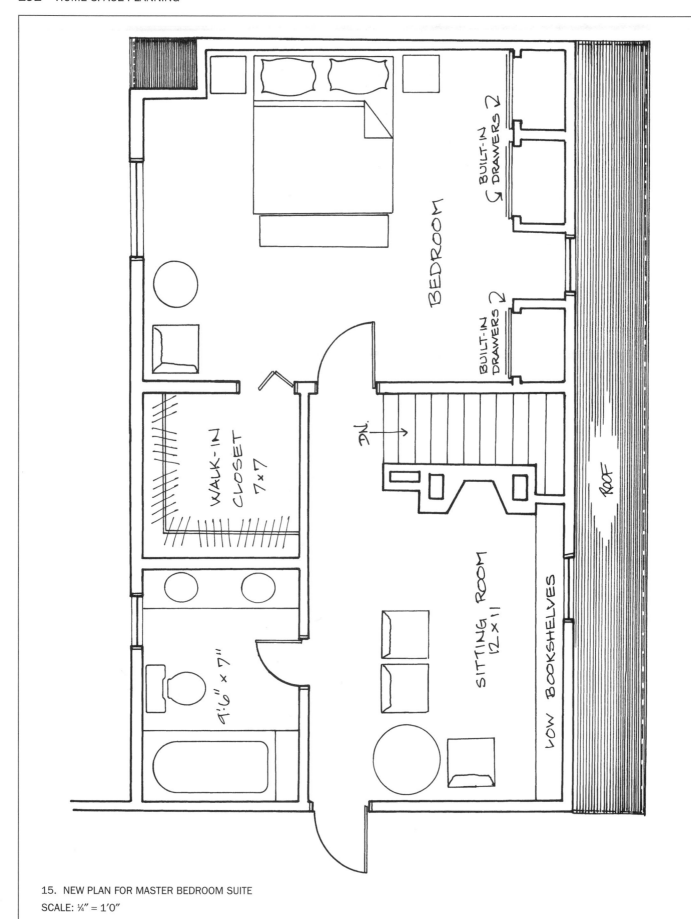

BUILT-IN DRAWERS 2

BUILT-IN DRAWERS 2

BEDROOM

ROOF

WALK-IN CLOSET 7×7

DN.

SITTING ROOM 12 × 11

LOW BOOKSHELVES

4'6" × 7"

15. NEW PLAN FOR MASTER BEDROOM SUITE

SCALE: ¼" = 1'0"

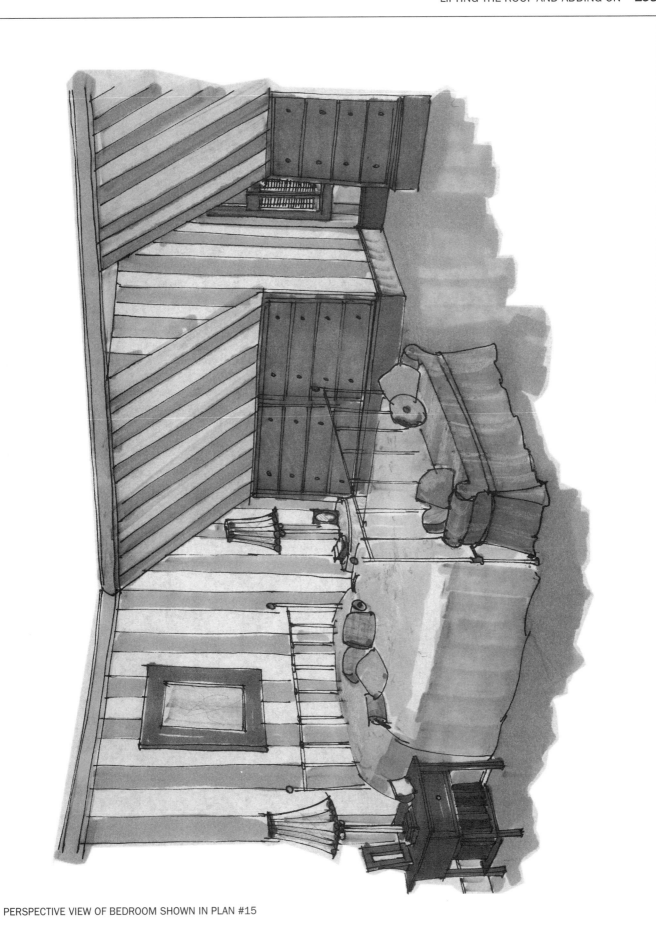

PERSPECTIVE VIEW OF BEDROOM SHOWN IN PLAN #15

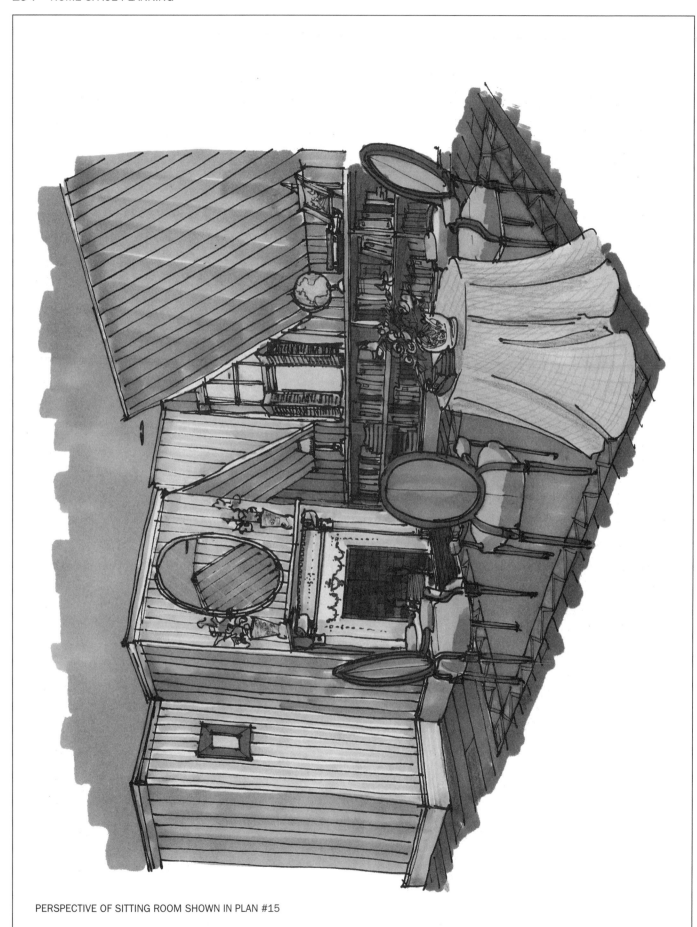

PERSPECTIVE OF SITTING ROOM SHOWN IN PLAN #15

PERSPECTIVE VIEW OF PLAN #15

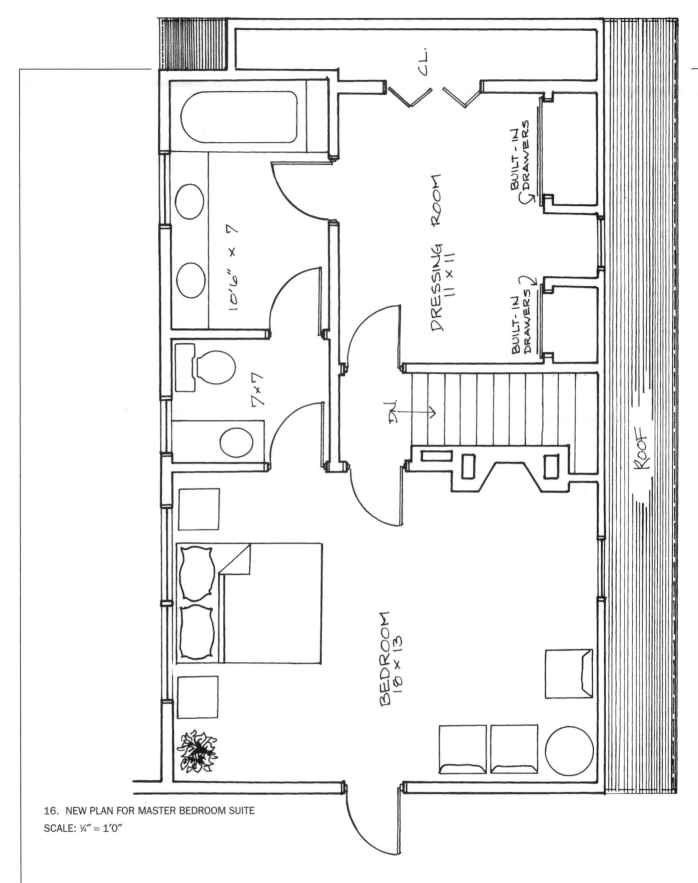

CL.

BUILT-IN DRAWERS

BUILT-IN DRAWERS

DRESSING ROOM
11 × 11

10'6" × 7

7 × 7

DN.

ROOF

BEDROOM
18 × 13

16. NEW PLAN FOR MASTER BEDROOM SUITE
SCALE: ¼″ = 1'0″

16 In this plan, the bedroom and sitting room spaces are flipped. The space to the right of the stairs becomes a dressing room, with the original closet and drawers left intact. The single bathroom is large enough to accommodate two people at once, and the bedroom, now enlarged to 13 × 18, takes up the rest of the space, with a sitting area at one end. If the bathroom were made more compact, it would be possible to install additional closets.

BIRD'S-EYE PERSPECTIVE OF PLAN #16

Improving the Children's Wing

The worst part of the design of the children's rooms above the garage was the architect's decision to install a bathroom without raising the roof in any way—even a dormer would have helped—so that the small tub is tucked under the slope of the roof, in an unpleasantly tight space with no natural light. The laundry appliances and bathroom sink are in the hallway. This arrangement, though unusual, worked fairly well, since the bathroom sink is the fixture most often used, and it was easily accessible. Another, less critical problem with the design of this part of the house was the discrepancy between the sizes of the bedrooms and the fact that the smaller of the two was only about 9′ × 10′.

Nina's goals in redesigning the children's wing were to provide it with a pleasant bathroom with natural light, and a standard-sized tub and vanity; to try to make the children's rooms of more equal size and to give cross ventilation to each (by making each a corner room); to maintain a space for washer and dryer; and, if possible, to create additional space for linens. At the same time, she wanted to keep costs down, so she decided that, in any case, the toilet would remain in its original location and also that by putting the laundry area across the hall she could access plumbing which was in the garage beneath.

Drawing #17, a section through this part of the house, shows clearly how the pitch of the roof at the front of the house means an enormous loss of usable floor space and how the only way to meet Nina's requirements was to raise the roof. Drawing #18 demonstrates how lifting the roofline—for example, by means of a shed dormer—creates needed floor space.

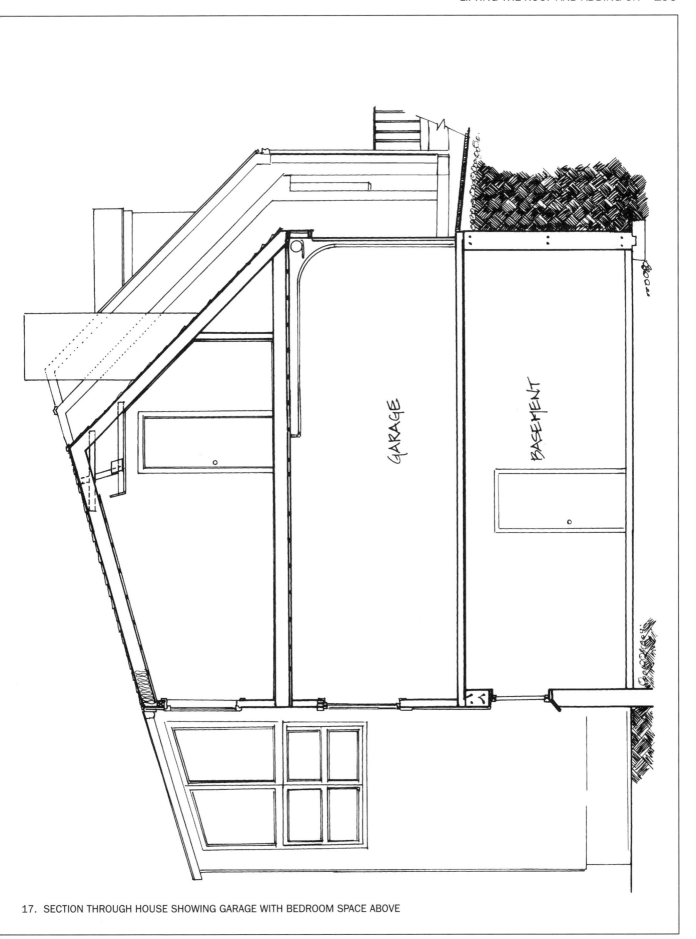

17. SECTION THROUGH HOUSE SHOWING GARAGE WITH BEDROOM SPACE ABOVE

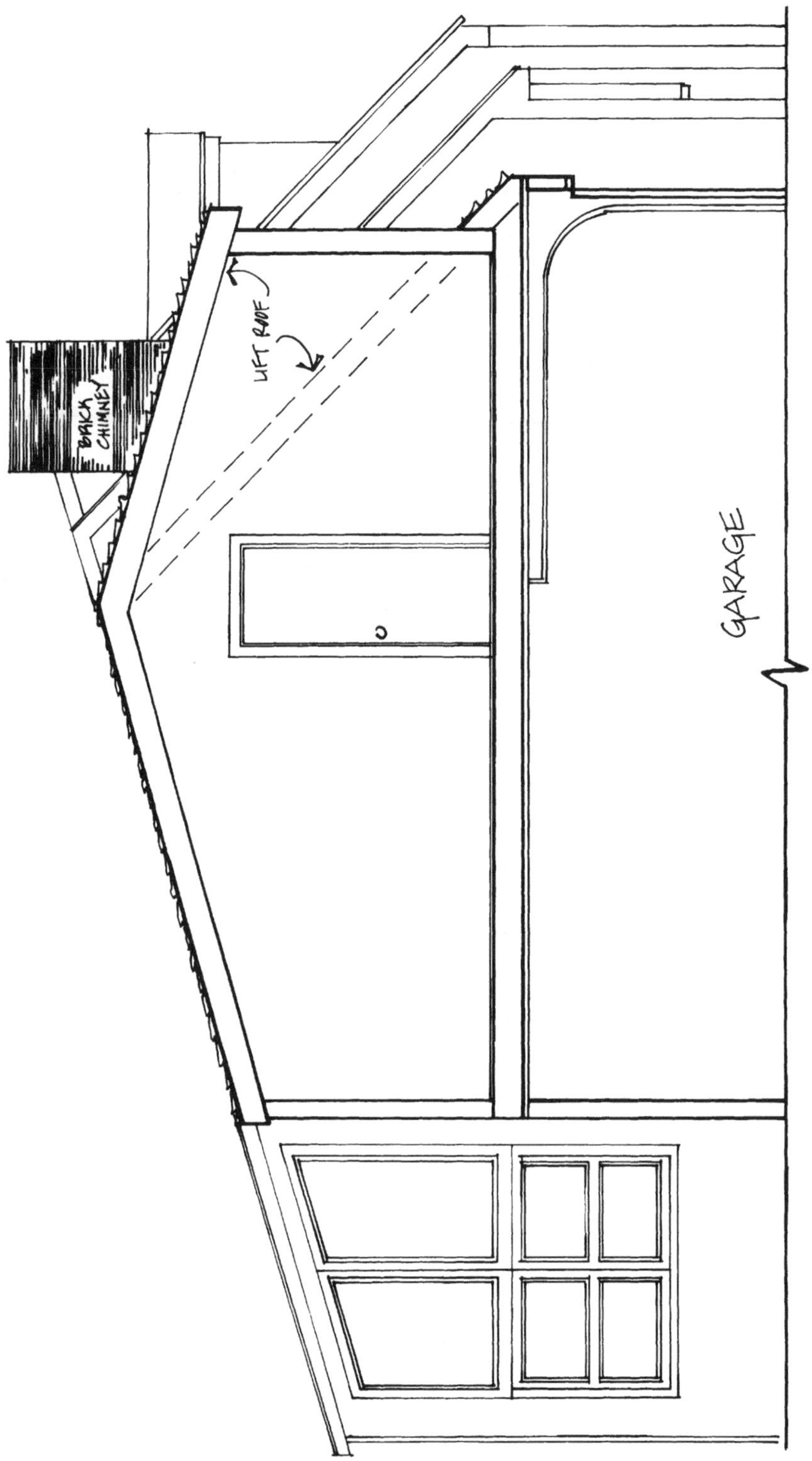
BRICK CHIMNEY
LIFT ROOF
GARAGE

18. SECTION THROUGH HOUSE SHOWING GARAGE AND BEDROOM AREA WITH RAISED ROOF

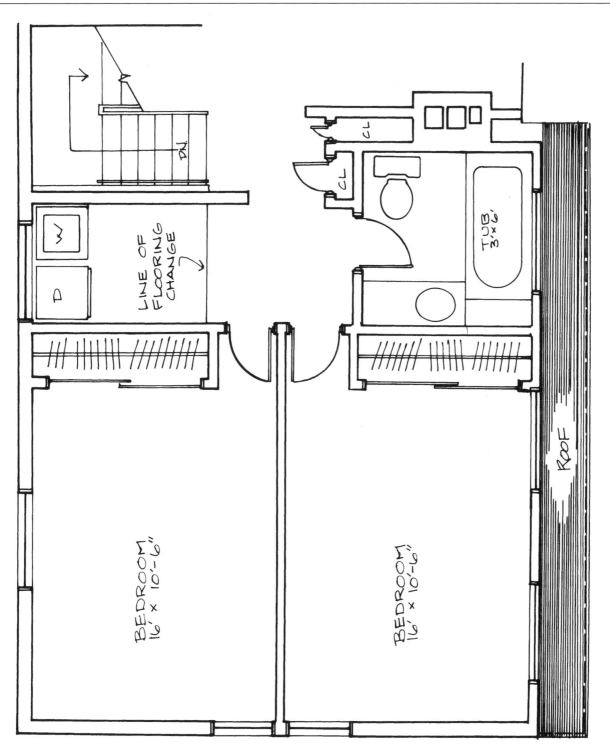

19. NEW BEDROOMS, BATH, AND LAUNDRY
SCALE: ¼" = 1'0"

19 Here is one possible layout for this area. All of Nina's goals are met: the bathroom is standard, the laundry center is across the hall, a second linen closet is created, the children's rooms are of equal size, and both are corner rooms.

A bird's-eye perspective shows how Plan #19 would look if built.

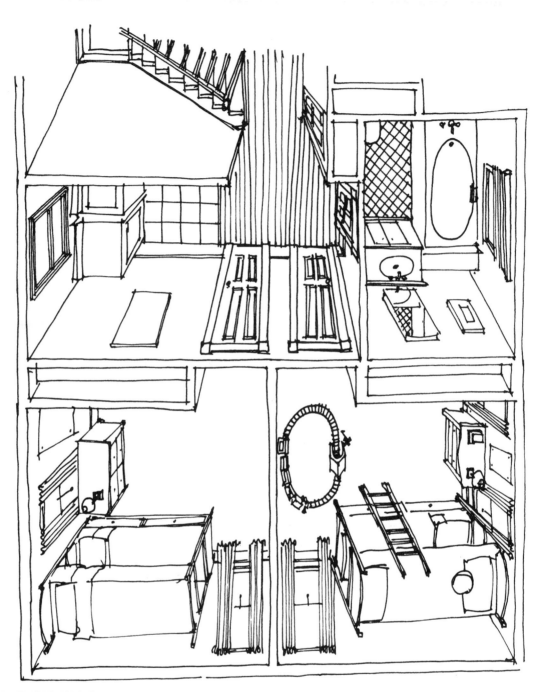

BIRD'S-EYE VIEW OF PLAN #19

20 In a variation on Plan #19, the bathroom is separated into two rooms: one with tub and sink; the other with toilet, sink, and laundry appliances. As noted on the plan, these two bedrooms could instead be made into a single large bedroom; this end of the house could actually be made into a master suite.

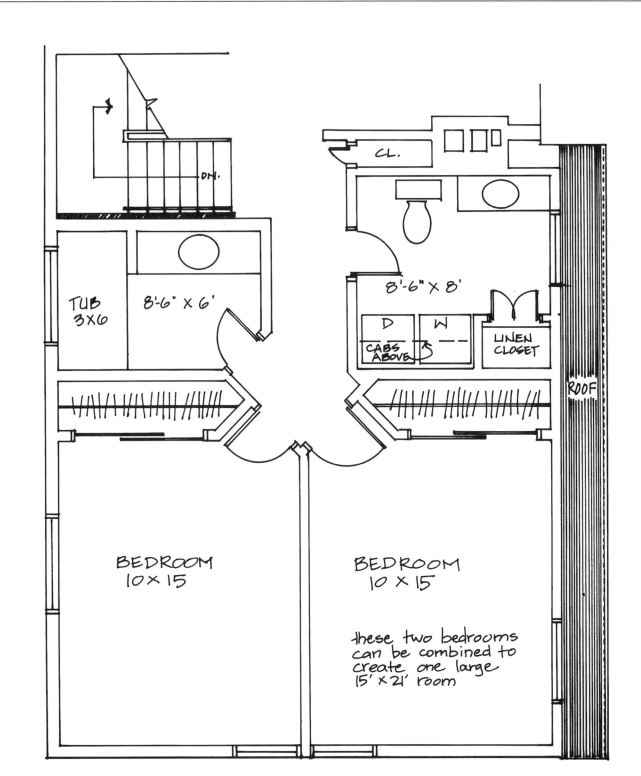

TUB
3×6

8'-6" X 6'

CL.

8'-6" X 8'

D   W

CABS
ABOVE

LINEN
CLOSET

ROOF

BEDROOM
10×15

BEDROOM
10 × 15

these two bedrooms
can be combined to
create one large
15' × 21' room

DN.

20. NEW BEDROOMS AND BATHROOMS

SCALE: ¼″ = 1'0″

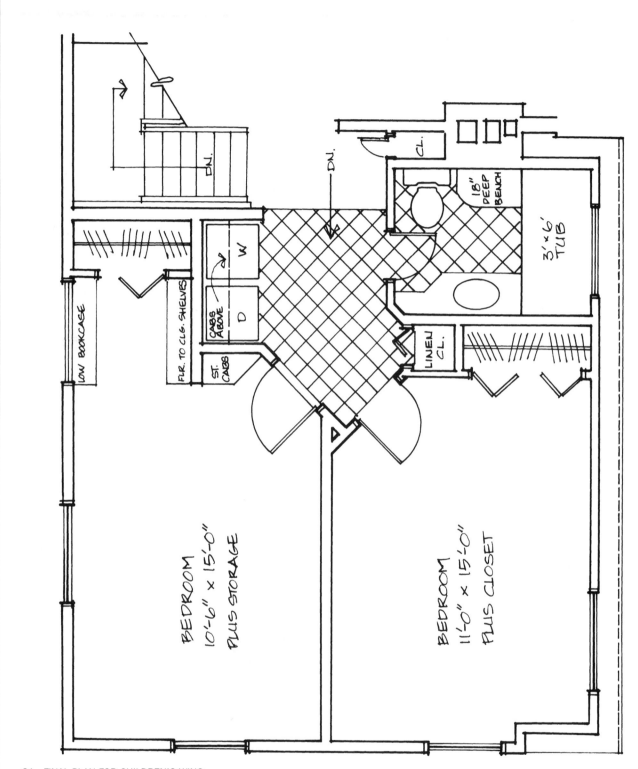

21. FINAL PLAN FOR CHILDREN'S WING

SCALE: ¼" = 1'0"

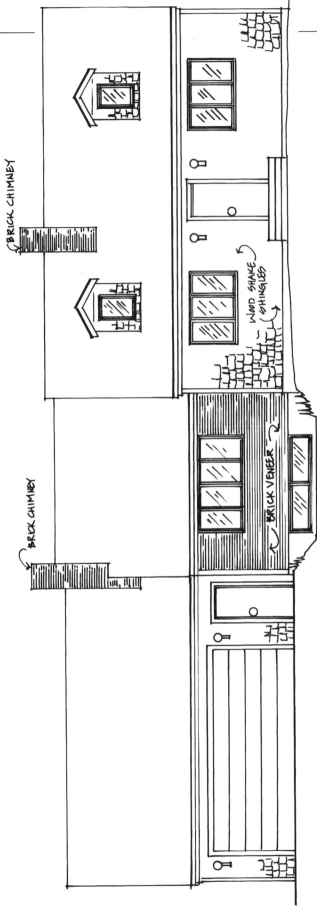

BRICK CHIMNEY

WOOD SHAKE SHINGLES

BRICK VENEER

BRICK CHIMNEY

22. FRONT ELEVATION

SCALE: ⅛″ = 1′0″

21 In the end, Nina chose to minimize the size of the bathroom and laundry area in order to give as much space as possible to the bedrooms. Here, the bedrooms are as large as possible, while still leaving enough space for sufficient closets, a three-fixture bathroom, washer and dryer, and a new linen closet. The hallway is more than 4-feet-wide, so that traffic flow is easy. The laundry appliances are brought forward towards the hall, though somewhat set back, so that the area behind them becomes a part of one of the bedrooms. This little alcove contains a closet and bookshelves.

22–25

These drawings show the elevations of the house before Nina's renovations took place.

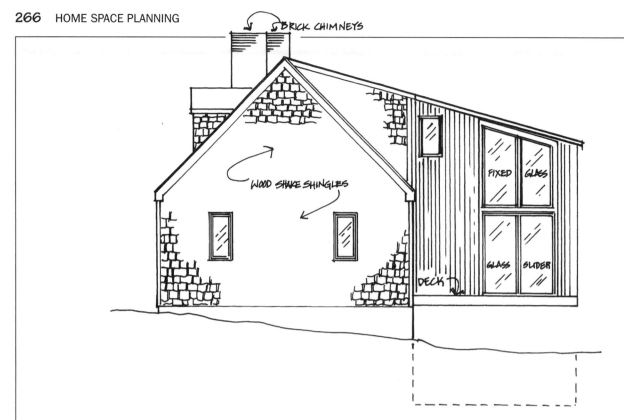

23. RIGHT SIDE ELEVATION
SCALE: ⅛″ = 1′0″

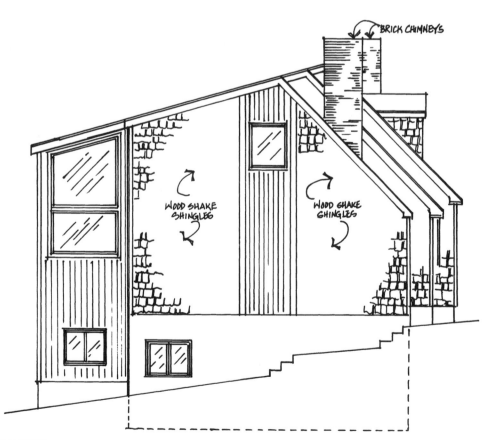

24. LEFT SIDE ELEVATION
SCALE: ⅛″ = 1′0″

25. BACK ELEVATION
SCALE: ⅛″ = 1′0″

26 This drawing shows the new front elevation, with the new roof over the garage. There are many design options for putting in windows.

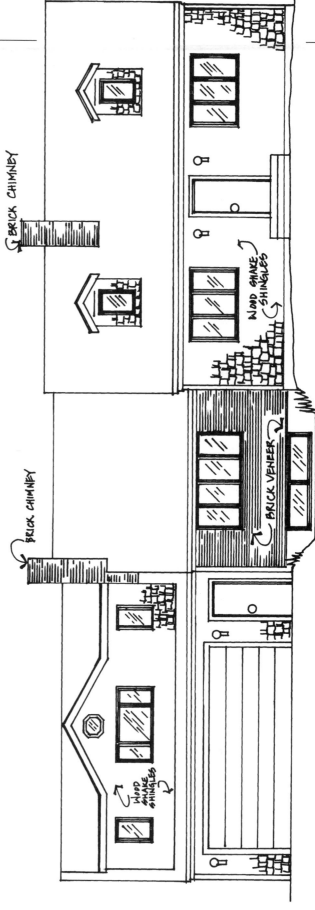

26. REVISED FRONT ELEVATION
SCALE: ⅛″ = 1′0″

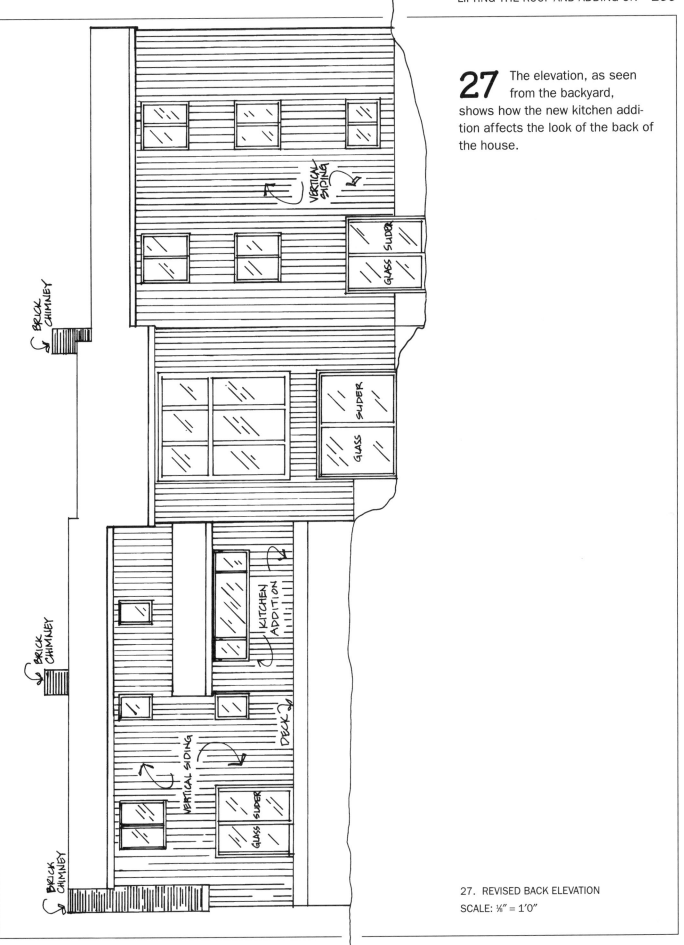

27 The elevation, as seen from the backyard, shows how the new kitchen addition affects the look of the back of the house.

27. REVISED BACK ELEVATION
SCALE: ⅛″ = 1′0″

Making Changes on the Lower Level

28 This plan shows the lower level as it was when Nina and Michael bought the house; the bedroom abutting the storage space was an addition which they arranged with the architect to provide. The workshop, as large as the garage above it, has sliders to the backyard and is a wonderful, light-filled space for Michael's woodworking tools. The large family room space is heavily used by the children. It is furnished with TV and stereo, big sectional sofa, piano, long tables with computers, and baskets of toys.

For several years, Michael kept a desk in the large lower-level bedroom's closet. This is where he kept track of household accounts, paid bills, and did his taxes. However, this meant that there was no storage for guests' clothing in this room. It also meant that Michael's computer, out in the big family room where the children played, was constantly in use by the children playing games; his file cabi-

net, meanwhile, had to be kept in the storage room. Michael wanted a compact but private home office for his desk, computer, and files. This room did not need to have natural light or be large, since he used it only occasionally, but he did want it to be complete and efficient.

Nina and Michael were often puzzled by the placement of two bathrooms back to back; this seemed a waste of space. They also found that, since they used the sides and back of their large garage for storage, as well as much of the workshop, the storage space which housed the furnace was larger than it needed to be. What follows are several redesigns which provide Michael with his home office, consolidate the bathrooms and storage, and maintain the guest bedroom.

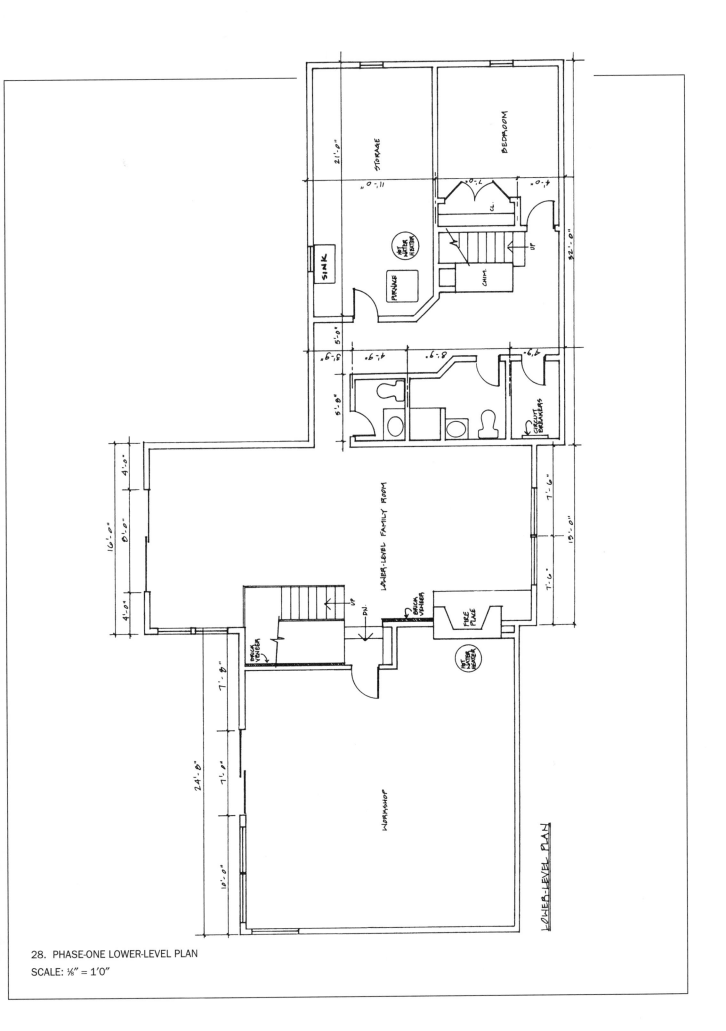

28. PHASE-ONE LOWER-LEVEL PLAN

SCALE: ⅛″ = 1′0″

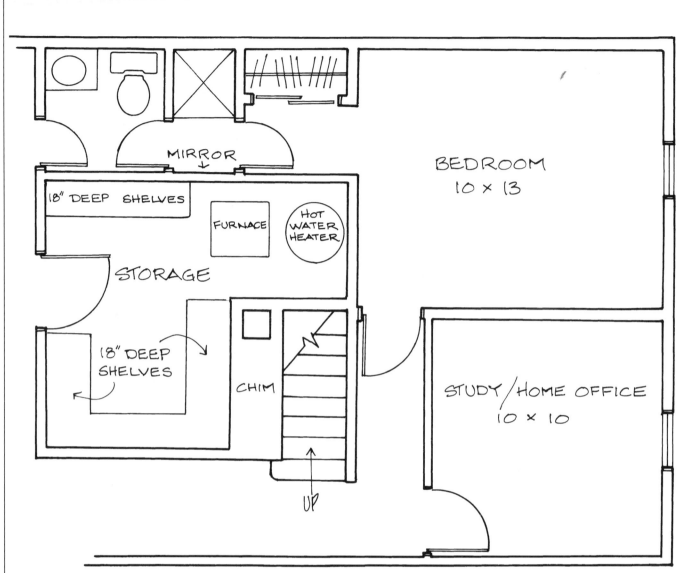

29. NEW LOWER-LEVEL PLAN WITH GUEST SUITE AND HOME OFFICE
SCALE: ¼" = 1'0"

29 In this layout, several changes take place which are effected largely by moving the bathroom. Here, a single bathroom serves both the guest and family rooms. The bedroom is carved out of what was storage space, and the home office exists in the original bedroom space; this arrangement allows the bedroom to abut the bathrooms. The furnace and hot water heater remain in their original locations, but the shape of the storage room has changed. A glance at Plan #28 shows how the hallway leading from family room to home office has been relocated in order to make the changes possible.

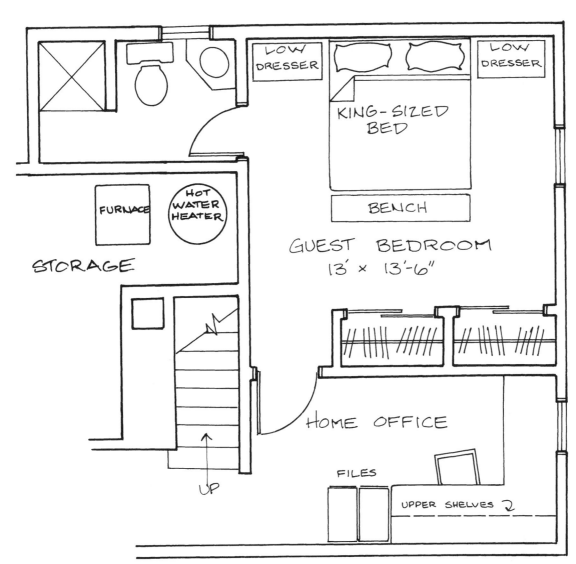

30. NEW LOWER-LEVEL PLAN WITH GUEST SUITE AND HOME OFFICE
SCALE: ¼″ = 1′0″

30 In a variation on Plan #29, there is a separate bathroom for the guest room; here, the shower remains in the same position, but the closet space shown in #29 is used for sink and toilet. The closets are relocated and the bedroom made larger by shrinking the home office. This office, in fact, would, if well planned, be quite adequate for Michael's purpose. The only drawback here is that it is open to view and to noise traveling from the family room.

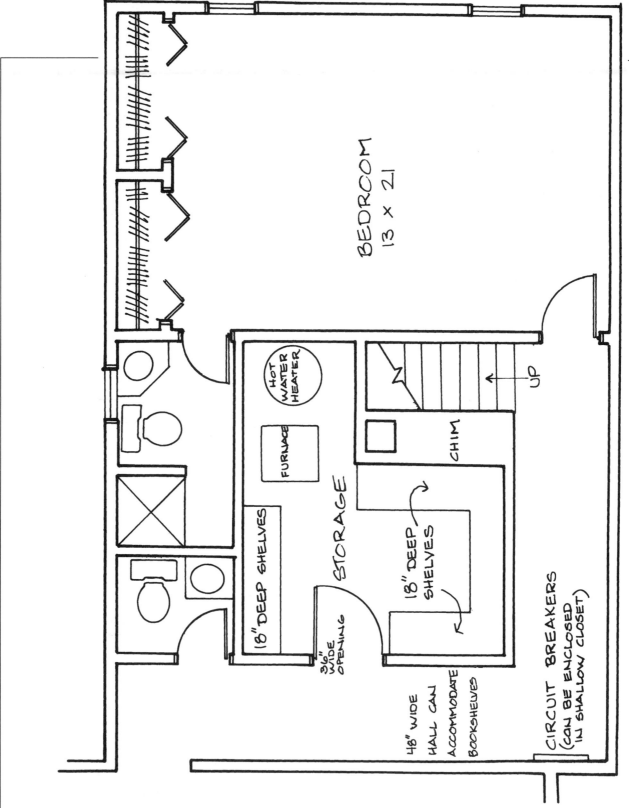

BEDROOM
13 × 21

HOT WATER HEATER

FURNACE

STORAGE

UP

CHIM

18" DEEP SHELVES

18" DEEP SHELVES

36" WIDE OPENING

48" WIDE HALL CAN ACCOMMODATE BOOKSHELVES

CIRCUIT BREAKERS (CAN BE ENCLOSED IN SHALLOW CLOSET)

31. NEW LOWER-LEVEL PLAN WITH LARGE BEDROOM AND TWO BATHROOMS
SCALE: ¼″ = 1′0″

31 If Nina and Michael wanted a large guest room—or if a teenaged child or au pair were to be occupying the lower-level bedroom—they could try to accommodate the home office by putting an attractive roll-top desk in the living room.

32 If, on the other hand, they wanted to keep the home office on the lower level, they could nearly eliminate the storage room (leaving it as a furnace room), take care of storage needs in garage and workshop, and build Michael's desk into the center of the space abutting the stairs, with two pocket doors which could be left open or closed for privacy.

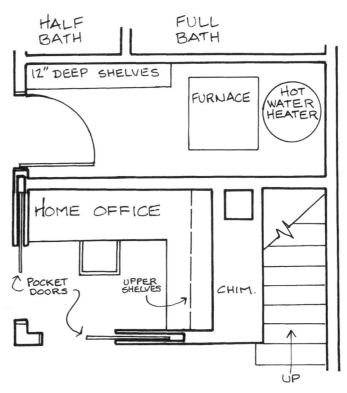

32. VARIATION ON PLAN #22 WITH HOME OFFICE

SCALE: ¼″ = 1′0″

Index

Index

About the Author

Nancy Temple is a space planner and interior designer certified by the National Council for Interior Design Qualification. She has taught courses in both architectural and interior design at several Boston-area colleges. She has a Master of Science in Interior Design and has also studied art history and textiles. She spent many years as a tapestry designer/weaver and still produces tapestries on commission for corporate clients. She has written numerous articles on tapestry design and is the author of *Interior Design Workbook*, a text for beginning interior design students.